# THE ENGLISH LETTERS OF
# BLESSED COLUMBA MARMION

# The English Letters
## *of*
# BLESSED
# COLUMBA
# MARMION

Angelico Press

This Angelico Press edition is a reprint of the work originally published as *The English Letters of Abbot Marmion, 1858–1923* by the Helicon Press in 1962.

For information, address:
Angelico Press, Ltd.
169 Monitor St.
Brooklyn, NY 11222
www.angelicopress.com

PB: 979-8-88677-050-6
Cloth: 979-8-88677-051-3

Cover design by Michael Schrauzer

# FOREWORD

"AS the Heavens are filled with stars, so does the land of Ireland abound in excellent men." This saying, from the *Fioretti* of St. Francis, though referring originally to the region of the Marches, could actually have been coined to express the merits of that Island of Faith among whose sons, so outstanding for their great goodness and lively intelligence, is numbered Columba Marmion, Abbot of Maredsous, native of Dublin. Abbot Marmion closed his work-filled earthly career on January 30, 1923, leaving behind a memory rich in holiness and doctrine. And the deep spirituality of his life still shines bright and vibrant in his writings.

The excellent education imparted by his Irish father and French mother laid the foundation for the thorough ecclesiastical formation he received, first in Dublin, then in Rome. After his ordination to the priesthood in June of 1881, he devoted himself for several years — and with distinction — to the care of souls and the instruction of future priests. But the combination of refined religious sensibilities and the attraction he felt for the unceasing round of adoring praise of God led him to the Benedictine life of the Abbey of Maredsous. Here in the silence of pure contemplation and deep prayer was formed the man wholly consumed by union with God and virile love of Christ, the unique Mediator; formed also the enlightened spiritual guide, the inspired preacher, the celebrated author of *Christ, the Life of the Soul.*

The profound Pauline concept of our divine sonship in the Person of Christ, who by His grace takes possession of the very essence and operation of our soul and becomes our life, willing and acting in us and through us, was expounded and recommended by Abbot Marmion to Christian souls of our day with that great profit of which all are aware.

With the praiseworthy intention of extending even more the circle of those already acquainted with the writings of the Irish monk, the American Benedictine Academy offers to readers in the United States this collection of the English Letters of Dom Columba Marmion, O.S.B. These writings have all the simple directness and cordial confidence of the familiar letter, the while retaining the elevated wisdom of a doctrine that has been deeply meditated and contemplated.

"I see more and more that the great point is to sink our personality and let Christ act in us and through us," he wrote to one correspondent. "The more I gaze at God, through the eyes of Jesus living in my heart, the more clearly I see that nothing can be so high, so divine, as as to remit oneself totally to God." To a niece eager to achieve perfection he put it, "Place your heart in that of Jesus and let Him will for you." — Clear expressions that are at the same time living and personal affirmations of the "For me to live is Christ" of St. Paul.

We are confident that this publication will prove most inspiring and fruitful, that it will assist the action of grace in clergy, religious, and lay people, thus directing souls to an ever more joyous and serene experience of that union with God which found its apostle and herald in Abbot Marmion.

Amleto G. Cardinal Cicognani

Rome, 24 June 1961

# CONTENTS

# ILLUSTRATIONS

# INTRODUCTION

The writer of these letters, Dom Columba Marmion, third Abbot of Maredsous of the Order of St. Benedict, is perhaps the greatest spiritual master of the past century. Among many other indications of the range of his influence, an American abbey bears his name, and a translation of his biography has just (in 1960) appeared in Japanese — not to mention the extraordinary proliferation of his works in more than twelve languages, European and Oriental, during the last forty years.

The great and profound good he has wrought in souls throughout the world has convinced many of his readers that he must have been a saint. But of course this title cannot technically be conferred on anyone without official or "canonical" investigation. The first steps in this process were undertaken in 1957 by the episcopal curia of Namur, Belgium, the diocese in whose territory Dom Marmion lived and died.

Before initiating this official process it was necessary to assemble all extant writings of the "servant of God" and submit them to the diocesan tribunal. This was the occasion for gathering together a veritable treasure, a collection of 1,700 letters, of which several hundred had been completely unknown. Among these letters over three hundred were written in English.

Letters are the most sincere and least studied expressions of the soul, and this is especially true of familiar letters, among which should be included letters of spiritual direction. When there is real friendship and *rapport* between the letter-writers, neither correspondent attempts to dissimulate his true self; he says what he is doing, what he is thinking, and what he feels. Dom Marmion was already well known through his vast personal influence and vast responsibilities, but it has remained for those who had not known him in life to verify the recollections of those who had. Those who knew him could see that he lived what he believed, what he taught. For those who did not know him, these letters will reveal better than anything else the degree to which his soul was penetrated with his teaching and how much it inspired his life.

Son of an Irish father and a French mother, Joseph Marmion was born in Dublin on April 1, 1858, with the most Christian blood of the Western world in his veins. Before he was seventeen he entered Holy Cross Seminary at Clonliffe, there to study philosophy and to begin theology by way of preparing for the priesthood. He pursued and finished his theology brilliantly at the Irish College in Rome (1879–81), where he was ordained priest.

After several years of pastoral work and seminary teaching in Ireland, he answered a call to the monastic life which he had felt strongly during his visits to the Benedictine abbey of Monte Cassino in Italy and to the abbey of Maredsous in Belgium. It was to Maredsous that in 1886 he came to ask for the habit of the "monks of the West." There he pronounced his religious vows on February 10, 1888.

His contemplative soul had found a favorable climate for its development. His professors at the Propaganda (whose classes the Irish College students attended) had given him a solid basis of classical theology. In the regular life of monastic silence marked by the canonical hours, he was to elaborate this material into a personal doctrine by his prayer and his life. Soon, however, various invitations to preach came his way, and these became more numerous as the years went by, stimulating him to build up a living synthesis that could be imparted to others.

It was at Louvain especially that these claims became more pressing; there, close to the Catholic University, the Maredsous community had founded in 1899 an abbey of which Dom Columba was one of the pioneer members. For ten years he was prior, and professor of theology to the young monks, as well as being responsible for their spiritual formation. He received many invitations from Belgium, England, Ireland, and France to preach retreats to seminarians, diocesan priests, religious, both men and women, of different congregations. He devoted to this work (to which he felt himself called more than to any other) all the time that his vow of obedience and his other monastic responsibilities allowed. It was at this time that he gained the confidence and friendship of the illustrious Désiré Cardinal Mercier, who had chosen him as his confessor, an example that was followed by many priests and professors of the university city. His outstanding qualities were soon to be given official recognition by his brethren of Maredsous.

This was seen when in September, 1909, Dom Hildebrand de Hemptinne resigned the abbacy of Maredsous to devote himself wholly to his duties as abbot-primate, and the monks of the abbey elected Dom Columba, prior of Louvain, to succeed him. From that moment he assumed the place and the role of Christ in a large community of monks, first and foremost as director of souls, then as administrator of a complete monastery with its different departments, each having its various tasks and obligations. He himself admitted to being at times "overwhelmed." And again, the years of his abbacy included the First World War (1914–18), a particularly anxious and difficult time. He was forced to seek a refuge in Ireland for the younger members of his community, and himself to stay there for nearly two years, far from his beloved abbey. For more than four years Belgium was occupied by an enemy that became more exacting as defeat drew near. And this separation of his flock into two parts was to have lasting consequences.

During the war, as throughout his priestly life, he never lessened his retreat work; this at one and the same time prevented him from being wholly immersed in material cares and kept him in that spiritual atmosphere where he felt truly at home. No one could seriously believe that he would have done better to confine his burning apostolic zeal strictly to the limits of his monastery.

He was to survive the war by only a few years. The Armistice was signed on 11 November, 1918, and the abbot of Maredsous died on January 30, 1923. He was not quite sixty-five, but his life had been a full one.

It is of the nature of great souls to be aware of the needs and aspirations of their time. For a writer or for an orator this is the secret of his influence and of his success. We should not be mistaken in describing Dom Marmion's time as one of Catholic renewal in search of "authenticity." It has been said, and with some justification, that the spirituality in vogue before he began preaching was one of *waiting for Christ*. That is to say, Christians had to be made aware of their membership in Christ, of the reality of their divine adoption by Christ, and of the exacting moral claim that Christ makes on them. Their souls had to be aroused to the echoes of the "mysteries" of Christ. The risen Christ had to be shown them, Christ still alive in the Church, a truth which St. Paul and St. John had already proclaimed, but which had so strangely been forgotten. Abbot Marmion adopted the teaching of this great doctrine, putting his hearers and his correspondents in direct contact with Sacred Scripture. He drew also on the liturgy with its revelation of Christ, who was at the heart of all his teaching. "It is only passions which make oratory convincing," said La Rochefoucauld; why not the love of Christ? And in this is the source of Dom Marmion's influence. He could have written books and built up a synthesis in the calm of a monastic cell; as it happened, however, circumstances demanded of him a great number of spiritual conferences, which led him to work out and assemble the elements of his spiritual synthesis.

Dom Marmion did his work by the spoken rather than by the written word. The strength of his convictions, the liveliness of his faith, the warmth of this speech struck all who heard him. Whether he spoke in French, which he learned when young, or in English, his mother tongue, he spoke with the temperament of an Irishman, with his sensitiveness, his good nature, and his sense of humor. One was compelled to listen to him, and he moved his hearers. He spoke "from his overflowing heart." The only writing he did in advance was by way of plans, sketches, outlines. Such notes will help the editors of his books, even though they use as their chief sources the work of those monks and nuns who faithfully recorded his words. For it was soon noticed at Maredsous that his teaching was so striking by its freshness and its depth that it deserved to be recorded and published.

This was the genesis of the now-classic *Christ, the Life of the Soul* (1918), *Christ in His Mysteries* (1919), *Christ, the Ideal of the Monk* (1922), *Sponsa Verbi* (1923), and, long after the author's death but based on original manuscripts, *Christ, the Ideal of the Priest* (1951).

From the copious surviving correspondence, a small number of his letters has already been published *in extenso*, in the biography of Abbot Marmion by Raymond Thibaut, O.S.B. Moreover, a fairly extensive anthology of the best spiritual passages of the letters known at that time was published in French in 1933: *Union with God, According to the Letters of Direction of Dom Marmion.* Soon afterward this was translated into English (1934). But in this work, which we owe also to Dom Thibaut, the extracts from the letters are skillfully worked into a systematic exposition of his spirituality. (It is noteworthy that the English translation of these two books benefited from the use of the original text of the English letters.)

To complement these well-known publications there is now need of something further. Our times have a taste for original documents, presented as they come from the pen and the heart of their author, and with the least possible textual editing. It is this that we have endeavored to do here: to reveal an original personality in the setting of his daily life, allowing him to speak in his own words to his intimate friends. And so we offer, in all their fresh spontaneity and their living background, the letters *written in English* first by Father Joseph Marmion, then by the monk and abbot, Columba Marmion. It is interesting to note that this is the first time original writings of Dom Marmion in the English language have been published. As will be seen, these letters are arranged in chronological order covering the whole of his priestly and monastic life.

It is still too soon to be able to prepare a complete and scholarly edition of the letters. Nevertheless, of all the letters judged suitable for publication we have endeavored to give the whole text; and it is with regret that we have had, here and there, for reasons of discretion, to make a few omissions, especially in certain series of letters where the preservation of the anonymity of the correspondents has been insisted upon. We are sure that the reader will understand this and accept it. We can state that the passages omitted are insignificant or too personal for publication. The text of the letters is always given according to the autographs, except in a few instances where the originals have been lost. The dates in brackets have been conjectured from events mentioned in the letters, for Abbot Marmion often forgot to give the complete date.

All the letters to the same correspondent are grouped in chronological order and bear a number in roman numerals. The different groups of letters follow one another, as far as possible, in the same chronological order, but with some unavoidable overlapping in the time sequence.

A great many spiritual letters are included in this collection. In them is to be found the most faithful reflection of his contemplative soul, of his loving heart. As with the Epistles of St. Paul (the main source of his inspiration), they speak with authority in spite of his personal humility. We find also a clear understanding of a great mission, the art of arts, as says St. Gregory the Great — that of leading souls to God. But Dom Marmion has a clear road, he follows an unfailing light: Jesus Christ.

But in order to reveal a prominent feature of a personality which made such a notable impact on those who knew him — that is, his tender and deeply human heart — we have also reproduced here a number of familiar, simple, friendly letters. Even in his letters of direction, however, the great soul of Dom Marmion does not divorce friendship from direction, for direction is not for him merely the relation of a father to his spiritual child in which he is the only giver, but a true, authentic, and friendly exchange, one from which he himself expects to receive something, too. It is a dialogue, a joint enterprise.

We wish to thank Anne Schuyler-Lighthall who has given us diligent and indispensable help in the English wording of the introductions and notes, and also in the preparation of the text of the letters; as well as Mary Ellen Evans, who added some notes for American readers. Likewise we are indebted to Doms Cuthbert McCann, O.S.B., of Downside Abbey, and Martin Varley, O.S.B., of Douai Abbey for their useful advice.

Finally, we are happy to entrust the publication of this work to our dear brethren of the American Benedictine Academy, whom we thank most fraternally.

Gisbert Ghysens, O.S.B.<br>
Thomas Delforge, O.S.B.<br>
Editors

# THE ENGLISH LETTERS OF ABBOT MARMION

# I. TO ABBOT-BISHOP RUDESIND SALVADO

## TWO LETTERS

*Dom Rudesind Salvado, O.S.B., Abbot Nullius of New Norcia in Australia, and superior of a mission to the inhabitants of that country, had come to Rome in 1880 for the purpose of obtaining helpers for this mission. Joseph Moreau, a young Belgian student at the Propaganda College, had promised to join him later in Australia. On his return to Belgium after ordination in Rome, Father Moreau went to the Abbey of Maredsous to make his canonical novitiate before going on to New Norcia.*

*While in Rome Moreau had become friendly with Joseph Marmion, a seminarian at the Irish College. So, when Joseph Marmion passed through Belgium on his way home to Ireland in July, 1881, he went to see his friend at Maredsous. This was the first contact that the future Dom Columba Marmion had with the monastery to which Divine Providence had secretly destined him, and he felt strongly drawn to it. (Ironically, Father Moreau shortly afterward had to abandon his intention of going to Australia, and even of entering the Benedictine Order. As Abbot Placide Wolter observed to Father Marmion at the time, "You have a much stronger vocation than your friend.")[1]*

*Thus the first attraction of Joseph Marmion was to the monastic life, but to a monastic life with an apostolic character — an emphasis that marked his vocation and became stronger with time.*

*For several reasons, however, he had to spend five years in pastoral work in the archdiocese of Dublin before he could follow his vocation. When he finally entered Maredsous on November 23, 1886, he was no longer thinking of New Norcia, but came to Belgium to live the life of a simple monk.*

*It is impossible to find out exactly why this change had occurred*

---

[1] *See* M. M. Philipon, O.P., The Spiritual Doctrine of Dom Marmion, *p. 31.*

*in the orientation of his life between 1881 and 1886. The references
to his religious vocation in his first letter to Dr. Dwyer, his bishop
friend (see Section III), do not throw sufficient light on this important point in his soul's evolution.*

*These two letters to Dom Salvado are placed at the beginning of
this collection because the first is the earliest of all the letters of
Joseph Marmion which have been preserved.*[2]

I.

✠ Pax                    Irish College, Rome, April 29th 1881
Very Revd. and dear Father

This letter will doubtless surprise you, as by it I wish to
acquaint you with what I believe to be my vocation to your mission
of Western Australia. I am at present at the termination of my
theological course, was ordained Deacon on Holy Saturday, & hope
to receive priest-hood on Trinity Saturday. During my entire course,
— that is for about the last eight years — I have continually felt a
great attraction for the religious state, & have made various attempts,
although strongly opposed by the members of my family, to accomplish my desire, but never succeeded owing to the refusal of my
bishop, the Late Cardinal Cullen. Last August, on occasion of a
visit to Monte Cassino, I felt all my old desires revive, & on my
return to College my Confessor told me that, although he had been
confessor to the Irish College for over thirty years, he had never
advised anyone to join religion; yet he said that the marks of my
vocation were so evident that he felt himself bound to tell me that
he believed it was God's will I should join religion, & as he believed,
the Benedictine Order.

As my bishop[1] came to Rome a couple of months after this, I
opened my whole heart to him, & as he is a man of great sanctity
he told me, after a day's consideration, that, although I had enjoyed

[2] *See Raymond Thibaut, O.S.B., Abbot Columba Marmion, pp. 26 f., for further
details concerning the circumstances of these two letters.*
[1] Archbishop Edward McCabe (1816–85), Cardinal Paul Cullen's choice for his
auxiliary in 1877. He succeeded Cardinal Cullen as archbishop of Dublin in 1879,
and in 1882 — within the year of Father Marmion's ordination — was elevated to
the College of Cardinals. (MEE)

a free-place in his diocese for some years, he would not be an obstacle to my fulfilling God's will, but that as it was a matter of great importance he thought it more prudent that I should spend a year or so as a secular priest in Dublin; & then if my vocation continued, he promised me his blessing & permission to depart. I accepted his terms, & continued my studies, etc., as before.

Although I always felt a great desire for the religious state, yet I felt, at the same time, a kind of uneasiness, or scruple, about joining the Benedictines, as God has given me an intense desire to labour for the salvation of souls; & I always felt myself greatly moved when I heard or read about the thousands, for whom Jesus shed His Blood, dying without knowing Him. So when I read about your mission, I felt it was exactly what I was called to, because I could satisfy my desire of being a religious, & at the same time labour for the *most abandoned* souls, & under obedience. I spoke about the matter to F. Joseph Moreau; & became more convinced. I then consulted my confessor, & he told me that it was quite plain Providence had called me to that vocation; & gave me permission to write this letter to your Lordship.

I have, Very Revd. Father, laid my heart open to you as much as I could; & I will now tell you the difficulties I must meet in accomplishing my vocation, in order that, if you think it well to answer this letter, you may be able to advise me how to proceed. In the first place, my bishop has given me leave to join the Benedictines; but I did not say anything about your mission to him, as at the time I knew nothing about it, however I don't apprehend much difficulty in that respect. Secondly, since my father's death [2] my family is not in good circumstances; & I promised one of my brothers, who is studying for the medical profession that I would support all the expenses of his studies when I return, as my mother is old & depends entirely on the interest of some money which is in bank, & which I don't wish to be put to any other purpose than her support. However, I expect that during the year I will have to spend in Dublin after my return, that I will be able to save sufficient to fulfil my promise, as I don't intend living very extravagantly. These are the only difficulties I apprehend, except, of course, the affection of my mother,

[2] April 9, 1874.

5

brothers & sisters; which, however, I think with God's grace I can overcome, especially as I will not let them know of my resolution 'till the last moment.

Having said this much, I place my case in your hands, & recommend myself most earnestly to your prayers.

I am, My Lord,            Your most dutiful Child,

Joseph Aloysius Marmion EDM[3]

P.S. If Your Lordship wishes to write to me, please send your letter to F. Moreau, as our letters coming here are opened; & I would expose myself to the certain opposition of my superiors here, & the mind of my bishop would be influenced by them.

II.

Dundrum[1] June 7th 1882

My Lord Bishop

I received your kind & useful letter, to which I should have replied sooner, but for the following reason: For some time past, there has been question of appointing me private secretary to His Eminence Cardinal McCabe, & while the matter was doubtful, I put off writing to you expecting every day that the matter would be settled, & that I would be able to tell you, & receive from you some advice regarding the line of action which I should follow, in case I were appointed. I was written to by the V.G.[2] in reference to the appointment; but when the Cardinal returned from Rome, my parish-priest pressed him not to remove me yet, & so the matter stands.

As regards the mission of Nova Norcia, my intentions are fixed as ever, &, I may say, more so; for my year's experience of a secular priest's life — though no doubt very useful to me — has given me an intense desire for the [cloistered] religious life; not that I may have

---

[3] The earliest letters of Father Marmion are signed this way. Joseph was his baptismal name; Aloysius seems to have been the patron chosen at Confirmation. The initials "EDM" signify "Enfant de Marie" (Child of Mary). This French expression is still used in certain circles in England and Ireland.

[1] Near Dublin. Father Marmion was appointed curate (assistant pastor) there in September, 1881.

[2] Vicar general of Dublin.

6

less work, but that I may work under obedience & be removed from the influence of the world, which unfortunately has great charm for me. Therefore I will just tell your Lordship most candidly — & *coram Deo*[3] — my position. I desire most ardently to go with you, & am ready to sacrifice everything most dear to me in order to go. My difficulties are just these. I am educating my brother for the medical profession, & I am in debt (about £70); & I would not like to leave my present position (which is lucrative about £200 a year) till my debts are paid. Also the Cardinal may make some difficulty; & I do not wish to speak of the matter to him till I am out of difficulties, lest he might place me in some position in which I might not be able to get out of my difficulties. I say all this subject to your approval, & will do exactly what you advise, no matter how contrary it may seem to my own views.

I remain                                    Your obedient child,
                                            Joseph A. Marmion EDM


## II. TO DR. KIRBY, RECTOR
## OF THE IRISH COLLEGE[1]

[Dublin] 2 Black Hall St.[2] August 10, 1881
My dear and most Reverend Father,
     Following the doctor's advice, I delayed on my way home, in order that on my return I might be able to commence work with renewed vigour. A most favourable opportunity presented itself; for a young friend of mine,[3] who is a novice in the beautiful Monastery of Maredsous, invited me to spend a few days with him in his beautiful mountain home.[4] I gladly availed myself of the invitation; and while recruiting my strength, I also made a beautiful retreat

----

[3] "In the presence of God."
[1] Dr. Kirby, Bishop of Lita and rector of the Irish College in Rome for 45 years, had ordained Joseph Marmion in the College chapel on June 16 of that same year.
[2] House where his mother lived in Dublin.
[3] Joseph Moreau, to whom an allusion is made in the first letter to Dom Salvado.
[4] Father Marmion came to Maredsous at the end of July.

7

of some days; hence my tardy arrival, and delay in answering your letter. Though late, I now, with all my heart, thank you, my dear Father, for your great kindness in thinking of me, and obtaining for me the papal faculties. I will always remember your fatherly kindness to me, who am — before God I say it — the most unworthy of your children.

As yet I have received no appointment. My work, for the few days I have been at home, has consisted in saying Mass for some priests who were obliged to take some rest on account of ill-health. However, I will not waste my time; but will study my moral theology, and administration of sacraments, etc. Even for the short time I have been in Ireland, I find the great utility of the little promise I made through your hands to the Madonna, as I have been pressed, and almost forcibly constrained, to partake of drink by *seeming* friends, on many occasions; but the promise I made to my dear Mother had always been such a protection to me that I found no difficulty on steadily refusing that for which my conscience would afterwards reproach me.

When I have been appointed, I will again write and tell you all about my new position; and I feel sure you will afford me advice on any points I may find difficulty in.

Till then, I remain, my dear Father,

Your affectionate child in J.C.
Joseph A. Marmion, EDM.

## III.  TO A BISHOP FRIEND

TWENTY LETTERS

*Born the same year as Joseph Marmion, in 1858, of an Irish family, but in Australia, Vincent Dwyer received his elementary and higher education in that country. As he had heard the divine call to the priesthood, he came to Europe for his ecclesiastical studies, first at Clonliffe Seminary (Dublin), then at the Irish College in Rome. It was in these two establishments that he met and became a close friend of Joseph Marmion, who was just one class ahead of him. Upon his ordination for the diocese of Maitland on March 4, 1882, in Rome, he returned to Australia, where he carried on a most varied and fruitful ministry more especially directed toward Catholic education. Appointed Coadjutor of Maitland in 1897, he was consecrated on June 6, the first native-born Australian to become a bishop. His solicitude to improve elementary education earned him the title of "The Children's Bishop."*

*The following is what the* Catholic Press *of Sydney wrote about him the day after his death on April 2, 1931:*

> *Personally, the deceased prelate was a man of commanding presence and splendid physique, of marked force of character and executive skill, and his administration in every office entrusted to him was characterised by energy, wisdom and discretion. In his private life he was wholly unselfish, kind and considerate to all with whom he was associated, and the charity of which many of his friends knew so little, because of its unostentatious nature, was almost boundless. He lived for his Church and his people. His sincerity of purpose, which was always so apparent, was evidenced in every action of his splendid life, and it endeared him to all.*

*The friendship which united the two "men of God" from 1881 was sincere and profound. Here is what Abbot Marmion wrote in a letter dated December 15, 1919: "My greatest friend perhaps in this world, — we were brought up together, — is Dr. P. V. Dwyer, Bishop of Maitland." And this Dr. Dwyer, for his part, wrote in 1927 a "Tribute of a Friend," the text of which, published here for the first time, will undoubtedly help to make better known the personalities of both correspondents.*

*My memory of the late Abbot Marmion goes back forty-six years to the days when we were both beginning our theological studies. It was in Holy Cross College, Clonliffe, Dublin, that we had the privilege of entering that* via sacra *which leads to God's holy Altar. The "Clonliffe" of those days housed about eighty students. It was under the direct personal patronage of the first Irish Cardinal, Paul Cullen, and had for rector Dr. Michael Verdon, afterwards first rector of our Australian College of Manly, and more recently Bishop of Dunedin in the Dominion*

9

*of New Zealand, and for vice-rector Father B. Fitzpatrick, now Vicar-General of Dublin. The small sheepfold was well cared for, and had the benefit of the Cardinal's secretary, Dr. Tyman, for professor of Dogmatic Theology and S. Scripture, and of the saintly Vincentian Fr. John Gowan, as spiritual director. To me, coming, as I did* de finibus terrae,[1] *from far-off Australia, such surroundings appealed with uncommon force; and the memory of them now often evokes the sentiment expressed in the words of the Psalmist*: funes ceciderunt mihi in praeclaris.[2]

*It was in such circumstances that Joseph Marmion and I first came to move in the same little sphere, and, as the sequel showed, to begin a friendship that was to last for life. Marmion had a lively and cheerful manner and good ability, but his chief characteristic was piety. An institution in the College encouraged by the superiors was known as "dogmatizing." It meant the custom of two students walking together at recreation and rehearsing to each other the portion of dogmatic theology which was the subject of the professor's next lecture. It was carried on in Latin, the language of the class-book and of the professor lecturing, as well as of the student repeating or replying to questions. Marmion and myself by some kind of affinity came to be the constant factors of one of these walking "binomials"; and every school morning found us during early recreation combining useful talking with healthful exercise and agreeable companionship. Our companionship was continued not only in our studies but also in the results as set forth in the annual prize list; and this lasted until in 1880 my friend went to Rome with Dr. Verdon who had just been appointed to the governing staff of the* Collegio Irlandese.

*Many were the points of difference in our characters, most of them, I think telling to the advantage of Marmion; but one occurs to me which often afforded to us and our companions an occasion of cheerful banter and harmless fun. It was a tendency to weakness in spelling English. I believe that even in later years, during residence in Belgium this weakness was always ready to show itself; and the learned author of treatises in French and lecturer of retreats to priests and others in that language would fail in the spelling of some simple English word. I distinctly remember the amusement caused by his announcement in a letter from Rome that he was to be ordained deakon.*

*I had the pleasure of following my friend to the Eternal City and of joining with him in study in the Irish College for a few months and then*

---

[1] From the ends of the earth.
[2] "The lines are fallen unto me in goodly places" (Ps. 15:6).

*of assisting at his ordination to the priesthood by the venerable Rector, Monsignor Kirby, who had shortly before been honoured by Pope Leo XIII, his former schoolmate, by being raised to the episcopate. It was a day of much happiness for me when I had the privilege of assisting in the capacity of "Ceremoniere" at the ordination in the College Capella, and of serving Father Marmion's first Mass.*

*The newly ordained priest soon left Rome for his missionary work in Dublin; and I think his first appointment was to a curacy in Dundrum, Co. Dublin.*

*In 1882, after ordination in Rome, I returned to my southern home in Australia; and thus our paths in life were as widely separated as the* orbis terrae *permits. Different too were the ways in which we were to use the sacred science studied together in College, and yet the difference was rather one of degree than of kind. It was a sincere pleasure to me to see the fruits of his study and living piety set out in the beautiful treatises on the spiritual life which the late Abbot has left as an enduring monument of a life of religious activity.*

*Since 1882 I had the pleasure of making two visits to Maredsous. On the first occasion, in 1896, another dear friend and College companion of ours in "Clonliffe" days, Monsignore Dunne, V.G. of Dublin and myself were privileged to enjoy a few days of pleasant companionship with Dom Columba who was then Master of Novices in Maredsous.*[3] *The second visit was made in 1914, just on the eve of the war; and my travelling companion — another Australian Bishop — and myself were the guests of Abbot Marmion during a brief but very pleasant stay in his beautiful monastery.*

*The last letter I received from the late Abbot came just two years ago. It shows him the same kind and constant friend I had known and loved for nearly fifty years. I may therefore be pardoned for setting down these few facts, of some interest to his friends, of very great interest to me, and, in doing so, of renewing towards his memory the strong affection I entertained towards his person.*

*The friendship of Christians has the advantage of looking forward to the future life for its completion and perfection. The death of Abbot Marmion brings no anxiety to us regarding his eternal happiness. It brings to his many friends the consolation of having a friend at Court, and to one of them the confidence that, it now being well with him, he will remember his fellow prisoner of the days that are gone.*

[3] A slight mistake: he was at that time assistant master of novices.

II

*In 1957, twenty-six autographed unpublished letters which the late Bishop had kept arrived from the Bishop's house in Maitland. Unfortunately they are in very poor condition: nine of them, which are only in pieces, are practically worthless; of the other seventeen, six are more or less mutilated. We are publishing here all that, in these letters, might prove of some interest to a better understanding of Abbot Marmion. For in them one sees above all a biographical document clearly revealing (even in the writing), the evolution of a character. Most spontaneous, familiar, written with great frankness and lack of restraint, these letters, chiefly the earlier ones, show an exuberant good humor that is typically Irish. One may say concerning them what the Editor of the* Spiritual Letters of Dom John Chapman *said of his subject: "Like St. Teresa or Blessed Thomas More, to both of whom he had a great devotion, Abbot Chapman thought that a man's religion was likely to be all the more sincere if he was able to make jokes about it. . . . To argue from these that the writer is dealing with serious matters in a flippant way, would be to do him a great injustice."* [4]

*All this could be applied equally well to Abbot Marmion's other letters.*

*Whenever it was possible to do so, we have attempted to fill in the above-mentioned gaps; this was the case when only the ends of the lines were missing: the conjectures were then highly probable.* [5] *We have also corrected the spelling mistakes — the author's besetting sin, according to the recipient himself.*

I.

Sacred Heart Convent. Dundrum, Co. Dublin.[1] [1881]
Dear Revd. Junk [2]
[. . .] you. I have shared your happiness & felt just as if it were my

[4] London, Sheed and Ward, 1935, p. viii.

[5] In this difficult task we have been greatly helped by Dom Cuthbert McCann, monk of Downside Abbey, to whom we must express our gratitude.

[1] The first and last pages are mutilated. Father Marmion had been assistant pastor at Dundrum since September of 1881. His friend Dwyer had been ordained subdeacon in Rome, where Father Marmion had been with him until June of that year.

[2] Nickname which Father Marmion usually gave his friend and which apparently applied also to his Australian compatriots.

own. I also offered the H. Sacrifice for you etc. I dined last evening with my fellow curate in Stillorgan. I met James there. He told me he had given you permission to remain another year in Rome & will have you ordained priest. [. . .]

I find it much easier to live *right* on the Mission than I thought. Indeed I find it easier to serve God than I even did in College. [. . .]

I prefer the hearing of confessions to any other duty. I never found any difficulty as yet although I have a great many penitents, even from other parishes & from Dublin. I believe that very much less "geny" is required than is generally thought; *great* kindness & patience are everything & the principle *sacramenta propter homines (et mulieres)*[3]: of course you must know that if a man steals a pound he must restore it, & that murder, drunkenness etc. are sometimes mortal sins; beyond this, you very seldom get a "casus." . . .

I am chaplain & confessor to the criminal Lunatic Asylum. I found it a little difficult at first but at present find no difficulty. I have got quite accustomed to listening to the details of the most horrible murders as many there are committed for that crime & it is strange to see how these poor fellows went from bad to worse; true, the devil so got possession of them that they were fit for anything & yet I assure you many of them are at present leading lives of real *perfection*, being for months without committing a deliberate venial sin. *Misericordias Dni cantabo in aeternum.*[4]

I say Mass every morning at the convent of the Sisters of the S. Heart.[5] The Rd. Mother is a woman of great sanctity & *common sense.* She has been Superioress in Poland, Italy & France. She comes to speak to me almost every morning & is *very* kind to me. When I was sick she sent me a dozen of rare spanish wine & sends the carriage for me, although I never asked her, & my predecessor often *demanded* it but never succeeded in getting it. However *Satis de to "Ego."* [6]

I met some Junks lately, they are very nice. The Hon. Dr. Mullen who was chief medical practitioner in Brisbane is a great friend of

[3] "The sacraments are for men (and for women)."
[4] "The mercies of the Lord I will sing forever" (Ps. 88:1).
[5] Mount Anville.
[6] "Enough said about me."

mine. He was a student for eight years in the Irish College Rome & had all his theology. He was a contemporary of Dr. Moran, Dr. O'Mahoney etc. . . .

How are all *your* Junks? I often remember Kathleen at Mass & sometimes say a Mass for her perseverance. . . .

I often wish you were my fellow C.C.[7] I would be then *too* happy for I have *indeed* found that in your case "absence makes the heart grow fonder." *Ma queste cose non saranno mai; ci vedremo in celo.*[8]

My confessor does not approve of my changing my state at all.[9] He says I am doing much good as a secular, & would not be following God's wishes by changing. *Come si fa?*[10], I am not changed in my inclinations. I sigh for quiet & absence of responsibility. *Cosa ne dici tu?*[11]

I must now wind up. This is a very foolish scribble, but I just wrote as I would speak to you. . . .

With affectionate regards to Mgr. D. Verdon, & the Camerata especially — I can't spell his name — to the fat bob, & Pat, Jim. I remain your affectionate friend in J.C.

Joseph A. Marmion E.D.M.

P.S. I am very anxious to get permission to give the papal benediction to give the nuns of Mount Anville on the 8th December. Could you get it for me? Perhaps O'Hanan would do me this favour. Let me have a line when you can & don't be ordained without letting me know the date, as I will say Mass for you.

II.

Dundrum, Feb. 28. 1882.[1]

Dear Rev. Junk

I got your letter this morning and though I have considerably more on hand than I can accomplish they must go to the wall for this time in order that you may have a line.

---

[7] Catholic curate (assistant pastor).
[8] "But that will never happen. We shall see each other in Heaven."
[9] I.e., by becoming a monk.
[10] "How can that be?"
[11] "What do you say about it?"
[1] Written several days before the ordination of his friend.

With all my heart I congratulate you on the happiness which is before you next Saturday and I will unite with you in thanking the good God for bestowing this the greatest mark of His love which He can give. The more I see of the life of a priest the more I love it & become every day more convinced that *Servire Deo regnare est.*[2] Only those who try to do their little best for love of that Sacred victim whom they daily immolate can know how God repays the priest for the slight sacrifice he makes in consecrating to Him all his joys & his labours. It is true that you will often find the old Adam showing his head & feel how unworthy you are of all the favours you receive, but nevertheless I am of the opinion that no one feels so well as the priest that God is all-merciful & is content so long as we *try* to please Him & do not *deliberately* fail in our duty. I say then *Prospere procede et regna.*[3] I will offer Holy Sacrifice for you on the day of your great oblation. I will try to assist you before the tabernacle as much as I can.

Oh, I am more convinced now than ever that a student can't set too high a standard of holiness for himself in College; and *take my word for it*, for I have seen it that those students who are considered "good," but don't go in for an unreserved service of God, would shudder if they knew what they would be, after about *one year* on the mission. The life of a priest is very much more lonely than we anticipate. I have often been for days without opening my lips to a mortal. This may seem very strange but it is true, & if we can't find our pleasure before *Gesu sacramentato*, we will, inevitably, go for consolation into society & then . . .[4] This may seem at variance with what I said to you some time ago about visiting, but it is not. It is quite a different thing to dine out occasionally with a *good intention* and to go into society because one can't bear to be alone.

*Eccomi:*[5] four pages given to a sermon! I am so accustomed to lecturing every one now that I had quite forgotten myself. You want to know how I am. Well, even since my last letter I had a partial relapse of my attack, but now D.G.[6] it is wholly & finally removed

[2] "To serve God is to reign." Postcommunion of the Mass for Peace.
[3] "Proceed prosperously, and reign." Psalm 44:5.
[4] Sentence left unfinished.
[5] And there I am.
[6] *Deo gratias*, "Thanks be to God." Often abbreviated as "D.G."

15

together with its effects & causes, & I am at present enjoying such health as I never had before, as you will guess when I tell you what my duties are at present.

I say Mass in Mt. Anville convent every morning at 7.10 and consequently rise at 5.45 every morning to prepare. I then do my *chronic* sick-calls & then go home for about an hour. Then visit the poor schools in which I give instructions for half an hour twice a week. I instruct the young ladies in Mt. Anville once a week & besides in Lent preach to them on the Passion every Friday. I preach twice *every* Sunday and three times every second Sunday, & on Wednesdays in Lent. Besides, I am spiritual director to the Ladies' Association of [. . .] of which I have the entire care, & have to preach to them, keep their accounts, settle their disputes! etc. I am also spiritual director to the St. Vincent de Paul society which meets once a week; chaplain to the Lunatic Asylum & finally Fag-in-general to anyone who wants me for baptisms etc. So you see I haven't much time to be idle. One great advantage of having so much to do is that it hasn't left the *ghost* of a scruple in my conscience, & I sometimes wonder how I could have been so foolish, *cosi vanno le cose mie.*[7]

I am delighted to see that Jem has cottoned so much to Rome. I knew it would exactly suit him & I expect he will pray for me as I flatter myself that my advice had something to do with his going; tell him that he is never forgotten in my prayers, & that whenever I have a spare Mass — which is very seldom, as I always have more intentions than I can satisfy, as you will *know* — he & some others, not to be mentioned, get the benefit.

I was delighted to get the "telegraph." I would not have believed it unless I had seen it a realized fact. I fear he is sadly degenerate. I expect to hear soon that he has taken shares in some railway Co.! it's wonderfully like him. Do you know I am very fond of him. I felt a real pleasure in looking at his holy old phis again. How is the "Boss?"[8] I see he got a bequest lately for the college. I wish some old maid would die & make me her heir, as I am in debt. I was thinking of giving a dose to an old one out here who likes me very much; only I fear she hasn't made the will yet, & that would spoil all.

[7] That's how things are with me.
[8] Rector of the Irish College in Rome.

I met [. . .] some time ago, he is expecting to be made a fellow of the new university, & the lads are persuading him it is a fact. It is more likely they will make him a butler in the new university hotel . . . , however, *chi lo sa?*[9] I won't venture on a new sheet as I have to instruct a large congregation of antiquated virginity this evening. I haven't put my thoughts together yet, so *basta.*[10]

I have just read that poor Tom Reilly of Maynooth is no more. R.I.P. Poor fellow, he is gone *straight* to Heaven. Would I were with him! However, we must not forget him as it is hard to be so spotless as to satisfy the envy of the All Holy.

Your affectionate friend in J.C.<br>Joseph A. Marmion, EDM.

*Salva la convenienza delle cose;*[11] this letter is terribly egotistical.

III.

Holy ✠ Seminary,[1] April 1883

My dear Vincy

I am sure you have thought many hard things of me lately; but I can assure you that my silence is in no way to be attributed to forgetfulness, as I often think of you, & I can say in truth that you are one of the very few upon whom I look as dear & sincere friends. I think with the exception of my mother, there are not more than four upon earth for whom I entertain a real affection, & you are one of the four & not the least; so you must not look upon my silence as a sign of change.

The reasons for my delay were chiefly these: my brother got suddenly ill & received the last sacs; went over in a hurry & stopped with him till he was able to swallow the H. Viaticum, & then administered It. He remained a long time at death's door. Every day I expected would be his last, & so, I was constantly with him except when at class; & I had to take the hours of the night when I should

---

[9] Who knows?

[10] That is enough.

[11] To call a thing by its name.

[1] In October, 1882, Father Marmion was appointed professor at Holy Cross Seminary at Clonliffe, near Dublin, where he had studied his philosophy.

be in bed for study & prayer. He is now out of all danger. Another reason of my silence was that I did not wish to send a *short* letter to you, & I would not have been able to send more than a page at most if I had written before; so now Vincy, you must forgive me and believe that I am unchanged. *De me ipso.*[2] I am still in Alma Mater, & never knew what real happiness was before. I have given up the world entirely, & am trying to live "all for Jesus." It appears when I say Mass, or kneel before Our Lord at Benediction, that He says to me "Joseph, lovest thou Me more than these?"; & I feel that the priest should be able to say from his heart "Lord, Thou knowest that I love Thee." And so I have cut entirely with the world: *omnia arbitrans ut stercora ut Xtum lucrifaciam.*[3] I am teaching Metaphysics, Greek & French, & am making some progress *considering* the difficulties under which I have been labouring. It is not impossible that you will see me in Maitland before many years: *chi sa?*[4] The life here is very happy. I pull splendidly with the others, & we are always in good humour. Dr. McGrath[5] sometimes gives lectures for our common good on temperance & politics, but they have not induced me to change my evil habit of taking wine at dinner. Oh, how I would wish you were here, for although our characters are entirely different, I never found anyone to whom I could speak with the certainty of being understood as to you! . . .

We had a great *miracle* here during the winter. F. Sam Dunnigan was driving through Dublin during the intense cold of the winter. He suddenly felt some strange feeling about his hand, & on taking off his glove, discovered that his index finger had disappeared. He searched fruitlessly in his pockets, the car, etc., & at last found the missing member in his glove. He said an aspiration, & it was miraculously joined to the stump again. *Sic ipse.*[6] He firmly believes this, & so do many priests in Dublin. It is admitted that he raised a man to life in order to give him the last *sacs.* I guess your country can't show anything to beat that!

[2] "Speaking of myself," or, "As for me."
[3] "Counting all as dung, that I may gain Christ" (Phil. 3:8).
[4] "Who knows?"
[5] President of Holy Cross College ("Clonliffe").
[6] "Thus he said."

Give my respectful regards to Dr. Murray [7]; also to your Mother, Father, etc., & believe, my dear Vincy, ever your sincere & affectionate friend in J.C.

Joseph Aloysius Marmion
goose
E.D.M.

IV.

Holy ✠ Seminary [August? 1883?]

My dear Vincy,

Although I am writing out of my turn you must not be amazed. I know you will be glad to get a line from the land of invincible, [. . .].[1] *Art. II. Quid dicendum de amicis Marmonii et Junkii? Art. III. Quid dicendum de Ipso Yunko et omnibus ad eum pertinentibus? Ad Ium. Respondeo dicendum:*[2] — I find myself exactly in the same position as when I wrote last. My health continues good; spirits excellent; & I like my *present* mode of life very much — for the *present*. Our year is just over. It will, I expect [. . .].

[. . .] a large dog: he turns out to be no good, but he amuses me by his stupidity. I should get something of the kind when he & you left. I bring him out daily for a walk through the grounds; he is an extraordinary animal; he has got diabetes, & when I bring him down to the river he occupies himself for over half an hour pumping water in & out of himself; most extraordinary brute! (I had written *bruit* but there ain't any noise).

I am glad the year is over. I intend, D.V., commencing the next year with great fervour. My Mother has been very ill, but is able to be up now. . . .

You may expect to see me soon if I live, as I intend going out to Australia; but no one knows this but yourself, so *serva sigillum, satis de Marmonio.*[3]

---

[7] Bishop of Maitland.

[1] A quarter of the first page is torn off.

[2] "Art. II. What should we say about the friends of Marmion and of Junk? Art III. What can be said of Junk himself, and all that concerns him? As to the first point, I reply . . ." Stereotyped expressions from the medieval Scholastics.

[3] "Keep the secret. And that is enough about Marmion."

*Art. II. R. dicendum . . .*

The papal circular is causing great commotion in ecclesiastical circles. I hear a great deal of wild — & to me disgusting talk — from priests about papal interference & things appear in the papers over priests' names which if the animal with tall ears could write would certainly be attributed to him. *Povero J. Christo, Povero Chiesa! Povero papa* what will he do? [4] He is utterly unprovided with the assistance of the [. . .] we must only pity him, meantime it would be good to make a subscription to buy fodder for some of these poor animals as if they found themselves before a well filled manger they might stop braying. That last remark of mine looks uncharitable, & I have a kind of scruple about it, but I don't like to tear this sheet; don't show it about. . . .

*Art. III. De Junko ipso. Dicendum.*[5] I hear you are some kind of a school functionary. *Cave, iterum dico, Cave.*[6] If you find yourself becoming anxious about your appearance etc. *Cave* . . . But leaving jokes aside, I will pray for you, because I consider that kind of work distracting, & not free from danger for a young priest. I am delighted, my dear Vincy, to see that you are getting on so well, & I feel sure that you will do great things yet for the glory of God & the salvation of souls. *Ma chi va piano va sano.*[7] Distrust your own lights, & keep close to obedience, & all will go well. Q.E.D.

Your affectionate brother in J.C.
Joseph A. Marmion E. D. M.

v.[1]

Holy ✠ Seminary April 28 1884

Dear Rd. Junk,

I ought to have written to you before this, but the fact is my heart was too heavy [2]; I know that dull letters would serve no useful purpose in your regard [. . .].

---

[4] "Poor Jesus Christ! poor Church! poor Pope!"
[5] "Concerning Junk himself, one should say . . .".
[6] "Take care, I repeat, take care."
[7] Slow but sure.
[1] This letter is badly mutilated. About half of each page is missing.
[2] By reason of financial crisis afflicting his family.

20

[. . .] say a little prayer for me. This last business at home has been an obstacle to arrangements all but completed. *Fiat voluntas Dei*. I found this the hardest part to bear. I am awfully sorry you are not somewhere near. I have no one whom I can call a friend here. I *like* all immensely, but I take to very few. God knows best. Jerry will be soon home, D.G. I am glad to see you are keeping[. . .] will keep you in union with Him. I say this because I imagine — perhaps erroneously — that a life of continual action like yours is apt to make one fix his attention more upon the magnitude of the actions themselves than upon the motive. Remember the widow's mite "she cast in more than all the others." [3] I will never cease to pray for you that you may reap a rich harvest of merit, & advance every day in [. . .]

I am hearing each confession solely for this sake: that as Jesus shed His Blood for that soul, that I will take all the trouble I can with each; & when I give absolution, I humble myself as I think that I am holding the place of the King of Virgins &c. &c. Also, a favourite devotion of mine is to offer myself mentally at the Consecration of the Mass every morning in union with the S. Victim to God to suffer . . . for His glory.

I ain't got no more time for no more. Write soon & don't bore me with politics, I don't care a d—— about them; they are a humbug, except in so far as the glory of God may perhaps be advanced by one kind of government more than another. However the matter about Irish Bishops in Australia is, I admit, important; but if you & I were [. . .] aim in life to look after these matters; consequently they don't want me to spend my time in fruitless speculations about politics, & therefore I don't. Them is my sentiments on politics, and they are very profound. Q.E.D. Love to ✠ James. [4] Affect. regards to Da & Ma Connice etc. etc.

J. A. Marmion   E.D.M.

[3] Mark 12:41–44.
[4] The cross before the name indicates Bishop James Murray of Maitland.

## VI

Holy ✠ College, Clonliffe Nov. 1884

My dear Vincy,

Although I received no letter from you since my last to you, I will not let Xmas pass without sending you a line; especially as I imagine I shall receive one from you about that time.

I often think of you & sometimes amuse myself by thinking of all you must be doing out in the bush for Our Lord's glory. How "many lilies you are causing to bloom before Him, who will day & night send up before His throne the sweet fragrance of their love" (*justus germinabit sicut lilium, et florebit in aeternum ante Dominum*).[1] You may be sure I will not forget to assist you by my prayers in that great & glorious work; but as I often think that even the most fervent are liable to lose that fervour & union with God, which is the one source of grace *Ego sum vitis, vos palmites, qui manet in me, et ego in eo,* HIC *fert fructum multum quia sine me* NIHIL *potestis facere.*[2] I pray fervently that God may give you the grace to advance daily in personal holiness, in the same proportion as you increase your labours of zeal for souls. For this end I am sending you by this post a book of "meditations for priests," from which I imagine I have derived great fruit myself. Accept it as a Xmas present & a pledge of my unalterable friendship for you.

Having preached my sermon I shall now do what I ought to have commenced by doing, viz., I wish you a very happy Xmas & through you I wish the same to your Father, Mother, Sister etc. whom I still hope to have the pleasure of seeing at some future time.

As regards news. First myself. I am, as you see, still at Clonliffe & though my desire to enter religion is stronger than ever, the same pecuniary difficulties still remain so that I must defer my hope. My classes are all very successful: two out of three presented for examination have passed the B.A., viz., Hatton & Pat Malone; & in the greek class *all* passed but two out of a large class. One of our students

---

[1] "The just shall grow like the lily and flourish eternally in the Presence of the Lord" (Osee 14). Gradual of the Common of Abbots.

[2] "I am the Vine: you are the branches. He that abideth in Me, and I in him, the same beareth much fruit: for without Me you can do nothing" (John 15:5).

got an exhibition (£15) having taken honours in physics, English, French & Latin so that we have been congratulated as having been very successful. Still my heart is not in the work, although I study hard for conscience' sake. (One of my students at the B.A. exam got honours in Metaphysics & Ethics), yet I would rather have one hour in the confessional than a life-time of successful teaching; yet I daily repeat the words of Pope Clement XI *Domine volo quidquid vis; volo quia vis; volo quomodo vis; volo quamdiu vis.*[3] No jokes will come this time; I fear they have been all squose out of me by family troubles, & others which were no less severe. *Satis de me ipso.*[4]

All the professors here are well. McGrath has written a *"document"* about the philosophical paper set at the R. University Exam. which has created a great *furore.* He is now looked upon as the great champion (potatoe) of Xtian philosophy in these parts. You have doubtless seen this "document" in the *Ecc. Record* for November. . . .

Wishing you every grace & joy of this holy time,
I remain your affectionate friend in J.C.

Joseph A. Marmion E.D.M.

P.S. Please present my respectful compliments to Dr. James[5] & wish him from me a Happy Xmas &c. Mr. Ed O'Reily has just asked me to remember him to you & to say he often thinks of you.

## VII.

✠ Pax                    Abbaye de St. Benoit, Maredsous,[1]
                          par St. Gérard, Belgium [1888?]

My dear Vincy,

Many thanks for the photo as also for the *Ordo* last year. The latter was much valued & appreciated here. I shall speak of the former later. The *Ordo* came during my novitiate. I think I asked

[3] "Oh Lord, I want all that you want; because you want it; the way you want it; and as long as you want it."

[4] "Enough about me."

[5] Bishop of Maitland.

[1] Father Marmion entered Maredsous on November 21, 1886, receiving the Irish name "Columba." His monastic profession took place on February 10, 1888, and this letter must have been written shortly after.

23

permission to write to you & was refused. In any case our faculties for letter-writing, usually limited, are almost suspended during novitiate. I won't waste any more time or paper on excuses. I will only say that my affection for you has undergone *no change*; & *no* day passes without a special prayer for you—according to promise—& the rosary every Saturday for the four.[2]

To begin from myself. I am convinced that I am where God wills me to be. I have found great peace, & am extremely happy: to use a euphemism, I wasn't success on the secular mission; & it is a singular mercy of God towards me that I am here.[3]

The monastery here is but a few years in existence. It is in its first fervour. It forms one of five monasteries which constitute the new Benedictine Congregation of Beuron. This Congregation was founded at the desire of Pius IX by two brothers—one of whom is our Abbot here. After suffering great trials, in consequence of the "May Laws,"[4] it seems to have received a very special blessing from God. We number now about 300 members, we have five Monasteries & four Abbots. I send you the photo of Maredsous in the background.

But you will ask me, what do you do? Well, we are up about $3\frac{1}{2}$ every morning. Matins commence at 4, & from that, till bedtime—about $8\frac{1}{2}$—in choir, in study, & in teaching & manual work. The chief object of our congregation is to carry out the S. Liturgy & the Chant of the Church with the greatest exactitude & splendour possible. We have therefore the conventual masses, masses of vigils & in fact everything prescribed. I had no idea that such riches & beauty were contained in the D. Office etc. How I wish you could spend a week here. I know you would be charmed.

I know almost nothing in the shape of news to tell you, as I very

[2] Four intimate friends.

[3] Here Dom Marmion in his humility disparages his service as a diocesan priest. In 1907 the archbishop of Dublin paid him this tribute, that he had fulfilled his functions as curate and professor in an exemplary manner and that he had received full recognition from his superiors for his outstanding zeal and genuine piety. The complete Latin text is cited in Thibaut, *Abbot Columba Marmion*, p. 32 (English trans.).

[4] May (or Falk) Laws, repressive measures against the Church designed to liquidate Catholic opposition to Bismarck's *Kulturkampf*.

seldom hear from any-body. I will tell you what I know. Poor Tom Brady going to attend a sick-call at night fell off his horse, broke his arm, put out his eye, cracked his skull & died after a couple of days without ever recovering consciousness. R.I.P. In reading the last sentence I see it is calculated to make you laugh; it was not meant in that way: it's my genius. The photo you sent me was a *real pleasure.* . . .

Somebody told me that there was a young Junk at Clonliffe. Is it the little one who made his genuflection at the altar backwards? I have wandered away from the photo. You are looking well & fat; your head taking the shape of the mitre. You have something like a pectoral — only it's in the wrong place — cross, hanging out your vest. The "nigger" seems to have got a dash of whitewash. Pierce is a very respectable looking clergyman & J. Burn very "distingué" as they say in French. If you ever go to Tasmania, try & see the Dominican nuns M. Gabriel & Sr. Paul. I take a great interest in them. They suffered terribly in Ireland, & I came in for my share on their account.

What a stupid letter; but I know you didn't want a sermon, & I have no news. If ever you come to Europe, pass this way; it's only a few hours by train from Antwerp. You would be charmed I know, & we could ramble across the hills & talk over old times. Present my most kind regards to Dr. James, Dr. Verdon, F. Hand. My affectionate regards to your father and family.

Your affectionate brother in J.C.<br>Dom Columba O.S.B.

VIII.

✠ Pax                           Abbaye de Maredsous,
                                par St. Gérard, March 19, 1890.
My dear Vincy,

I just have a few minutes leisure to-day, & so I shall treat myself to the pleasure of a little chat with you. I suspect you will say to yourself that if I mortify myself in all other pleasures as I have done in this I must soon become a saint. I can say, however, in all sincerity, that though I have changed in many respects, I have not in the sincerity & warmth of my friendship for you; & that a line from

25

you, or any indication that you have not forgotten me, is a source of deep joy & a veritable treat.

Talking of indications: the *Ordo* was *very* welcome. It is brought out in splendid style, & does credit to the *rédacteur*, whom I suspect I know. The state of the Australian church as indicated there, is really quite a revelation for us here. F. Abbot has been under the impression that there were four or five bishops, and was astounded to see the flourishing & imposing hierarchy which has been established in so short a time. In your last letter you were a little bitter on His Em. He has a terribly cold nature, but he is certainly a *homo Dei*, and is a great credit to the Green Isle; & then he is the first Cardinal of the Mother Country.

How is "James"?[1] Does he still glide along with his green silk-lined biretta? I have a very great veneration for him. He was my confessor for a time in Rome; and I shall never forget his kindness in calling to see me when I was sick in Dublin after my return from Rome. Kindly give him my most humble and respectful compliments. While I am asking for people: how are your parents and Sr. Columba (isn't that your sister's name?)[2]

The Junk at Clonliffe is doing well. Tom Watters described him in a letter to me as a "calm, cool, studious fellow, just like the brother." If so, that will work. I suppose you have the intention of giving him the final brush up in the Eternal City. Without saying anything derogatory about the Coll. Irlandese, if I were you, I'd send him to the Prop.[3] as I am sure one gains more real advantage there. I *insist* on his giving me a call before going back to the mother country. Need I say how I shall try to make him at home etc. *propter te.*[4]

Frank Wall & John Waters are ordained at the Prop. since before Xmas. I saw a letter from Frank who is burning with fervour and devotion. *Esto perpetua*, I pray.[5] A host of little fellows who were in their lay clothes, or under the tender care of the fourth prefect when

---

[1] Bishop Murray of Maitland. Father Dwyer became his coadjutor in 1897.

[2] Father Dwyer's sister was a Dominican nun.

[3] Irish College; Propaganda College.

[4] "For your sake."

[5] "I pray that these dispositions may be lasting."

we were at Clonliffe, are being ordained now; & I begin to think that I am just about to begin my 10th year of priesthood. The few years which remain won't be long about flying, & then the long rest & union of dear friends in our Father's Home.

I never forget the promise which we made (James Dunne, You and I); and I am faithful to the little practices which we undertook, & sometimes I think what a joy it will be for us to find, after a few years, that we have contributed to save each others' souls; and I feel that God will bless, by a closer union of our hearts in heaven, that spiritual union commenced for His love here on earth. And after all, my dear Vincy, as I reflect here in the solitude of the monastery; & look back on my life since my ordination; I find that the simple, almost boyish, ideas we had as students, & which, while in the world I was sometimes tempted to look on as foolish, were the true ones. To love God is the beginning & the end of wisdom; & if we have laboured for any other, and "even tho' we should give our bodies to be burned & give all our goods to feed the poor,"[6] it would be all lost time. Therefore, I pray for you, that in the midst of the distractions to which the position in which God has placed you, expose you, in the midst of success & praise, you may always keep the eye of your soul fixed on God *si oculus tuus mundus est, totum corpus tuum lucidum erit,*" i.e. *si intentio tua pura est omne id quod facis, vultus divini lumine illuminabitur.*[7]

As regards myself D.G., I am in excellent health and *very, very* happy. I am well occupied; & well protected against myself by the walls of the monastery, I am able to occupy myself usefully. I have a class of Dogma & Moral & three classes of English in our school; besides choir work which lasts about four hours every day. Besides this, I have sundry other *jobs* which obedience imposes from time to time. As I am beginning to speak french pretty well, I will soon, I think, be allowed to hear confessions. So you see I won't grow musty for want of work. You said in your last that you scarcely hoped to visit Europe, & that I would probably not have the happiness of seeing you again *inter vivos.*[8] I look on it as certain that I

[6] I Cor. 73:3.
[7] "If thy eye be single, thy whole body shall be lightsome'" (Matt. 6:22).
[8] "Among the living."

shall see you again, i.e. that you will come to Europe; for I am *firmly persuaded* that before many years you will be making your official *ad limina* visit.[9]

Satolli is a bishop I think; and has been sent to Washington as representative of the H. Father. Aliardi is also a bishop, and takes snuff through one nostril still; your great friend & model Galimberti [10] is *in carriera* [11] somewhere near a cardinal's hat; if he hasn't it already.

I'm so glad you are president of the Sacred Heart College. It is just the place for you; you can do so much good there, & will not be distracted as if you were on an outlying station. Is it an ecclesiastical college, or species of St. Gall's establishment?

I've just heard that Satolli has been named cardinal, *prosit* say I. Practical resolution "study D. Thomas if you want promotion." [12]

Clonliffe very seldom writes me. James Dunne has never sent me a line since I came here. I hear he is studying *on ne peut plus*.[13] He is professor of all the Greek taught in Clonliffe together with Philosophy & Plain Chant. He would be a great acquisition to your establishment.

How is the little pudge O'Callaghan getting on? Making a row, I'll be bound, where ever he is. I would like to know how poor Joe Farrelly died. We were friends. His parents were poor, and I used to take him with me during vacation for little trips, so that we were rather intimate; but I never heard of, or from, him since he went to the Antipodes.

There is one thing for which I must ask your pardon: it is this. During his stay in Ireland, I did not show myself as hospitable &

[9] "To the Apostles' thresholds," a bishop's official five-year visit to the Holy See.

[10] Satolli, Aliardi, Galimberti — Dom Marmion's former professors at the Propaganda. Satolli was assigned to Washington in 1889, becoming first Apostolic Delegate to the United States in 1892. According to Philipon, of all young Marmion's professors Satolli "had the most influence on his intellectual development. . . . To the end of his life Dom Marmion would recall with emotion the admirable teaching of this beloved master" (*op. cit.*, p. 29). It was Satolli who introduced him to the *Summa Theologica* of St. Thomas. (MEE)

[11] "On the way."

[12] Actually, Satolli was not named cardinal until 1895, while still in Washington.

[13] "The best he can."

kind towards F. Hand as I should have liked to have towards a friend of yours. I felt this all the more, as personally I took a great fancy to him, & should have liked very much to have been in his society. The fact is, precisely at that time owing to family difficulties, my purse was quite empty. I was even considerably in debt, & being unable to act the part of a host, I rather avoided him; though perhaps it was pushing delicacy too far. . . .

I must conclude. You'll write soon? Give my affect. regards to your Father, Mother & family.

Yours very sincerely & affect. friend in J.C.

Père Columba Marmion, O.S.B.

IX.

Abbaye de S. Benoit
Maredsous
Belgium. August 10. 1892

My dear Vincy,

Wasn't it a pleasure to see your hand again? When I got to recreation, they remarked that I looked happy. I explained that I had just heard from one of my dearest friends. You should not think that a monk is a kind of dried-up [. . .] who is so wrapt up in the prayer[?] that he forgets his friends. I never allow a day to pass without praying specially for your intentions, & I look forward to the day when I shall have the joy of kissing your ring, when you come to make your visit *ad limina*. I shall [. . .]

Well I am nearly 6 years a monk; last year I made my solemn & final profession. I am extremely happy, & daily thank God for the great grace He gave me in bringing me to a place where I have a chance of saving my soul; since in the world I was sure to have lost it [. . .] from any exaggerated idea [. . .] but from the knowledge & [. . .] of my own frailty [ . . .]

[end of fragment]

July [1896]

. . . Later on, it is my conviction, you will have a more extended
sphere in which to exercise your activity. But we can talk over the
matter when you come to make your visit *ad limina*. (Must stop now,
God knows for how long.) July 22. I have been beyond my ears in
work these days. Some of my pupils have been up for their University exams & have not done marvels [?]. D.G. Want of success after
a year's hard work is the very best way of purifying our intention
& showing how foolish it is to have any object in view beyond *Dieu
seul!* A magnificent ideal, but very hard to act up to.

Our Lord Abbot[2] has been made primate of the whole order.
He is a very holy man, and very talented. When a young fellow,
although a nobleman & very well-off, he went out as a simple zouave
to fight for Pius IX. After a few years he came home dying; became
a monk here. Since his election as abbot & primate, God has given
him back his health so wonderfully that we can say: *Digitus Dei
est hic*.[3] Unfortunately we shall lose him as he will leave us to take
up his permanent residence in Rome as soon as our new College
is completed.[4]

I don't see any prospect of my going to Rome. Any thing I know,
I know very superficially; & with us solid study & erudition are the
great requirements[?] in a professor, & I am incapable of these,
partly owing to health, partly lack of vigour of character. However
I have no desire to go to Rome, but am perfectly happy here in
Maredsous which becomes dearer & dearer to me every day.

I am very fond of the Belgians, they are far the best missionaries
in the world. St. Francis Xavericus was always writing to S. Ignatius:
*"Da mihi Belgas."*;[5] & now that I know the *priests* more intimately,

----

[1] Mutilated letter. The first page is entirely missing; the second lacks a vertical
strip, but the meaning can be reconstructed. This holds good also for letters 12, 13,
and 14. Missing portions are indicated by [. . .].

[2] Dom Hildebrand de Hemptinne.

[3] "The finger of God is there."

[4] Sant' Anselmo, on the Aventine, one of Dom Hildebrand's achievements (see
Section X).

[5] "Give me Belgians."

I think it would be hard to get better. [. . .] In Flanders you may judge of the formation[?] of the priests when I tell you that not only are *all* the classes in latin, but even the conferences[?] of the clergy, & all the correspondence with the authorities.

Our Congregation [6] has received the mission from the Pope to reform our order in Brazil. [. . .] fathers have just returned and bring tales of the deplorable state of religion in certain parts of the country. It seems the level of morality has fallen so low that the people has no reluctance to accept the ministration, & attend the offices of a married clergy, looking[?] on such things as pardonable weakness[?]. It is not impossible that I might be sent. If it were God's will, I should be delighted to cooperate in such a glorious work, & even if need be, give my life in such a cause. The bishops[?] — who are very good —, are most anxious to have us, but the devil is placing formidable obstacles to our [. . .], & we are not quite sure yet if we should go or not. I recommend this to your prayers, & I wish you to keep it for the present *entre nous.* [. . .]

I am more convinced than ever that in these matters [7] there is nothing like a pure child-like faith; & that all the *higher-criticism* is a lot of high humbug. I have come in contact with many "high critics" as they call themselves, & they are very often but little removed from protestantism. *Nisi efficiamini sicut parvuli,* etc.[8] is as true now as in the time of Our Lord.

Dear Vincy, let us grow in *personal* love for Jesus. It is the great joy of this life, & source of durable[?] peace. It is only through Christ that the angels can praise God; & only in so far as we are united with him, are we pleasing(?) to the Father, who looks down on us saying[?]: *Hic est filius meus dilectus. . . .* [9]

Affect. regards to Str Columba.

[. . .] affec. brother in J. C.
D. Columba O.S.B.

---

[6] Beuronese Congregation, to which Maredsous belonged at that time.

[7] I.e., in the new so-called "progressive" biblical criticism shaping up during this period.

[8] "Unless you become converted, and become as little children, . . ." (Matt. 18:3).

[9] "This is my beloved son'" (Mark 9:7).

✠ Pax

Abbaye de S. Benoit
Maredsous
April 1st 1897

My dear Lord

When I heard of your appointment [2] I confess that I felt a double sentiment: one of great & very sincere pleasure, & the other almost one of sadness. Your appointment was a very sincere pleasure for me; because the honours & favours bestowed on those we love are as if conferred on ourselves; & you know that twenty years have not diminished the friendship & affection I had for you when we were students together at Holy Cross. Besides I always felt that God had destined you to fill the position. [. . . ] to find that God has approved my previsions.

I confess that at the same time I felt at first a kind of sadness. For the thought came to me that in gaining a bishop I was losing a friend; for friendship requires a certain equality; & I felt at first that your elevation must necessarily change my friendship into some other sentiment more in harmony [. . .] *jam non dicam*[3] [. . .]

[. . .] if He could stoop to consider these poor sinners as His *friends*, why my old friend can do the same; & there is no need of any change in our relations, except an increase of respect on my part for the sacerdotal character now existing in its plenitude in my friend; & an increase of affection on his part towards me, arising from the increase in him of the spirit of the good Pastor.

You may count on my poor prayers during this time. [. . .]

[. . .] very sincere compunction & humility, & a complete abandoning of yourself to the guidance of the H. Spirit to carry out His will, & glorify Him according to His designs.

I am not going to write a sermon. I haven't received the mission to instruct the pastors of the Church; but I just write as if we were chatting together. [ . . .]

[. . .] offer a suggestion, I would advise you to read habitually

---

[1] Mutilated letter, of which only two horizontal strips remain.
[2] As coadjutor bishop of Maitland.
[3] "I will not now call you servants . . . but friends" (John 15:15).

the lives of those great modern bishops who were raised up by God to give an example of episcopal sanctity in contact with modern civilization; e.g. *"Vie de S. François de Sales,"* par Hammon; *"Life of S. Charles Borromeo,"* by Capecelatro, etc; & also *"Vie de S. Alphonse de Liguori,"* par le Cardinal de Villecourt. These lives I have read & reread; & although I have not got an episcopal vocation [. . .]

If I can be of any service to you (finding out for you names of books on Canon Law, Theology, etc, etc) you know I shall only be too glad to help.

I have no news. Our life here is so uniform that the only changes are those which I suppose must occur in our invisible world *regnum Dei intra vos est.*[4] The only event worth mentioning is that I [. . .]

[. . .] & very dark. I ran a great danger; but my angel guardian, whom I did not cease to invoke, aided me; & I was able to arrive at the village to which I was going, say my Masses, & get back all right.[5]

You are receiving congratulations & presents, I am sure, from all sides. In my poverty, I can only offer you this chronogram; which I am sure you will keep for my sake as a pledge of the very sincere & respectful [. . .]

XII.[1]

✠ Pax

Abbaye Regina Coeli
Mont-César
Louvain
3 April [1900]

My dear Lord

I am sure you must be displeased with me for interrupting my turn. I am beginning to wonder if my last letter to your Lordship

---

[4] "The Kingdom of God is within you" (Luke 17:21).

[5] Early one morning Dom Marmion had to go on foot to a village some distance from the monastery. It was winter, and the countryside was thickly covered with snow. He had great difficulty in finding his way in the darkness.

[1] Dom Marmion was one of the group of monks of Maredsous chosen to found a new monastery at Louvain in April, 1899, under the direction of Dom Robert de Kerckhove, who subsequently became abbot there when the priory was made an abbey on August 6 of that year, and immediately appointed Dom Marmion prior and prefect of the clerics. See Philipon, *op. cit.*, pp. 47–49.

got to its destination. You asked me to write out for you all the particularities concerning the struggles for religious[?] education here in Belgium. [. . .] [2]

Since I wrote, I have been named Prior, & I have a deal of responsibility; but I am very happy. I find that when one gives one's self without reserve to God, leaving to Him full control over our acts, & seeking His glory in all things, then He helps wonderfully; & even He supplies where talent or knowledge [. . .] are wanting. This kind of life of study, teaching[?] and contact with the University is [. . .] according to my natural tastes; but as I have not chosen it, I am sure it is God's will for the present; & I succeed very well in it.

Our little community here is very fervent [?] & our Abbot is a man of great humility[?] & union with God. He is looked on by many, not alone in the monastery, but throughout the country, as a saint; & I who know him more intimately than most others, know the beauty of that soul. It is such a consolation to be placed under the guidance of a man who seeks *God alone* in all that he does. I hope, my dear Lord, that one day you will come and pass a few days here with us, & then you can judge for yourself.

Almighty God has just sent me a severe trial: my brother-in-law, who was in the full strength & vigor of manhood[?], was struck down by the inf[luenza?] and died in four days.[3] Thank God. He always[?] had lived as an excellent catholic; but he leaves my poor sister Mary with 10 children, many of them very young. God certainly shows a most wonderful care for them, as at first [. . .]
[. . .] but divine Providence has most admirably arranged all; giving extraordinary courage to my poor sister, & raising up friends in a most unexpected manner.

I am teaching the treatise *de Ecclesia* [4] at present. It often brings back memories of the past, when we sat together listening to the wisdom[?] of the great *Toss*.[5] I read an article written by your Lordship in an Australian newspaper in reply to a Protestant minis-

---

[2] The lines that follow are impossible to reconstruct.
[3] January 31, 1900.
[4] Theological treatise on the Church.
[5] Father Tynan, professor of theology and Sacred Scripture at Clonliffe.

ter, & recognized many of the "points" as having been taken down from the notes of the great man.

My friendship & affection for your Lordship are as fresh as ever, more [. . .], friendship founded in God increases as we draw nearer to Him. I pray for you every day; & I most humbly recommend myself to your prayers, that I may most perfectly[?] fulfil all God's designs on me.

With most profound respect I remain

very affectionately yours in J.C.
Columba Marmion O.S.B. Pr.


XIII.

✠ Pax
Mont-César Louvain
Nov.[?] [1902]

My dear Lord

It was really so kind of you to write to me, though it must seem to you as if I had forgotten. In all truth I have not forgotten; for daily I beg our Lord to bless & keep you in His love & service; & you will believe me when I say that the souvenir of your faithful friendship is one of the sweetest things of my life.

I have been working very hard, being prior, & professor of theology; & having many other occupations as confessor, etc. and during the vacation I gave 3 retreats: one in Belgium, an other one at Douai to our English Benedictines; & a third at Metz to the ecclesiastical personnel of the diocese. The explanation of my going to this place is that the bishop [1] is a monk[?], knowing me well personally; & asked me to preach to his priests. I got knocked up after the last retreat, & was obliged to give up head-work. And so when I got back to work, there was such a quantity of necessary things to get through that I was forced to let this letter stand over till today.

I am delighted to see our Lord is continuing to bless you; & that you feel such a strong desire to live up to the perfection of your state. I am more & more convinced every day that in the spiritual life: *fundamentum aliud neme ponere potest, praeter illud quod positum est,*

[1] Bishop Benzler, monk of Beuron, former abbot of Maria-Laach.

*quod est Xt Jesus.*[2] St. Basil says: [. . .] *est imitatio Verbi secundum* [. . .] *Incarnationis.*[3] In fact J.C. *est imago Dei invisibilis,*[4] & the more we study Him, the more He reveals Himself to us. *Qui videt me, videt et Patrem.*[5]

For myself I find that the spiritual life becomes wonderful when one has made up his mind to give one's self without reserve to J.C., for then He becomes our light, our life, our all: *Xtus factus est* nobis *sapientia a Deo et justitia et* sanctificatio *et redemptio.*[6] You ask me to refresh your soul with words of edification. I know nothing better than to recommend you to identify yourself as closely as possible with the *Pastor animarum.*[7] It is His great desire for us, as we see by His sublime prayer to His Father: *Ut omnes unum sint sicut et nos*; ego in te et in me, *ut sint consummati in unum.*[8] But this is especially for those whom He has chosen to carry out His work on earth. For this I do pray for us three,[9] & I beg you to ask the same grace for me. [. . .]

I was to have gone over to [. . .] this Summer to prospect;[10] but to the great disappointment of my Sisters, I could not for many reasons. Perhaps next year. In such matters I allow myself to be guided solely by obedience, & try not [. . .] a wish of my own.

I was sorry your Sister Columba had been ill; with nuns & monks, illness is often a part of God's plan of sanctification; & they must take it as such. Tell her I pray for her.

In Louvain there is a great spirit of study. The young priests, after

[2] "Other foundation no man can lay, but that which is laid: which is Christ Jesus" (I Cor. 3:11).

[3] Unrecoverable text.

[4] "Image of the invisible God" (Col. 1:15).

[5] "He that seeth Me, seeth the Father also" (John 14:9).

[6] "In Christ Jesus, who of God is made unto us wisdom and justice and sanctification and redemption" (I Cor. 1:30).

[7] The Shepherd of souls, Jesus Christ.

[8] "That they all may be one, as Thou, Father, in Me, and I in Thee: that they also may be one in Us" (John 17:21). The New Testament texts quoted in this letter are frequently repeated in Dom Marmion's preaching.

[9] The two correspondents, together with a third friend, James Dunne, a priest in the Dublin archdiocese.

[10] Text unrecoverable. There seems to be a question of a foundation in Ireland, and it is in this connection that Dom Marmion speaks of his eventual trip to that country.

3 or 4 year's theology in their Seminary, come here & follow the courses for 3 years. The standard is very high; but, *entre nous*, in some branches, v.g. H. Scripture they are very advanced, & German Protestant authors are much esteemed.

I use the *Summa*[11] as text-book[?], & am greatly pleased with results. P. Billot S.J.[?] an *excellent* help, though I don't follow all his opinions. I have the advantage to be in relation here with some great theologians, like P. Dummermuth O.P.[12]

With sincere respect

[. . .] affection ever yours in J.C.
Dom Columba Marmion O.S.B.

XIV.[1]

Louvain. [April, 1902 or 1903]

My dear Lord,

It is a long time since you heard from me, but as I so often told you before, you are daily remembered where remembrance counts; for hearts once united in God's love cannot be separated by distance. I often think of you & all you are doing for our emigrants. There are two roads to perfection, i.e. to perfect love. One is to seek God continually in the person of our neighbour, the other is to seek Him by contemplation; provided we seek Him, & rest united to Him in perfect love, it little matters by which of these two roads He wishes to lead us. He has chosen to lead you by the same road as He led His only Son the Saviour . . . by presenting Himself to you in the souls of those who are committed to your care. He expects me to go to Him by prayer & contemplation. It seems to me that this difference is well illustrated by the two ceremonies which are the starting points of our respective routes. On the day of my monastic profession I con-

[11] The *Summa Theologica* of St. Thomas Aquinas.

[12] Well-known Master of Theology at the Dominican house of studies in Louvain, and author of two large volumes numbering nearly twelve hundred pages and in Latin, on the subject of physical premotion. The esteem Dom Marmion bore him in no way inhibited his sense of humor. During an official dinner that brought together many prominent personalities from the university, he declared in the presence of the formidable Dominican: "If you suffer from insomnia there is an infallible remedy: just read Father Dummermuth."

[1] A vertical strip has been torn from this letter.

secrated myself to God, & on the day of your consecration you offered yourself entirely to your flock. Let us pray for one another that we may be very faithful in our respective spheres, I as a *Conf. non Pont.* you as a *Conf. Pont.*[2]

I was greatly pleased to receive the account of your splendid Cath. Congress, & to read the paper which your Lordship prepared. What we are losing here in old Europe, where *principes convenerunt adversus Dominum, et adversus Xtum eius,*[3] you are gaining in those new countries where the faith is growing strong and bearing fruit. For the moment the devil seems to have the upper-hand here in Europe. In Belgium, the Catholics are still in power, for the faith is still strong among the people. But I think Socialism & irreligion will soon become so potent that the acts we are deploring in France, Spain & Portugal at present will be repeated here.

While awaiting these events I am trying to accomplish my little bit as perfectly as I can, for God will not leave us to face these trials, of which I have spoken, when their hour comes. I am still teaching dogmatic, & it is a most enchanting study, when one goes into it thoroughly. I am beginning to understand how very little I knew when I had finished my course; & what an immense blessing it is for the students here at the University, who, after a 3 year course in their seminary, arrive here to begin a further course of higher studies for 3 or 4 years more. [. . .]

Besides my teaching I am Prior of our new foundation, and have our young scholastics to form; and am chaplain to a Convent of Holy Carmelites; so you can see I am not idle. I am, however, living in great peace, for I find my happiness in being united to our dear Lord. He takes all on Himself; although at times He may make you wait for Him in faith *Revela Dno. viam tuam, et spera in eum, et ipse faciet.*[4]

I told you in my last that my brother-in-law, Stephen, died suddenly leaving my poor sister with a very large family. D.G. *He* has done wonderfully in providing for all. . . .

---

[2] "Confessor not a Bishop" and "Confessor Bishop" — designations used in the Common of Saints in the Missal.

[3] "The princes met together against the Lord and against His Christ" (Ps. 2:2).

[4] "Commit thy way to the Lord and trust in Him: and He will do it" (Ps. 36:5).

Please remember me to Sr. Columba and the other members of your family, especially to Joseph.

I remain with profound respect & affection

yrs in Xto.

D. Columba Marmion O.S.B. prior.

xv.[1]

[. . .] so the new school would take Kant; but all the water in the ocean couldn't baptise Kant, nor make his philosophy christian. Loisy of whom so much has been said & written, is simply a victim of this false philosophy.[2] Kant distinguishes between the *phenomenon* (things as they appear to us) & the *numenon* (things as they are in themselves); & he asserts that there is no necessity for the one to correspond with the other. Loisy distinguished also between *Christ phenomenon* i.e. Christ as faith presents Him to us; & he admits that every christian must admit that *ideal* Xt; & *Christ noumenon,* i.e. Xt. as an historical personage; & he differs absolutely from the first. A large portion of the French clergy is infected with these ideas; & those who don't admit them feel their influence.

Since my class of theology was finished,[3] I have been occupied — through obedience — with the study of mystic theology; & I give one or two conferences weekly to the community. It is a [. . .] study [. . .]

xvi.

✠ Pax                    Mont César, Louvain. 30 Oct. 1904.

My dear Lord,

Since I wrote my last letter, I have received another letter from

[1] Fragment of a badly mutilated letter.

[2] Alfred F. Loisy (1857–1940), leader in Modernist heresy, former priest and professor of Sacred Scripture at Institut Catholique of Paris, from which he was suspended for espousing Kant-inspired "higher criticism" and the accommodation of revealed Truth. By the time of this letter (1904), Loisy had terminated a five-year professorship at the Ecole des Hautes Etudes; his excommunication for heresy followed in 1908. See *Catholic Encyclopedia*, "Modernism." (MEE)

[3] Dom Marmion taught theology to the young monks at Louvain from 1899 to 1903 — one complete four-year course. He was then relieved of these classes because of his many other all-engrossing activities.

my sister in which she tells me of your great kindness to my nephew. I am most grateful to Your Lordship & shall never forget what you have done for him. . . .

We are again at work. The great question at present is the nature of biblical inspiration. It is certain that the old explanation of Franzelin,[1] though true as far as it goes, wants completeness. Loisy, & I think Lagrange,[2] goes too far; but I am of the opinion that the whole question requires revision. When the bible tells us that the sun stood still for Joshua, etc., we answer that the inspired author only used the language of his time, *having no intention to teach astronomy*; & when (as very grave authorities assure us) the sacred books narrate events which are historically inexact, they answer that, *not having the intention to teach history*, they narrate the current belief as a means of teaching religious & moral truth. Of course this is *very slippery ground* & I have not as yet made up my mind. One of the best professors of S. Scripture, member of the Biblical Commission & professor here at Louvain, a holy priest & a most clear-headed man, is propounding principles such as I have just expressed. When they are all given I shall get a copy of notes of one of the pupils, &, if it interests you, send it on to you. I am *very conservative* in such matters; but yet there *are* difficulties in the sacred text which it is very

[1] Johann Baptist Cardinal Franzelin, S.J. (d. 1886), a pioneer in the 19th-century restoration of the primacy of speculation in theology, but in the field of Biblical scholarship, particularly on the question of Inspiration, his conclusions were inadequate for the times, as Dom Marmion recognized. See R. T. Murphy, O.P. (ed.), *Père Lagrange and the Scriptures* (Milwaukee, Bruce, 1946), Chap. I, "The Old Testament — Semitism," by J. Chaine of Faculté Catholique of Lyon. (MEE)

[2] Marie-Joseph Lagrange, O.P. (1855–1938), eminent Scripture scholar and founder (in 1893) of his Order's Ecole Pratique d'Etudes Bibliques (St. Stephen's) in Jerusalem, can hardly be bracketed with Loisy, although his conferences at Fribourg in 1897 on the authorship of the Pentateuch, and his exegetical publications of 1903, particularly the *Méthode historique* (2nd ed., 1904, year of Marmion's allusion), caused a furore in orthodox circles. Recognizing that biblical scholarship utilizing only the traditional argument from divine inspiration was powerless in the face of rationalistic attacks of the day, Père Lagrange simply applied the same rational criticism of the Church's enemies to his work of vindicating the Bible's value as historic document — but always in the light of his strong faith in the "divine character of the Bible." His approach is basic to Catholic Scripture study today, but in his day he was blazing a perilous trail, and suffered accordingly. See Murphy, *op. cit.* (MEE)

hard to explain on the old principles; & I am in search of a *"Working theory."*

This year, besides my ordinary work as prior, & prefect of studies, I have a class of exegesis. I am explaining the gospel of St. John which I did nearly 30 years ago with Tynan. Do the Australian Bishops never visit the *limina?* It ought to be nearly your time now.

A new book has just come out published by one of our Fathers.[3] It is all the new ecclesiastical legislation regarding the religious congregations of simple vows. It is *very complete* & well done; only it is in French, as it is destined not only as a guide for the bishops, but as a manual for the religious themselves.

I pray, as ever, every day for your Lordship, & remain with profound respect and affection, Yours most devotedly in J.C.

Dom Columba Marmion O.S.B. P.

XVII.

✠ Pax                  Mont César, Louvain. 12 Feb. [1908]
My dear Lord

I am most grateful to you for your kind remembrance of me, & should have answered sooner; but that I am just recovering from a heavy attack of influenza accompanied by fever & lung trouble. I am still very weak. It is a very great consolation for me to see that our friendship, begun so many years ago, & founded on God, is like Him unchangeable, & I hope eternal. We are getting on towards the evening of life. I shall be 50 in April, & you some months later; & the great truth which comes out clearer & clearer every day is that nothing is eternal but God, & what we do for Him *opera in Deo facta*.[1]

I very often think of you before God; for I must say in all sincerity that I have found no sincerer or dearer friend up to this. James Dunne never writes, but he remains a fast & sincere friend. I told him I should like to receive the new Theological Review published

[3] Dom Pierre Bastien, O.S.B., professor of canon law at Sant' Anselmo, took part in preparation of the New Code of Canon Law.

[1] "The works done for God." Council of Trent, 6th sesssion, chap. 16.

41

at Maynooth, & he always subscribes for me, so that I receive it very regularly.

You seem to think I have a very quiet life. God has arranged otherwise. Besides being prior & prefect of studies, I am invited to give a great number of retreats. I gave, I think, about 12 last year in Belgium, England & Scotland. Besides this, a great number of priests, professors of the University, etc., come to confession, & take up a lot of my time. Then I am the confessor & intimate friend of the Cardinal,[2] who gives me a deal to do in many ways. (Commission of Vigilance, examen of books, different odds & ends in a diocese of 2,500,000 souls).

The Cardinal is a saint. He lives a most mortified life, & a life of prayer; & yet does a prodigious amount of work. Since his consecration, besides the active government of his vast diocese, he has given a series of magnificent conferences to his students, which is being brought out in book form. Then he sees them all individually; invites them to dine with him; & is a real father to them. Although a broad-minded man, he is strongly orthodox, & carries out the Pope's instructions in that respect with great vigour. He is one of the three Cardinals (Rampolla, Maffi, Mercier) charged by the Holy See to constitute the "International Scientific Institute." Some weeks ago I was in England, & in his name, waited on some of the foremost scientific Catholics in order to arrange preliminaries.

I suppose you have no modernism out in Australia. It is simply the effect of trying to baptize Kant. St. Thomas did up Aristotle, baptized him, & made a very respectable Christian of him. The Germans, & the Neokantists in France, have been trying to do the same for Kant, but it won't do. Grace supposes nature; & just as you can't baptize an ape, so you can't baptize Kant's system, because it is radi-

---

[2] Désiré Cardinal Mercier, (1851–1926), former (from 1882) professor of theology at Louvain, consecrated archbishop of Malines in March, 1906, and elevated to the College of Cardinals the following year. The two friends had met first at Maynooth's centenary celebration (1895) at which Dom Marmion represented Maredsous, and Mercier, Louvain. According to Philipon (p. 57), after the Benedictines were established at Louvain, Mercier consulted Marmion regularly and was "a constant visitor and a faithful friend to Mont-César. It was there that he received formal notification of his elevation to the cardinalate; there also that he composed in 1914 his famous letter: 'Patriotism and Endurance'." (MEE)

cally false. The University of Louvain is showing itself very correct in the present crisis. There is a very great sentiment of loyalty & submission all through Belgium towards the Holy See; & once all the professors sent a declaration of sincere adhesion to the Pope's ideas.

It is not easy to see exactly what one *ought* to think on certain points; for my own part I would willingly give my life for the faith, and welcome with sincere joy every declaration of authority. Yet on some points, v.g. the nature of inspiration, my mind is in a muddle. Up to this I had always held Franzelin's explanation as very satisfactory. Yet it seems to me difficult to admit that inspiration always guarantees historical truth; & yet if it doesn't, of what practical use is it? I give you an instance of what I mean. It is evident that the *substantial fact* of Our Lord's baptism is true, & falls under inspiration; but are the *details* guaranteed by inspiration? For it is really very difficult to reconcile the description of this same fact as given by Math. 3; 14 sq. & Jo. 1; 31, 33. In Jo. 1, 31 St. John says *Ego nesciebam eum* etc.[3] & that he did not know Him till *after* the dove had descended on Him, v. 33; where as in St. Math. we are told that St. John knew Him before the baptism *Joannes autem* prohibebat *eum*,[4] etc. v. 14. There are numbers of places like that: v.g. in the description of the resurrection by the different Evangelists, in which it is very hard to be sincere with oneself, & admit that there is no difficulty in reconciling the details. I don't give this as an opinion, but simply say I don't see clearly; & am waiting for some authentic teaching on the point; & others like it.

I see you have plenty of work; & I expect coadjutoring has some analogy with prioring; & if so, it requires at times patience & a strong spirit of faith. I see by your "Almanac" — for which *thanks* — that religion is making great strides in the colony. What a pity that God's work should depend so much on questions of money, & yet practically so it often is.

Please give my sincere love to members of your dear family, & tell them I do not forget them before God. Pray for me, that I may live

[3] "I knew him not" (John 1:33).
[4] "But John stayed him" (Matt. 3:14).

up to the high ideal of our Benedictine life, & Believe me ever with sincere affection & respect

Yours in J.C.<br>Dom Columba Marmion O.S.B.

P. S. My very respectful regards to your excellent Bishop.

XVIII.

✠ Pax            Mont-César, Louvain. 12 May 1909.
My dear Lord,

I was about to begin this letter by one of the hackneyed phrases of worldly politeness & tell you how sorry I was at your father's death; but I really cannot; for I am too convinced that such a death ought to be a subject of rejoicing & not of sadness. A long life spent in the service of God & of the sacred cause of Catholic education; his efforts and prayers to bring up his own family as he has done; his intense interior life nourished at the source of sanctity by daily communion; & crowned by such a holy death, gives us the certitude that he is in that *home* of peace towards which all our desires tend. You will convey to Fr. Joseph, Sr. Columba and the other members of your family, the expression of my profound sympathy. I am saying 16 Masses for him (there is no difficulty for us as being *exempti*. Our *ordinarius* is the Abbot, and not the Bishop).[1]

Poor Dr. Murray![2] He has lived his time, & could help you more now by his prayers in heaven than by his presence on earth. I won't forget him, as he was very kind to me years ago in Rome when I needed counsel & encouragement. James Dunne came over to Louvain some months ago with Pivers & Mivers; or rather these last remained at Spa, & James came on here & we spent the day together. He is just the same as we knew him years ago, a model priest. We spent a *very happy* day together. In fact he declared that it was the happiest he had spent since we three spent the day together at Maredsous.

Do Australian Bishops *never* visit the *limina?* I know at least one

---

[1] Since the Council of Trent, religious orders are exempt from jurisdiction of the diocesan Ordinary in local, personal matters. (MEE)

[2] Bishop Murray of Maitland had recently died.

who has not been to Rome for over ten years. I often think that when you do come I shall get James over, & we could spend a day together as of old.

Since I doubled the cape of 50,[3] I often think of eternity; though to be candid, I am feeling stronger & better than I was when you saw me last. I do a lot of active work giving retreats, conferences to priests, confessions; & get back to the monastery to get up fervour when it is waning. Of course I pass the greater part of my time in the monastery as my abbot does not accept half of the invitations, but yet I have a deal to do. I am not *at all* a preacher, but something in the style of old father Gowan [4]; & as I have a good deal of experience I am able to help souls, especially priests & nuns.

I don't know how things will get on here in Belgium. I fear sooner or later, perhaps very soon, we may be in the same state as in France & then it would fare badly with us monks. Good people in Belgium are *very good* just like good Irish Catholics; but bad people are *diabolical*, & if the government once got into the hands of our *liberaux*,[5] we should be stamped out without mercy. In which latter case I should be applying to His Lordship of Maitland for a place as chaplain to finish my days in peace & prepare for eternity.

I suppose you have no modernists over in the colonies. There is not much of it in Belgium, but it's in the air; & that simple faith, which looks on the Church as Christ living in our midst *"usque ad consummationem saeculi,"* [6] is changing into a critical attitude towards all dogmatic guidance. I have read a good deal of theology, & mixed much with all kinds of *savants*, & I have a reputation for being

[3] To pass one's 50th birthday, an expression possibly derived from the nautical feat of sailing around the Cape of Good Hope.

[4] A Vincentian and Joseph Marmion's spiritual director at Clonliffe. Thibaut has more on the subject (*op. cit.*, pp. 16 f.). Of his "style," to which Dom Marmion likens his own, Philipon writes: "Humble and austere in himself but impassioned when in his celebrated conferences he spoke of God, of the Passion and Death of Christ, or of the other divine mysteries, he required the same supernatural spirit from his penitents, asking of them a generous acceptance of crosses and humiliations and a fervent devotion to the sufferings of Christ. . . . It was under his guidance that Dom Marmion formed the resolution to make the stations of the Cross every day, a practice to which he remained faithful to the day of his death" (*op. cit.*, pp. 27 f.). (MEE)

[5] In Belgian politics the Liberal party is generally anti-Catholic.

[6] "Until the end of time" (Matt. 28:20).

45

a large-minded man, but I am convinced that light & truth are to be found in humble docility to Christ's Vicar.

With all respect, Your ever affectionate

*Joe.*

## XIX

✠ Pax        Abbaye de Saint-Benoit, Maredsous [1] par Maredret.

le 6. XII. 1919.

My dear Lord,

I was really delighted to get your letter; for our old friendship has not changed &, as years pass & eternity approaches, I find that ours has been one of the sincerest & most enduring. I spoke of eternity; I have had once or twice the *responsum mortis*,[2] & it has a very sobering effect even on those who live in the peace & calm of the cloister. I had heart trouble (tired out heart), some three years ago, as a result of the anguish & horrors of the German occupation. We were in the middle of it here, & being responsible for my flock, and in daily danger of all kinds, it wrought on my heart, & one night I thought the end was come. That passed away as there is nothing functionally wrong, but just fatigue. Again, some months ago I had an attack of gravel. It is the greatest pain one can endure, & I had it during nearly 3 weeks for 15 or 20 hours at a time. I am now quite cured and all that remains to do is to be careful about diet, & so I am living principally on fruit & *raw* vegetables. It is not nice, but very wholesome. So much for myself.

I don't know if you received the 2 vols. I sent you: *(Le Christ Vie de l'Ame & Le Christ dans ses mystères)*. It has had a most astonishing success. The 9th edition is already almost exhausted, & the Pope [3] has given me a very nice letter of approval. I know also that he uses it for his own spiritual reading. The reason of the success is that there is practically nothing in these works from me. I simply make Our Lord, & St. Paul, & St. Benedict speak; & explain their doctrine.

[1] Dom Marmion had been elected abbot of Maredsous on September 29, 1909, and governed the abbey until his death in 1923.

[2] "Answer of death" (II Cor. 1:9), i.e., a close call.

[3] Benedict XV.

46

I saw James D.[4] several times this year. I got my attack of gravel when passing through Dublin & had to lie up at St. Vincent's. Batty came to see me daily, & James very often. Both were most kind. . . .

I dined several times with the Vice (Dr. Hagen). He is a *very strong* patriot. Although quite of his opinion in theory, I felt that such ideas are outside the region of *practical* politics. Poor Ireland! I don't know what will become of her — yet when you live in the midst of these people they are unlike all others in their faith, their love of the priest & their purity.[5]

I have been preaching at Westminster & giving a retreat to the cathedral clergy. I am sorry Maitland is so far or I should also ask to preach to yours, *omnibus debitor sum* [6] even to the natives of the colonies. Poor Jack Hoey died like a saint. He was a most holy priest; an oddity up to the last, but he left a great reputation of charity & zeal. In fact almost all our old Cloncliffe companions have turned out well.

Best regards to Sr. Columba.

Tuissimus in J.C.

✝ Columba Abb.

xx.

Pax        Abbaye de Maredsous, par Maredret. le 22. V. 1921.
My Lord & very dear old friend,

Your letter just received was a great joy & consolation for me. It is so long since we have written to each other & yet it is not forgetfulness, for I have been very faithful to our contract of daily prayers & weekly rosary.

I saw a good deal of Jem, as I was laid up in Dublin for weeks, at Vincent's hospital, some two years ago. He & Batty, faithful old friends, came constantly to see me and cheer me up in my sufferings

---

[4] James Dunne, their mutual friend.

[5] See Letter 20 for clarification of Dom Marmion's position on Ireland. The date of the present letter is a scant year after the victory of Sinn Fein candidates in the Irish elections, whereupon Sinn Fein members in the old House of Commons had constituted themselves the Dail Eirann under Eamon de Valera (January, 1919), and David Lloyd George was preparing his campaign of reprisal in which Black and Tans would be turned loose on the countryside, local leaders murdered, and towns (including Cork) set afire. (MEE)

[6] "I am a debtor to all" (Rom. 1:14).

(stone). I suffered *a deal*; but it is now passed & perhaps has served to atone for a part of my very heavy debt towards God's justice & sanctity. St. Francis de Sales said that no order has produced so many saints as the episcopal order. Bishops having received the plenitude of the *Holy* Spirit, have helps which we have not: *Mittam eis* doctorem justitiae.[1] They have the H. Spirit as their professor of sanctity. He gives them such light, such graces, such help that they are in the state of perfection here on earth & shall be high above us in heaven. Abbots have the responsibility, but not the wonderful help & grace of bishops.

There was some talk of my being named a bishop in Wales or England, but the reports were false; or perhaps the information given to the Prefect of the Consistorial not satisfactory. In any case they came to nothing. I think it likely that Jem Dunne may be A.B.[2] of Dublin. I hope it with all my heart. He is so holy, so wise & so enlightened.

Poor Ireland is in a sad plight; & unless God gives very special help & light, I don't see any way out. England will never give us a republic as long as she has a soldier to carry a gun; & Ireland won't be satisfied with anything less. I am not for separation from England, nor for a republic; but I desire a very large measure of "self-determination," such as you have in Australia.[3]

I am glad you liked my conferences. The pope said to me at my last audience *"Vous avez écrit un très beau livre"*;[4] and I know from one of the Cardinals that he uses it for his daily meditation. This is a consolation, a guarantee of orthodoxy. The Vols. have been trans-

---

[1] A reference to "He hath given you a teacher of justice" (Joel 2:23).

[2] Archbishop.

[3] By this time Ireland was virtually in a state of civil war. After bitter guerrilla fighting between Irish and British forces, Lloyd George had invited De Valera to discuss settlement. Michael Collins and Arthur Griffith were dispatched to London, and returned with the Anglo-Irish treaty of 1921, which guaranteed home rule and dominion status to Ireland. Although the treaty was ratified by the Dail after protracted and violent debate, De Valera refused to accept it, and his left-wing "Republican" party split with the forces of the more conservative provisional government formed by Collins and Griffith for the period of debate until the right wing prevailed in 1922, after much violence and bloodshed. The Republic of Ireland was not formally inaugurated until 1949 — long after Dom Marmion's death. (MEE)

[4] "You have written a very beautiful book."

48

lated into English, German, Italian, Polish, Dutch, and have passed through 12 editions. Live Tynan, Satolli, & old Kirby! Dr. Mani made great noise over here.[5] He is a great man & a strong man. He was very badly treated in England.

Please tell Sr. Columba I pray for her & for your brother Joe. If you had a quiet spot where I could go & prepare for death, (an Abbot has not a moment: I have 100 monks, a college, a school of art etc.), and weep over my sins; I think I should bolt. May God bless & love you,

Ever your affectionate.

✠ Columba Marmion Abb.

P.S. The enclosed photo of Her Majesty [6] may interest you. We are quite chummy. She gave a chalice worth over £1000.

## IV. TO AN IRISH NUN

Holy ✠ Seminary. August 20, 1884.

My dear Sister,

I had the happiness of assisting at a most beautiful death in the Redemptoristine Convent;[1] & as the details are edifying, I will give you some of them. However, they are only for yourself & the Sisters, as the nuns here don't like to have such things spoken of.

One of the novices, who was about a month from her profession, was taken ill last week; although the malady appeared insignificant, she knew from the beginning that she would never recover. Her confessor, (F. Walsh, S.J.), happening to be away, I was delighted to hear her confession, assist her in her agony, & if necessary receive her religious profession. On Sunday evening I heard her confession & anointed her. She was enjoying great peace & consolation; & though suffering intensely, did not seem near death. I slept in the extern house

[5] Cardinal Satolli had died in 1910.

[6] Queen Elizabeth of the Belgians. See another mention of this visit in Section XIX, Letter 41.

[1] Father Marmion was at this time chaplain of the Redemptoristine convent in Dublin.

49

of the convent, & about 3½ on Monday morning, I was called, as she had become much worse; it happened most providentially that just at that time she had a good interval, without vomiting, so I was able to give her the H. Viaticum; & she made her holy profession, received the black veil & ring. Her agony commenced then & lasted till 10½ on Monday night. Although enduring the most intense pain, (the doctor said it was the most terrible that could be borne), she was filled with consolation. She made the most beautiful acts of love & resignation, & never showed a *shadow* of impatience. She displayed in the midst of her greatest agony a most wonderful obedience on the minutest things to Rd. Mother, & was as simple as a little child.

I *very* frequently got her to make a general accusation of her sins, & gave her absolution; & prayed quietly with her; as she was perfectly conscious all through. This lasted till about 6. in the evening, when she seemed to lose consciousness for a short time. I thought she was departing; after a little she recovered & turned to us with a smile, & said she had seen our Lord & His B. Mother; she asked them why they did not take her with them then, but Jesus said: "You have had too much consolation, you must suffer now"; almost immediately after, *all* consolation was removed, & from that till a few minutes before she died (10½) she endured such sufferings of body & soul as I never witnessed before. Four strong nuns & I had sometimes to hold her down in the bed; & the expression of her face, (which before had been very beautiful), completely changed, & was replaced with one of intense terror & anguish; but never a shadow of impatience &, as consciousness returned after each paroxysm, absolute obedience & resignation. I stood by her all the time, sprinkling holy water & applying the relic of St. Alphonsus, which seemed to give her great peace.

A few moments before death, complete peace returned; & with great happiness, calmly, as though going to sleep, she breathed forth her soul as we were reciting the Hail Mary round her. "Precious in the sight of the Lord is the death of His saints," [2] & she was truly one. R.I.P. She was admitted on the very day of her espousals to the nuptials of the Lamb. [. . .] [3]

[2] Ps. 115:15.
[3] The rest of this letter is missing.

# V. TO AN IRISH SISTER OF MERCY[1]

## THREE LETTERS

### I.

Holy ✠ College. April 29, 1885

My dear Child,

As you have got no name of your own yet,[2] I suppose you consider tomorrow your feast.[3] I will pray very specially for you, that you may receive the grace of resembling your holy patron, especially in the generous oblation she made of herself to her Divine spouse. Your life at present should be a perpetual oblation of yourself to the S. Heart, & as the Holy Sacrifice is being offered at every moment during the day, you can unite yourself with our Lord at every moment, & thus be sure your offering will be accepted.

When you have got the habit of nuns living in a state of perpetual oblation, it becomes a matter of absolute indifference to you, what you are engaged at; as your only desire is to accomplish the will of God, which is manifested to you at every moment by obedience. The more generous you are in endeavoring to arrive at this state of holy indifference & detachment from your own inclinations, the more perfectly you will taste that peace, which is the "hundredfold" which our Lord promises to those who have left all things for His love.[4]

Your father is persevering in the same fervent life; or rather making rapid advances in sanctity. He never omits Benediction nor Mass, etc. Duff is getting a fine big girl, & just as prim as ever; she won't be a nun. I fear Patrick has changed his mind about coming to Clonliffe. I am tormenting all the saints for Rev. Mother. I hope she will soon get better. My nuns had commenced a novena for her, & are very much concerned about her illness; tell her she must take care of health, as it is not God's will she should die till she has been able to do something for Him.

[1] Three of Dom Marmion's sisters were members of this congregation.

[2] I.e., a name in religion.

[3] St. Catherine of Siena (April 30), patron of Mother Catherine McAuley and her foundation, the Sisters of Mercy. (MEE)

[4] Matt. 19:29.

Tell the other Sr. Katie that I will put her name in my message
to heaven tomorrow. Give my love to Rev. Mother & all.

Believe me, your very sincere friend in J.S.

Joseph A. Marmion
EDM

II.

Holy ✠ College Clonliffe. Nov. 27, 1885.

My dear Child,

I must not let Advent commence without letting you have a line.
I have been so occupied that I found it difficult even to send a line to
Rd. Mother, & I knew that she would let you know the contents as
far as they could be of any interest to you. I pray very fervently for
you daily at Mass, that God may give you the grace to persevere; as
I don't think you are suited for a life in the world. You must do
your part generously with God, & He will not fail to assist you.

Each religious order is like a flower in the garden of Jesus, & just
as each flower has its own peculiar odour & beauty, so each order
has its own beautiful spirit & characteristic virtues which delight the
S. Heart. Therefore, no matter how good or virtuous we may be in
ourselves, if we have not the peculiar spirit & training of the order
to which we belong, we are out of joint in the community, & can
never be a good religious, nor truly delight the Heart of Jesus. It was
because our Lord saw all the sisters in the little convent of Avila
animated with the one, true spirit of their order that he said to St.
Teresa: "daughter, this convent is the paradise of my delights, in
which my Heart finds delightful repose & protection from the out-
rages of men."

But, you ask me, "how am I to gain that spirit, how am I to know
if I really have it?" Well, I answer, this is precisely the purpose of
the novitiate; the spirit of the order of Mercy is handed down from
the holy founders, through the Superiors; & all you have to do, is to
leave yourself *absolutely* in their hands, like wax in the hand who
moulds it; & at the end of the novitiate, the germs of that spirit will
have been planted in your heart to bud forth into perfection later on.

This, with prayer, is the only means of acquiring the spirit of your state. It is often hard to nature, to be thus cut, & plumed; but otherwise we can never hope to be pleasing to the S. Heart.

If I were joining religion tomorrow, I would enter with the determination of leaving myself absolutely in the hands of my superiors, to let them cut away *mercilessly* all the excrescences of my character, so that I might be fit to be presented, as a clean oblation on the altar of God's love; & even though nature might repine, I would try to bear all for the love of Jesus crucified; & I presume, that if I were but faithful, I would soon acquire the true spirit of my order & thus "reap with joy, what I had sown in tears." [1] Our Lord makes no exception: "if *anyone* will come after me, let him *deny* himself, take up his cross & follow me." [2] This is specially true of religious, who try to *follow* our Lord so closely; & consequently, if we reject the cross, if we repine when it presses on us, we are not following Jesus, but ourselves.

These, my dear child, are a few thoughts which strike me when I pray for you, as I know your character so well, I think, if you reflect on them. And the other sisters might like to know "Uncle Joe's" views about a novice. Well, in a word, my idea of a good novice is this: — A good novice is one:

1) who enters religion in order to glorify our Lord, by rendering her soul, & those of others as pleasing to the S. Heart as possible.

2) who, in order to effect this, will spare herself in nothing; & consequently is ready to suffer pain, & humiliation, & even death itself to please God.

3) who is not content with ordinary christian virtue, but through fidelity to her spouse, aspires to render her heart a very furnace of divine love; & who does all this under the guidance of obedience in accordance with the spirit of her order. Oh, how the S. Heart would rejoice, if He could behold such a paradise as this! That Dunmore [3] may be the realisation of this, is my constant prayer.

Matty & I dined yesterday in D'Olier St.; all are well. Your father

[1] Ps. 125:5.
[2] Matt. 16:24.
[3] Convent of the Sisters of Mercy.

53

never was better in every way. You have great reason to rejoice & to thank God.

I hope to be with you at Xmas; but you must pray that God may arrange matters.

Love to all.
Your very sincere friend in J.C.
J. A. Marmion EDM

III.

✠ Pax                                                   Louvain. July 2, 1896
My dear sister Alphonsus,[1]

I received your letter this morning just before starting for Louvain where I am to stay for a few days. I was very sorry to hear of poor Sr. Stanis. death. I say sorry, because you are so few in number that you cannot afford to lose anyone. For her, it is a favour to be for all eternity with God, in peace & love, free from sin, secure from temptation, knowing none of those miseries which dog our steps as long as we remain here below. I shall pray for her, & have had her recommended to the prayers of my brethren; for although hers was a simple, holy soul, yet God's sanctity is so great that even "in His angels He finds imperfection."[2] Please tell Rev. Mother how sincerely I condole with her in this trial; & that I shall beg God to send you others to take her place & do His work. I was very much pleased to see by Mother Columba's[3] letter that Sr. Evangelist was so much better. God grant her the grace to use this new term of life which He gives her, solely for His glory & for His love.

Every day I live, I see more & more that there is but one thing which is worth living for, & that is God's glory. In all that He does, He seeks His own glory, (to do otherwise would be contrary to His sanctity, & an imperfection); & for us, what can be nobler than to unite our will with His in seeking His glory purely in all we do. In seeking His glory, He seeks our good, for God's glory as regards His creatures consists in communicating His love & grace & joy to

---

[1] This is probably to the same sister.
[2] Job 4:18.
[3] Dom Marmion's sister, founder of the Dunmore Convent of Mercy. (MEE)

54

them. And we can glorify God by our actions, for although in themselves they are very little & mean, united with those of Jesus Xt, they give an infinite glory to the B. Trinity. And all the infinite riches of His S. Heart *are ours*, more truly than any thing we possess in this world, if *we are united* to Him by divine grace. Oh, my dear child, I would wish to engrave on your heart, in letters of gold, this truth, that no matter how great our misery, *we are infinitely rich in Jesus Christ*, if we unite with Him, if we lean on Him, if we realize constantly by a firm living faith that all the value of our prayer, & of all that we do, comes from His merits in us. All this is contained in two texts: "Without me you can do *nothing*." [4] "I can do *all things* in Him who strengtheneth me." [5]

Try, then, to become a saint, by acknowledging to yourself the full extent of your past miseries, present unworthiness, & the possibility of future infidelity; & at the same time, honouring "the Father through Jesus Xt" by reposing with the most absolute confidence on His infinite merits: "By Him, & in Him, & with Him," as we say daily in H. Mass, all glory is given to the B. Trinity. And even the praises of the angels do not ascend to God except through J.C., as we sing daily in the preface of the Mass "*by whom* the angels praise Thy Majesty." Therefore the acts of praise, of oblation, of adoration, of acceptance of humiliations & contempt, made in union with Jesus, especially after H. Communion, are infinitely agreeable to the H. Trinity.

August 4. This letter has been interrupted for more than a month, we have been up to our ears in examinations, university, etc., so you must excuse. We have had two of our young people ordained priests last Sunday, your feast. They are to say their first masses on August 6 & 7th. I shall have your name put on the pat. They are full of fervour; & as they came here quite young, they know very little of the world's wickedness except from books. What a joy for Jesus to enter into such pure hearts entirely consecrated to Him, knowing no other affection, & yearning to make Him known & loved by others.

We old fellows, after our long years of priestly life, are nearly

[4] John 15:5.
[5] Phil. 4:13.

dried up like old cabbage-leaves; but these young hearts are full of unction & fervour; so I'll get them to pray for you & for dear Dunmore.

From what I hear, I am to have very little to do next year. These young people will take up some of our work, & the old pots will be laid up on the shelf as rare specimens of antiquity; so I will bury myself in the S. Heart, & try to make some little progress in prayer & the interior life; pray for me for that intention.

My affect. love to M. Columba; & my affect. regards to R. Mother, & all the sisters.

Your father in J.C.
Dom Columba Marmion
O.S.B.

## VI. TO HIS FUTURE ABBOT

Dunmore East,[1] Co. Waterford, Ireland.

Very Rev. dear Father [2]

The Archbishop has now appointed my successor who is to take my place in the college tomorrow. I have obtained the necessary paper *ad ingrediendam religionem* [3] which I enclose. I will be retained here for some days to arrange some business matters, and will, D.V., arrive in Maredsous about the middle of this month.

Dear Father, continue to pray for your child, till I am safe in the house of St. Benedict.

I remain, most respectfully, your obedient child in J.C.

Joseph Aloysius Marmion, EDM.

P.S. My present address is:

Rev. J. A. Marmion
Dunmore East, Co. Waterford, Ireland.

[1] Convent of Mercy founded by his sister Mother Columba. See Letter to a Young Priest (Section IX).

[2] Dom Placid Wolter, first abbot of Maredsous. This undated letter must have been written in 1886, at the beginning of November, for Father Marmion entered Maredsous on November 21, 1886.

[3] "To enter religion." This is an expression of a definite decision on his part.

## VII. TO HIS SISTER FLORA

✠ Pax    Abbaye de St. Benoit, Maredsous. par St. Gérard
                                                    [Nov., 1889]
My dearest Sister,[1]

As I know a few lines from me will add to your feast-day joy, I come to assure you of my unchanging affection; & to repeat again, what I have so often told you, that many times each day I carry your intentions & desires with me into the Divine presence, & try my best to obtain for you the grace to become the saint that God would have you. I never told you, I think, that I think you are the only member of our family who resembles me: there is no purgatory for us two — as a very holy Jesuit assured me some little time before I came here, we must go either to heaven by a most fervent love of God & perfect detachment, a *very close* union with Him, or be lost forever. Srs. Peter or Columba [2] could save themselves, & even get a very respectable position in heaven, without leaving the world; at least that's my opinion; but for us, we must keep very close to God, never let go His hand for a moment, lest we fall. I sometimes sigh for the day when the sight of God will confirm my poor weak soul in His grace & love & render sin no longer possible.

But now about your feast-day. Your Saint isn't known over in these countries, we celebrate on the 13th of this month the feast of all "the Saints of the Benedictine order," (40,000); & on the 14th, your feast, we have "the Commemoration of all the deceased Benedictines." What I'll do is this: I'll offer everything that day for these poor souls, & tell them to do their best for you as you are my sister. I find the poor souls do great things for me at times.

I sent you the notice of the death of poor brother Fridolin.[3] We were great friends. He had been dying of consumption for the last two years. He was a very perfect soul, *most obedient,* simple &

---

[1] Flora, a Sister of Mercy whose name in religion was Sister Lorenza and whose patron saint was St. Lawrence O'Toole, an archbishop of Dublin in the twelfth century. November 14 is his feast day. Sister Flora died a happy death in 1892. See Thibaut, *op. cit.,* p. 6.

[2] Two other sisters of Dom Marmion, also Sisters of Mercy.

[3] Brother Fridolin, lay brother of Maredsous, who died on November 4, 1889.

57

charitable. Some days before his death, I got leave to go see him. He was unconscious & did not recognise me; when I went away he got better and asked the infirmarian who had been there. He said Père Columba. He sent me word to return. When I came to him he said, "oh, *Père* Columba, I desire so much to die!" But he added, I leave that entirely in God's hands. I said to him, my dear brother, in a few hours you will see God face to face. I want you to ask two special graces for me. Indeed I will, he said, but added immediately, but you know, I am but a poor sinner & we must fear till the last breath. He died most peacefully & beautifully. We were *all* present when the Abbot anointed him. He said he was never so happy, it reminded him of his profession. His is the third grave now in our little church yard.

I was so glad to hear Sr. Peter was in Dunmore. It would be a gratification to me to get a line from her giving me her personal impression of the place, &c.; as you know how great an interest I have always taken in the foundation, & Columba [4] scarcely ever writes to me now. I tell them that the new P.P. [5] with — doubtless — his velvet waist-coat and gold chain, has got inside the poor Benedictine who wears no waist-coat & sports a boot lace for a chain. However, for the honour of the order, I must say that all these defects are hidden by the habit, for though a Benedictine should yield to no other religious in the love & observance of the vow & virtue of poverty, he is obliged to be scrupulously clean & neat in his person, & even respectable &, as the French say, "distingué" in his bearing. I have had *croaks* innumerable on that subject. [. . .]

Say all kinds of nice things to Rev. Mother, M.M.G., M.M.A. &c. for me. Tell Rev. Mother when she writes for prayers I get all the Community to join, & do my best for her tho' I can't write. Tell Sr. Ryan to be a good child, & to keep very close to God, & to try to forget herself as St. Benedict says "seeking rather what is useful to others than to herself"; [6] if she does this she would do well.

fr. Columba, O.S.B.

[4] Sister (Mother) Columba, Dom Marmion's sister who had founded Dunmore.

[5] Parish priest, or, in American usage, pastor.

[6] Rule of St. Benedict.

## VIII. TO HIS SISTER ROSIE

FIVE LETTERS

I.

✠ Pax                                    Maredsous. Oct. 17. 1891
My dear Sister,[1]

You must excuse my delay in answering your letter. It is a real privilege to aid anyone to love our dearest Lord, & nothing conduces more to this than peace of soul.

As regards your questions. Your being a professed religious need not in any way hinder you from making the act of offering for poor sinners, which is very agreeable to our Lord. When a religious makes such an act, the condition is always understood "as far as my obligations as a religious permit"; so that, in practice, you make this act once for all, & renew it from time to time, & then go on just offering your actions for the intentions prescribed by obedience, & for your own wants, etc., *just as others do, who have not made this act,* & our B. Lord will arrange the details; that is, He will reserve in your actions what obedience & your obligations towards yourself or others require, & apply the rest to sinners. Just as a priest, who is a religious, is obliged to offer H. Mass daily for the intentions indicated by the superior; but this does not prevent him from offering it for any other intentions he may wish, as he only offers it for those last intentions as far as his obligations permit. In one word, act in this matter without *any anxiety*; make the act with your whole heart, & then just go on as before.

As regards various intentions in prayer, there are many souls who find that great precision, & nicety in specifying various intentions in prayer, interferes with the unity of their prayer, & is a cause of anxiety & distraction. For such souls the best thing is to specify these inten-

---

[1] Rosie, in religion Sister Peter, Sister of Mercy. During Dom Marmion's childhood and youth, Rosie was his confidant and the favorite companion of his walks and games. (See Thibaut, *op. cit.*, p. 10f.) He wrote her numerous letters that would have thrown much light on the evolution of his soul as child and young man, but unfortunately Rosie herself destroyed most of these valuable letters. (See *Ibid.*, Preface, p. xi, n. 1.)

tions only from time to time, for example, *once* in the morning, & then a single glance of the soul is sufficient to recall them at the beginning of prayer. However, in all this, my dear Sister, *follow the attraction of the H. Spirit* with great peace; as all anxiety is the mortal enemy of that disposition which the H. Spirit wishes to find in that soul which He calls to a great union with Him. If there is anything you don't take in, in what I say, write when you like, & I will answer, *when I find time.*

Your 3rd question is regarding the sisters with whom you like to be at recreation. Well, my dear Sister, your attraction to speak of God, & to be with those who are fervent, & to go often to choir is an excellent sign of the state of your soul, & shows that the spirit of God is guiding you, & calling you to an intimate union with Himself; however, I don't like the idea of your searching out special sisters to be near during recreation, even though the motive be most excellent; unless it be only from time to time. In a Community, charity is *so delicate*, that any preference shown to others is sure to wound it, & then the eye of love is so quick, that with the utmost precautions, your secret will get out in the end, & you will have wounded our Lord in the apple of His eye by saddening the heart of some sister, who thinks herself less loved, less esteemed by you, than others, & this would be specially the case with less perfect sisters.

I don't mean to say that you may not love in J.C. some sisters more than others, or find more pleasure in the company of those who are edifying & kindred spirits from time to time; but it is certainly more perfect, more pleasing to our dear Lord to associate yourself freely with those whom you find yourself with; & this practice will have a great power of detaching your heart from all merely human consolation & fixing it in the S. Heart. However, in all this there must be nothing strained or violent, no closing yourself up in yourself; but each day as you advance in love of J.C. & in union with Him, your heart must expand more & more in love towards all your sisters.

I would like you to read this portion of my letter to Rev. Mother — if you like — as what I have said depends in a great measure on the manner in which recreation is taken in the Community. Understand me well. What I have said does not mean that it would be against perfection to be united by a *spiritual* affection, or even to enter into a league of pious practices & prayers with sisters who had aspirations & desires similar to yours. — St. John Berchmans had entered into such a league — . But it would be contrary to perfection to do anything which would lead any of your sisters to suspect that they occupied a lower place in your affection & esteem than others.

As regards your desire & attraction towards a more intimate union with God, for a spirit of prayer, I feel, from the various points you indicated, that it is the H. Spirit who has inspired the desire; & that if you are faithful & patient, He will, in His own good time, work in your soul what is for His greater glory, & your perfection. Theologians teach that when God inspires us with an ardent desire of some gift, such as that of a spirit of prayer; & that we often feel, when praying for it, a great peace & confidence, it is a certain sign that He means to accord it.

Your habit of frequently turning to God during work, & of purifying your intention, are excellent aids towards the formation of this habit, in so far as it depends on us (for never forget that a spirit of prayer is a *gift* of God). You must be very careful to possess your soul in peace, as the evil one will probably make great efforts to prevent you acquiring this spirit of prayer. As a general rule, you ought to regard as coming from the enemy any thought which agitates you, throws you into perplexity, which diminishes your confidence & narrows up your heart. The best thing in such cases, is just to put the matter which perplexes you out of your mind, saying, "when I have the opportunity I shall ask the solution of this difficulty from some priest"; then go on in peace as you were before.

Finally, my dear Sister, never forget that Jesus Xt. is *everything*, & we are agreeable to the Father just in proportion as we are united to Him. When celebrating H. Mass lately, I was greatly struck, while reading the Preface, with the thought, that the Seraphim & Cherubim & Angels & Archangels in all their perfection burning with love as they are, can praise the Divine Majesty only "through Jesus Xt." (*per quem majestatem tuam laudent angeli*, etc.) He is the golden bond of union between all creation & the Adorable Trinity; as our dear St. Gertrude says He is the harp through the chords of which all praise must resound in order to be an agreeable harmony to the

Adorable Trinity. This is why the Canon of the H. Mass ends with these mysterious words, *per ipsum, et cum ipso, et in ipso, etc.* "through Him, & with Him, & in Him, is all honour & glory to thee Eternal Father, etc." Therefore, my dear Sister, in every action, try to unite yourself intimately with Jesus, who is ever in your heart, with His dispositions, His designs on you & on others etc. & you will thus raise your actions to a value they would not otherwise have. I have the habit of uniting myself thus by repeating very frequently, in the depths of my heart, "My Jesus, Mercy." However, in all this follow the attraction of the H. Spirit.

I would like you to show this letter to Rev. Mother. There is nothing in the new decree which would prevent her from reading it, (but do as you like). Pray for me, as I have many miseries of soul & body.

Yrs. in J.C.

fr. Columba O.S.B.

II.

✠ Pax     Abbaye de Saint-Benoit, Maredsous. 28. III 1922
My dearest Sister,

I have just got back from *Malines*, where I had been to see our Cardinal.[1] I find dear R. Mother's letter announcing your serious illness. May God's holy will be done: but He could not ask me a greater sacrifice than to lose you. You know how our hearts are united, & *one*, in Him. I shall say H. Mass for you tomorrow with my *whole heart*, begging our Lord to place your heart in His, & to assume & take on Himself all your pains & your languors, to make them Divine; crying out to the Father, as the Voice of His Son, as a continual prayer & immolation in His presence. Our Lord has said that what we do to the least of His members we do for Him, & so in the hour of your weakness, the voice of your suffering is as the voice of His own Son crying out for pity. As on the occasion of my last visit I offered the Infinite Sacrifice to supply for all that may have been wanting in your past life, to thank him for all he has

---

[1] Désiré Cardinal Mercier, Archbishop of Malines.

62

done for you, to atone for all your sins & purify you in His blood, so shall I do tomorrow.

I must finish for the post. I remain in close & continual union with you.

May God bless & love you as I do.

✠ Columba Abb

P.S. Dear R. Mother, a thousand thanks. Please let me know at once if any change comes.

III.

✠ Pax

Bruxelles. 47, Avenue des arts
21. IV. 22

My dearest Sister,

Just a line to wish you a happy & holy Easter. I should have done so sooner, but I have been very busy indeed. It is a great joy — in fact my greatest Paschal joy, — to know that God has spared you to us, & especially to me. You will be glad to know that I am in good health, & have been able to celebrate all the Pontifical offices without difficulty. God is very good to me. He shows me more & more that our great treasures are our weaknesses & our miseries, for He has espoused them at the moment of the Incarnation. *Vere languores nostros ipse tulit* [1] St. Paul says, "What is weakness in God is more powerful than all human strength, & what is folly in God is wiser than all human wisdom." [2] He did not take on Him a glorious body like that of the Transfiguration, but came clothed in a body which was like that of us poor sinners *in similitudine corporis peccati* [3] & He sanctified, & rendered divine all the weaknesses of that poor fallen nature. So St. Paul glories in his weakness, for this glorifies God & fills us with His power. [4]

I am here at Brussels spending a couple of days with the Marquis I . . . one of our highest families. All the family were at H. Communion during my Mass said in their oratory. When good, the

[1] "Surely He hath borne our infirmities" (Isa. 53:4).
[2] I Cor. 1:25.
[3] "In the likeness of sinful flesh" (Rom. 8:3).
[4] II Cor. 12:9.

Belgians are excellent. I am on my way to Tournai, where I have important business to transact. I am praying for you, dearest, & for all. God is so good to me I live now on my daily Communion. All the morning "I walk in the strength of that divine food," [5] & from the afternoon I live in the thought of the following Communion; for He strengthens us according to our desires & preparation.

Our Lord has promised that "He who eateth me shall live by me." [6] His life becomes ours, the source of all our activity.

May God bless & love you as I do, from my heart of hearts,

Love to R. Mother & all

✠ Columba Abb

IV.

✠ Pax                                                        Maredsous.
                                                             29. XII 22

My dearest Sister,

I was really longing to answer your loving letter for Xmas; but you have no idea of the life of an abbot in a large monastery, having a big college, & school of arts & trades, a convent of nuns, to provide for; & then I have got to be known by so many people that I have a crushing correspondence. Every morning at H. Mass I place you in our dear Lord's heart, & I beg Him, as He enters into the "Holy of Holies" (His Father's bosom), through the veil, which St. Paul tells us is His crucified humanity,[1] to take us with Him, & present us to the Father. "Xt has died for all," says St. Paul, "in order to present us to His Father. He, the Just one, for us sinners, having died in His Flesh to be filled with the force & strength of His Spirit for us." [2] *What He* presents to the Father is ever most acceptable, however miserable we may be. You have this every morning, & at Xmas the 2nd Mass was for you, Matty, Mary,[3] & some spiritual children.

I see our dear Lord is just introducing you into the last stage, through which your soul has need to pass before going to Him. Our

[5] III Kings 19:8.
[6] John 6:58.
[1] Heb. 6:19–20; 9:11–12.
[2] This text is not from St. Paul, but from St. Peter, First Epistle, 3:18.
[3] Matty, his brother; Mary, his sister.

Lord has taken all our sins on Him, & has fully expiated them & this expiation is applied to us by *compunction*, & absolution. But besides this, He has taken on Him all the infirmities & incapacity of His Spouse. Before going to Him, she must *see*, & *feel* & *know* that all come to her from Him, & that it is our misery, poverty, & imperfection which having been *assumed* by His S. Humanity, is raised to a divine value in Him. This is a great secret which few understand. St. Paul expresses it in these words: "Willingly do I glory in my infirmities, in order that it be Xt's virtue et strength which dwells in me. This is why I take pleasure in my infirmities." [4] When I make my Stations daily, & contemplate *God* the *Infinite*, the *All Powerful*, crushed by weakness, & trembling in Gethsemani; I see instead of taking on Himself a glorified body, He has assumed "a body like unto that of us sinners," [5] *in order to render our weakness divine in Him*. This is what you are passing through at present, in order to destroy & eradicate entirely from your soul the last traces of confidence in yourself, or the talents or qualities which He gave you, & on which you have perhaps leaned just a little up to this. "His left hand supports your head & His right hand encircles you in your weakness." [6] He has been showing me this in my soul for some time; & I am never so happy as when prostrate before His Infinite Mercy, & I showing Him my misery, weakness & unworthiness; but I keep looking all the time, not at my misery so much as at his infinite Mercy. Just like a little girl who having fallen into a pool of dirty mud, runs to her mother showing her pinafore & crying until it is cleaned.

I am laid up at present with a kind of bilious flu; but it is getting better. I have to go to Brussels next week & meet all sorts of people, bless a marriage, meet Mary, etc. My monks wish to have my portrait painted in oil by one of our great artists, as I am the 3rd Abbot of Maredsous.[7] The R. Mother of Tyburn [8] was at the *last* extremity

[4] II Cor. 12:9.

[5] See Rom. 8:3.

[6] See Cant. 2:6 and 8:3.

[7] This portrait was painted at Antwerp by the artist Joseph Janssens, in January, 1923. It was finished less than a week before Abbot Marmion's death (January 30).

[8] Mother Mary of St. Peter Garnier with whom Abbot Marmion had a long and very beautiful spiritual correspondence in French. See Section XXIV.

last week; but the Infant Jesus came & cured her (this is a secret).
Love to R. Mother, & all. from my heart of hearts

☩ Columba Marmion Abb.

v.

### Two Fragments of Lost Letters

[. . .] If we only had faith, we should *see* that by offering H. Mass
we *really* present, by the hands of the priest, a gift and an immolation
to God, which is beyond our debts, because it is infinite.[. . .]

[. . .] One of the highest and most perfect forms of charity is that
of consenting to govern others for God's love. God has chosen you
because you are so weak, and small, in order that whatever good you
do, may be clearly seen to come from Him. (St. Paul): "Divine folly
is wiser than the wisdom of men." [1] I pray that God may give you
the grace to abandon yourself entirely into the hands of Jesus Christ;
for when we abandon ourselves with absolute confidence, and without reserve, to His wisdom and love, He takes a most zealous care
of every detail of our life; for, says St. Paul, "Jesus Christ is our
wisdom, our sanctity, our patience, our justice and redemption from
God." [2]

"Reveal thy way to the Lord and hope in Him, and He will do
the rest." [3]

## IX. TO A YOUNG PRIEST

Abbaye de St. Benoit, Maredsous,
par St Gérard, Belgium. [November, 1889]

My dear Frank,[1]

I have been for a long time anxious to write to you to congratulate
you on the priceless grace God has bestowed on you in calling you to

[1] I Cor. 1:25.
[2] I Cor. 1:30.
[3] Ps. 36:5.
[1] One of his former pupils at Clonliffe, now studying in Rome, as Dom Marmion had
done. See Thibaut, *op. cit.*, pp. 40 f.

the priesthood.[2] I could not tell you how happy I felt when I heard you and John Waters were ordained. — You know, John was one of my spiritual children, in whom I take a special interest. — A priest can do so much for God if, in offering the H. Sacrifice, he unites the oblation of himself, his life, his love, all he has, with that of the divine Victim. He can obtain priceless graces for all mankind, can stay the anger of God, and gain powerful aid for the Church, not to speak of the great merit he gains for himself. Let us try to be faithful and loving towards Our dear Lord. It is in the heart of the priest He expects to repose, when He is outraged by sinners; and also, He so often finds even there but coldness and ingratitude.

I must thank you from my heart for your great kindness to my poor sister.[3] Poor thing, she is a stranger in the diocese of Waterford. She is almost without friends since my departure; and her little foundation has to struggle against very great difficulties and trials. And your kindness procured them a real joy, as the things of God are their only happiness. I hope, later on, when you have time, you will pay them a visit. It would be such a pleasure.

Talking of visits, I fully expect you will pass by here. It is scarcely out of your way; and the monastery is really worth a visit. Need I say, how great a happiness it would be to see you. — Of course, all this applies to John Waters too. — As for myself I am *extremely happy*, and enjoy excellent health. I had an attack of influenza; but it is now passed away. I get letters regularly from Tom Waters. I could not tell you how happy I am to get a line from my old Alma Mater.[4] She is prospering; and I believe there is a very good spirit there now, D.G.

Have you ever seen Mgr. Kirby of the *Collegio Irlandese?* You know he ordained me. I have always retained a great veneration for him, as I regard him as a real saint; but I fear he looks on me as a kind of apostate, for having left the secular mission. However, I heard the words: *Magister adest et vocat te*[5] and I should obey. I

---

[2] The ordination took place on November 1, 1889 — which allows us to fix the date of this letter.

[3] Sister (now Mother) Columba, who had just undertaken the foundation of Dunmore Convent of Mercy, near Waterford. See references to her in preceding letters.

[4] I.e., Cloncliffe.

[5] "The Master is there and calls thee" (John 11:28).

should be glad to get some details about the Prop. and *Coll. Irlandese*, the classes, etc.; as I always look back on Rome as one of the happiest epochs of my life.

. . . . . . . . . . . . . . . . . . . . . . . . . . . .

The Pope, when Bishop of Perugia, published a little pamphlet: *La pratica dell'umilità.*[6] F. Abbot gave me leave to ask you for it; if you can get it for me, I should be very grateful. I want you also to find out for me, if the faculty I received from the Prop. to substitute the 15 mysteries of the Rosary for the Office in case of illness, etc., ceases by my becoming a Benedictine. I was ill lately, and dispensed from the Office, but was so glad to be able to say the Rosary *in nomine Ecclesiae.*[7]

I recommend myself earnestly to your prayers, especially on the feast of St. Benedict. I will ask you and John Waters to give me a special *memento* in your Mass on that day in memory of old times. . . .

Write to me soon and give all the news of Rome you can. One of my brethren is making his studies in Rome. He is in the new college of St. Anselm *Piazza Scossa Cavalli*, near *Castel St. Angelo. Frère Pietro* is his name. If you come across him, tell him you know me.

Believe me, your affect. friend in J.C.

fr. Columba Marmion, O.S.B.

# X. TO ABBOT-PRIMATE

## HILDEBRAND DE HEMPTINNE

### NINE LETTERS

*The abbot of Maredsous to whom the following letters are addressed is Dom Hildebrand de Hemptinne, a Belgian, who after serving with the Papal Zouaves, went to Beuron in Germany to ask for the monastic habit. He was to play a most active part in the foundation*

[6] "The Practice of Humility."
[7] "In the name of the Church."

of Maredsous, and was elected its abbot on August 9, 1890. But scarcely three years later he was also appointed, by Leo XIII, first Primate of the Benedictine Order. This entailed residence for at least eight months each year on the Aventine in Rome, in the Abbey of Sant' Anselmo which he had built. In spite of his remarkable gifts of personality, such a situation could not last indefinitely. In 1909, therefore, he resigned the abbacy of Maredsous, and Dom Marmion was elected to succeed him. In 1913 the Primate returned to Beuron, the monastery of his profession, there to die.

The letters here published make clear the attitude of the young monk toward his abbot, who holds for him the place of Christ. They also show his own conception of the abbatial function according to Benedictine tradition. The simplicity with which he opens his soul to his spiritual father is especially noteworthy.

Until the death of the Abbot-Primate, Dom Marmion continued a regular and abundant correspondence with him, particularly after he succeeded him in the abbacy of Maredsous. These letters are full of interest, but often too private to be published. Moreover, being written in French, they have no place here.

I.

✠ Benedicite [1]                          Maredsous. 9.1.90. [1891] [2]
Very Rev. and dear F. Abbot,

You told us on the day of your election,[3] that the abbot receives, as a special grace of heaven, a very tender and paternal love for his childen, a kind of reflection of the Divine Paternity. I will not listen therefore to the thought which suggests itself to my mind, viz. that knowing as you do my past, & how unworthy [4] I am to be numbered

[1] In the Beuron Congregation the custom was to greet superiors with this word, *Benedicite* (Bless me), at the beginning of a conversation or a letter.

[2] From the contents of this letter it may be conjectured that the date 1890 should be 1891 — an error not too surprising at the beginning of the year.

[3] August 9, 1890.

[4] Concerning this humble deprecation of his past, read Note 4 to his Letter 7 to Father (Bishop) Dwyer (Section III), with its reference to Thibaut, *Abbot Columba Marmion*, p. 32.

amongst your children, words of congratulation from me could not add to your joy. No, dear Father, I will act towards you, as I try to do towards my Father who is in heaven. I will cast myself in spirit at your feet, & while acknowledging my unworthiness, will tell you that I feel you love me, & that in return I shall try to love you with that true affection of which our H. Father speaks. During these days I offer all my actions to God, that He may bestow every grace & spiritual light on you; & that, if it be for His glory, & your spiritual advancement, He may restore your strength, & establish you in robust health.

I commenced the course of Philosophy today.[5] The young clerks were very attentive & seemed to follow intelligently my lecture & explanations, which were all in latin. I will begin the class of Theology this evening with Br. Joseph; but I am doubtful, whether, with my classes at the school [6] & other occupations there, I could continue to give the two courses of Theology & Philosophy in a satisfactory manner. However, I will make the trial.

I shall be counting every day now till you come back to us again. The house is not the same when the father is absent.

Asking your blessing, & a little remembrance in your prayer at the tomb of our H. Father,[7] I remain your unworthy, but affectionate child in J.C.

fr. Columba O.S.B.

II.

✠ Benedicite.                                           Maredsous. [1894?]
Very Rev. and dear F. Abbot,

During our exile here below, we cannot see our Heavenly Father, nor hear His voice; our greatest consolation is to speak to Him and assure Him of our love; so also, during your absence, as I cannot see you or hear your words of encouragement, it is a great consolation to write a few lines to assure you of my unchanging affection. Many times each day, I pray our Heavenly Father to console and strengthen

[5] To the young student-monks of Maredsous.
[6] To the abbey's secondary school.
[7] St. Benedict's tomb at Monte Cassino.

70

you, and to give you all the light and grace necessary to carry out the great designs He wishes to accomplish through your means.

I am, thank God, well and happy, and living in great peace. F. Prior has given me permission to read the works of St. John of the Cross. This *lecture* [1] is a perfect flood of light for my soul, and I am beginning to understand what it is to live by faith, to pray the prayer of faith, and to make no account of the changes of time and temperament. At the same time, I see now more clearly than ever before, what danger those run who trust to their own judgement, and allow themselves to be guided by any light except that of the teaching of the Church, and the revealed word of God.

I have nothing to add about the novices. F. Master [2] and I are living in the greatest union; and a most beautiful spirit of charity and holy joy reigns in the novitiate. . . .

I was at Louvain [3] some days ago. It is a *real* consolation to go there now. They are very much in earnest, and take a great interest in philosophy. Philosophical discussions are their ordinary subject of conversation. Felix [4] was the best; but the others did very well indeed, except the two of the 2nd year [. . .] who had not worked as well as they might.

Asking your blessing, I remain with profound respect your loving child in J.C.

f. Columba, O.S.B.

III.

✝ Benedicite.  Maredsous. 8 Dec. 1898.
Right Rev. and very dear Father Abbot,

Having finished my retreat at St. Scholastica's [1] to-day, I wish to render account of my two retreats, and of my occupations.

---

[1] This reading.

[2] Dom Benoit d'Hondt, who had been a special trial to him during his novitiate. Dom Marmion was then *zélateur des novices* — that is, assistant to the novice master.

[3] Dom Marmion was responsible during this period for preparing graduates of Maredsous Abbey's School for their examination. These students lived at the hall the abbey had recently established in the university city.

[4] The future Dom Jean de Hemptinne.

[1] To the Benedictine nuns of Maredret, near Maredsous.

At Louvain[2] Our Lord protected and aided me in a very special manner. When I commenced and saw the members of the various faculties present, I was really afraid; but I said to myself: I am here through obedience, and God must aid me. Like St. Placid *vidi abbatis melotem supra caput meum*.[3] I found a great facility to express myself, and I received the most encouraging assurances of the entire satisfaction of the hearers from Mgr. Lami, Mgr. Moulard, etc.; and several of the young priests asked me to become their director when I should be at Mont-César. The vice-president having been obliged to leave during one of the conferences, came to ask me to supply what he lost as he did not wish to lose anything. I tell you this in all simplicity, as I wish you to know exactly how things were. In one of the conferences, I spoke *very strongly* against the spirit of extreme criticism and naturalism, taking for my text the words *sapientia hujus mundi stultitia est apud Deum*,[4] and although several professors, who are known for their advanced ideas, were present, no one was hurt. . . . The foundation at Mont-César is well received, and they are anxious for us to come.[5]

At. St. Scholastica's, I was *extremely* edified. In fact the retreat has done me almost as much good as the Religious. They seek God so simply and so generously. I felt really quite confounded that I, so impure and so unworthy, should be employed by God to communicate His light and grace to such pure souls. I felt like a hawk amongst doves; but it shows the grandeur of the christian priesthood which is ever a channel for God's graces despite the unworthiness of the instrument.

I am happy to say the clerics[6] are giving me satisfaction. Unfortunately they are all more or less weak, and are not able for as much work as I should like; but still it is *very satisfactory*, and in my

---

[2] Dom Marmion had preached the retreat at the University College of the Holy Spirit, where young priests, theological students, and several professors were in residence.

[3] "I saw Father Abbot's mantle over my head" — an allusion to St. Benedict's miracle, as related by St. Gregory the Great in his *Dialogues*, Bk. II, chap. 7. The young Placid, saved from drowning by the monk Maurus, who had been sent to his help by St. Benedict, declared that he had been saved by the saint in person.

[4] "For the wisdom of this world is foolishness with God" (I Cor. 3:19).

[5] See Note 1 to letter 12 in Section III.

[6] The young student-monks (or "clerks").

branch I am really pleased. . . . We have the most delightful summer weather at present; but of course that may change.

As regards my person, I am well and very happy, though *almost* astonished at times to see how full I am of vanity and of desire to please men.

With profound respect and sincere affection, your Paternity's most unworthy child.

f. Columba, O.S.B.

IV.

✝ Benedicite.          [Mont-César, January, 1900] [1]
Right Rd. & dear Father Abbot,

Please accept my best & most sincere wishes for a holy, happy & peaceful New Year. My most fervent prayers shall be offered to God that He may bless all your undertaking for His glory. All here goes well. I am satisfied with the studies of our clerks & also with their spirit which is excellent. Brother Athanasius is preparing with fervour for his solemn profession which he hopes to make on the 15th January.

There is a young Irish-man at our house at Louvain at present. He is son of [. . . .], a very nice, pious young fellow. I am praying that God may give him a vocation. He spent some days here at Christmas, & made a very good impression on all who came in contact with him. God is giving a great blessing to our monastery at present. There is great fervour & a most flourishing novitiate. It is God's way of recompensing us for the sacrifice we make in living separated from our beloved father. I feel more & more that God is the source of all *real* good; & that we are capable of doing good in the measure of our submission to Him, & union with His will.

I am glad our entry into Louvain has been put off, as it would be a very great happiness to have your Paternity present at the new foundation & receive your blessing on our work.

Humbly begging your blessing & prayers, I remain your unworthy but affectionate child in J.C.

f. Columba O.S.B.

[1] Dom Marmion had been appointed prior of Mont-César in September.

73

✝ Benedicite.                    Mont-César, Louvain. 2 June 1902.

Right Rev. and very dear Father Abbot-Primate,

Allow me to wish you from my heart a joyous, holy feast. As I have frequently told your Paternity, I very often pray for you; but on this feast-day, I shall do so more fervently, in order that God may bless and prosper you, and your undertakings for His glory. I take this opportunity of thanking you for your paternal letter; and I shall certainly study to avoid in future every thing which could cause you pain.

I have been explaining in class the treatise on original sin; and I have been extremely struck by the relation which St. Paul reveals between the disobedience of the first Adam, and the obedience of the Second Adam, Jesus Xt. I have felt drawn almost continually for the last few weeks to meditate this truth; and I have understood, as I never did before, that the beauty and strength of our monastic life consists in our association, as His members, to the obedience of Jesus Christ. I see more and more that the more completely and perfectly we embrace with J.C., and after His example, every manifestation of the divine will by a most perfect submission to Superiors, the more perfectly we become His members and partake of the effects of His redemption. I had always been persuaded of this truth; but lately God has given me the grace to see it so clearly, that it seems as though I had never known it before. And I find now a great suavity and docility of heart in accepting even what is most humiliating and repugnant to nature.

I tell you this, most reverend father, because you were good enough to tell me that what concerns my soul interests you; and also in order that you may know that by God's grace you will find me entirely disposed to acquiesce, not only externally, but also with entire docility of heart and judgement in whatever you may see fit to impose in future. In fact, for some time past, I feel a very great detachment in my heart from all persons and things in this world, and have but one desire: that of belonging without reserve to God, occupying myself *solely* with Him, and with these persons and oc-cupations which He may wish to confide to me; ready to quit them and take up others just as He may make known to me by obedience. This is my real disposition of heart at present; and I regard it as one of the most precious graces God has ever given me.

According to your instructions, I was at St. Scholastica's for the quarter term. I found that dear Community in great peace, serving God *in gaudio et simplicitate cordis*.[1] Here all doing well. . . .

I humbly ask your paternal benediction, and beg you to believe me most respectfully and affectionately in J.C. your unworthy son,

f. Columba, O.S.B.

## VI.

✠ Benedicite.                                    Louvain. May 23rd 1903.
Right Rev. and very dear F. Abbot-Primate,

St. Francis de Sales says that the most agreeable gift a child can make to his father is that of his affection. On the occasion of your feast, I wish to assure you once more of my respectful and filial affection. A few weeks ago, you asked me to fix my stability[1] at Louvain. I did so without hesitation, because I am persuaded that it is God's will and yours; but it was one of the greatest sacrifices I have ever made for God's love. Still, as Primate, I am sure you will still allow me to look on you as my father, and continue as heretofore to take an interest in my life.

Thank God, all is in perfect peace here.[2] Dom [. . .] is very quiet, and much more recollected and pious than formerly. I found in his case that also in general kindness is that great power of a superior; still, in certain cases a certain firmness is necessary. At the first *séance*[3] of the professors, he was arrogant and selfish, wishing to arrange everything his own way. I immediately spoke with authority, and acted with firmness; and ever since then he is meek and docile as a lamb. He had a long chat with me yesterday about his future, and I am quite persuaded that a few years of quiet in Italy (p.e.[4] at

[1] "With gladness and simplicity of heart" (Acts 2:46).

[1] At the time of his profession at Maredsous, Dom Marmion took the vow that all monks take — of perpetual "stability" in his monastery.

[2] Dom Marmion was director of the student-monks, as well as professor of dogma on the theology faculty.

[3] Meeting.

[4] *Par exemple*, the French equivalent of "e.g."

Cava,[5] as he seems to desire it so much, and they are willing to receive him) would do him an amount of good.

Dom [. . .] is still fluctuating. He is an excellent professor, and most agreeable *confrère*; but I feel he will never be at rest till "he has had his folly out," until he has seen *for himself* that a solitary life is not made for him. He is now confessor to the Little Sisters of the Poor. Perhaps the interest he takes in them, and their prayers, may attach him to our foundation.

The clerics are very good. . . .

I was invited lately to preach an English sermon at Brussels. All the English colony was there. I preached in the Church of the Servites, rue Washington. The congregation was greatly pleased, and I was introduced to quite a number of English, Irish and Americans. The next morning I said Mass in a convent. The Superioress has a great reputation for sanctity. She sent for me after the Mass. She told me she felt impelled to consult me about her soul. She is favoured by God with the highest gifts of contemplation and intimacy with Our Lord; yet a most simple, joyous soul, just like a child, and yet, despite great suffering, governing her Community with a most remarkable prudence and success for long years. She is 40 years of age. I told her I had no personal experience of such things; but I had no difficulty in seeing that she is led by the Holy Spirit; and so I told her to be in peace, and to follow the Spirit which is guiding her. I have had no further relation with her; for I understand very clearly now, what I did not before, that although real love of Our Lord must fill us with a most ardent love and zeal for all His members, yet we may not devote ourselves *in particular* to any soul unless He Himself puts us in relation with her by the ordinary way of ecclesiastical or religious obedience. This of course is strictly for your Paternity alone.

I am to go to Maredret in the beginning of June. After that I shall write again to your Paternity.

I remain with profound respect and sincere affection your unworthy child in J.C.

f. Columba, O.S.B.

[5] A Benedictine monastery in southern Italy.

## VII

✠ Benedicite.                              Mont-César. 27 May 1904.

Right Rev. and very dear F. Abbot-Primate,

As I am giving a retreat to a number of young religious, belonging
to one of the Congregations expelled from France, who are to be
raised to holy orders at Malines to-morrow, I have but a moment to
wish you from my heart a most holy and joyous feast. It is needless
for me to assure you of my prayers; but I take this opportunity of
expressing once more my filial affection, and to tell you that I am
more and more intimately united with you in the bonds of holy and
sincere charity.

I was at Jupille, and also at Lede, lately. F. Abbot[1] made no difficulty. Both these Communities are, I am sure, very pleasing to the
S. Heart of Our Divine Master. They certainly have all the marks
of His most abundant benediction. The Superioress of Lede is really
a superior person; and I find her greatly improved in every way.
In order to understand and be compassionate with others, a Superior
must pass through trial; and so it has been with her. The Superioress
of Jupille *looks* much better; but I feel she is getting ripe for Heaven.

I am off to Woolhampton on the 23 July; and at Jupille I shall be
from 30 August to the 8 September, on which date I hope to meet
your Paternity for the Profession of D. Laurent's niece, and of many
others.

Here all are well. Dom [. . .] is quite unhinged, and gives no
more class. I think he requires a change. A monk must find *all* his
consolation in God; or otherwise he will often be unhappy. . . .

With profound respect and filial affection, I remain ever your
unworthy son in J.C.

f. Columba, O.S.B.

## VIII

✠ Benedicite.                     Louvain. 15 August [probably 1907]

Right Rev. and dear F. Abbot-Primate,

The letter I sent yesterday was written while waiting for the
return of the Cardinal. It may interest you to know that, in an inti-

---

[1] Dom Robert de Kerckhove, abbot of Mont-César.

mate conversation which I had with His Eminence, I asked him: "What would be your Eminence's attitude in the event of the Abbot-Primate's being proposed for the Cardinalate?"

"J'y serais tout à fait favorable. Je ne pense pas devoir faire une démarche positive dans ce but; mais si l'on demande mon avis, je serais tout à fait favorable." [1] He told me he has no fear of his prestige, etc., being diminished by the nomination of a second Belgian Cardinal.

· · · · · · · · · · · · · · · · · · · · · · · · · · · · · · · · · · · · · · ·

Ever your dutiful and affectionate son in J.C.

f. Columba, O.S.B.

IX.

Benedicite.                                  Mont-César, Louvain. 9 Jan. [1908]

Right Rev. and dear F. Abbot-Primate,

Please accept my very sincere and affectionate wishes for this New Year.

I had the happiness last March to receive into the Church a young Jewess; and, with your permission, I received her as an Oblate of St. Benedict. Her novitiate should end the 16th April, but she is dying, and I don't think she can live more than a few weeks now. I should be very grateful if you would authorize me to anticipate her profession if necessary. She is a most beautiful soul; pure as an angel; and in *continual* suffering so as not to have more than about half an hour's sleep in 24. The light and union to which God has admitted her are surprising.

You will be glad to know that Br [. . .] is on the good road, and making *real* progress; I have no hesitation in recommending him for profession. Perhaps it might be better to wait still a couple of months. May I present Br [. . .] for the subdiaconate in Lent?

I add, very confidentially, that my impression at . . . was sad; in fact I was delighted to get away, and return to Mont-César. There seems little cordial union between the Abbot and his Community.

I have not been to St. Scholastica since May, and so have no news from that quarter as no one ever writes to me now.

---

[1] "I would be altogether in favor of it. I do not think I should take any steps to this end; but if my advice were asked, I would be altogether favorable."

I have been named a member of the "Commission of Vigilance" by His Eminence. I must acknowledge that to be selected to watch over the purity of the Faith in this diocese is a very great joy and consolation for me. As your Paternity is probably aware, I shall be associated with very distinguished men in this capacity.

With profound respect and affection, I remain your very devoted son in J.C.

f. Columba, O.S.B.

P.S. The name of the Jewess is Violet Agnes Susman.

## XI. TO AN UNKNOWN CORRESPONDENT

✠ Pax                            Abbaye de St Benoit, Maredsous.
                                 Sept. 11, 1897.

My dear Child,

Your letter was a joy for me; for I see that despite your unworthiness, God is guiding you, and is full of mercy and love in your regard. Your great object ought to be, to become very humble. This is the sure road to God's love; for He is so powerful that He can change even our corruption into the pure gold of His love, if He finds no obstacle in pride. Believe me, my dear child, if you are sincerely humble, God will do the rest. To become humble, a practice I have may aid you: it is to make three stations every day.

1st. station: Consider what you *were*. If you have once sinned mortally in your life, you have merited to be cursed for all Eternity by Him Who is Infinite truth and Infinite goodness. And that curse would have brought with it, separation forever from God; eternal hatred for God, and for all that is good, just and beautiful; and to be trampled for all Eternity beneath the feet of the demons. And this punishment would have been just, and have been pronounced by Him Who is Goodness itself. Oh, my dear child, we have perhaps merited all this; and if we be not there now, it is an effect of God's infinite mercy, and of the sufferings of J.C. Can anything be bad enough for us? can anyone do us injury in despising us?

2nd. station: what we *are*. It is *of faith* that we are incapable of a good thought without God, "without me you can do *nothing*"[1]; that is, we cannot make one step towards God without Him. Then our daily infidelities, our sins, our ingratitude, our best actions are very miserable indeed.

3rd. station: what we may *become*. If God takes away His hand from us, we are perfectly capable of becoming what we were before, and worse. God sees this. He knows what depths of treachery we are capable of. How can we be proud?

But after these stations, we must never forget another, and it is this: we are *infinitely* rich in J.C., and God's mercies are to our miseries what the ocean is to a drop of water. We never glorify God more than when we, despite the sight of our sins and unworthiness, are so filled with confidence in His mercy and in the infinite merits of J.C., that we throw ourselves in His bosom, full of confidence and love, *sure* that He cannot repell us: "a humble and contrite heart, oh God, Thou wilt not despise."[2] [ . . .][3]


# XII. TO DOM GERALD VAN CALOEN, ABBOT OF OLINDA

## FOUR LETTERS

*Dom Gerald van Caloen, member of a noble Belgian family, was the first postulant to seek admission to the Abbey of Maredsous, on the very day of its foundation. Twenty years later, when the few surviving monks in Brazil had asked for help from their brethren of the Beuronese Congregation, Dom Gerald was chosen to organize the revival of these unhappy monasteries ruined by persecution. He began with Olinda Abbey, of which he became first, prior, then in 1897, abbot. He had brought with him several companions from Maredsous, and others followed later. At one time there was even*

[1] John 15:5.
[2] Ps. 50:19.
[3] The end of this letter is missing.

*a possibility that Dom Marmion himself might be sent to Brazil. But divine Providence had other plans for him.*

*Dom Gerald van Caloen had a strong and adventurous character and he was successful in his enterprise. In 1906, when abbot of Rio de Janeiro, he was appointed bishop with jurisdiction over the Indians of the Rio Branco. He returned finally to Europe only in 1919, and died there on January 16, 1932.*

*The first of the letters that follow was written at the time when Dom van Caloen was prior of the Abbey of Olinda. These letters should be compared with the one written in July of the same year, 1896, to Father Dwyer.*

*These four letters were recently found among the archives of the Abbey of Saint-André, and have been kindly loaned to us by Dom Nicolas Huyghebaert.*

I.

✠ Benedicite                                    Maredsous, May 8, [1896]

Very rev. & dear Fr. Prior,

Please accept my most heartfelt sympathy, & the promise of my fervent prayers for the repose of the soul of your dear father. I had not the honor of knowing the baron personally; but as we are all brothers in J.C., I shall now look on him as one of my parents, & intercede for him with my own. For us who have left all things to assure our eternal happiness, our great consolation is to see our parents die happily in order that we may be sure to meet them again in our Father's home, never to be separated from them for all eternity. R.I.P.

Although I do not write often, it is not that I lack interest in your work at Olinda; on the contrary, I have your success very much at heart; & if Providence has destined me to labour here in a more modest sphere, I envy those who have been thought worthy to devote their lives to such a glorious cause; & I try to aid you by my prayers, since I may not do so by my presence.

Thank God, we have every mark of the divine blessing here at present. I have never seen such fervour & such union. Our novitiate [1]

---

[1] Dom Marmion was *zelator*, i.e., assistant to the master of novices.

is not numerous, but the elements are excellent. Besides, two excellent postulants are coming to us, & have been already accepted. Fr. John [Felix de Hemptinne][2] is really a model novice, & a *most* enthusiastic admirer of the monastic life; in fact, he finds it difficult to understand that his former companions, — Joseph del Marmol,[3] Ch [. . .], etc. —, can remain in the world, which to him seems so unworthy of them. I am sorry that what I said about publishing his mss. hurt Dom Willibrord.[4] It was said in pure fun. He ought to know me well enough to see that I was not serious.

Please tell Dom Feuillen that I spent a week with the Canon de Wouters, & that we have become great friends; though of course he can never reconcile himself to Dom Feuillen's departure.[5] The Canon told me all about your voyage to Jerusalem, all his difficulties, etc. He is a most interesting man; & I spent some very pleasant hours with him. Please present my most affectionate & fraternal greetings to all the dear brethren, & believe me with much respect, yours most devotedly *in Corde Jesu*

fr. Columba O.S.B.

II.

✠ Benedicite                              Maredsous, May 10.97
Right Rev. & dear F. Abbot,
It was very good of you to think of writing to me. I take a very sincere interest in the success of our workers at Olinda; & I daily pray our dear Lord to give you all His divine peace & joy & to console you all in the midst of the privations & sufferings attached to your present position. As for myself, you know me sufficiently to be assured that if my superiors thought I could be of any service at Olinda, they would encounter neither opposition nor the slightest hesitation on my part to obey. On the contrary I should regard their order as an indication of God's will; & should devote any energy or talents I have to your work. But I would not, for any thing, make

[2] Later he became prefect, then vicar-apostolic in Upper Katanga.
[3] In fact, Joseph del Marmol entered Maredsous some months later and became a monk under the name of Dom Boniface. He was for more than thirty years a missionary in Katanga.
[4] Dom Willibrord van Heteren, monk of Maredsous, sent to Brazil.
[5] Dom Feuillen Lhermitte, monk of Maredsous, sent to Brazil.

any move in this matter myself, lest I might be going against God's designs in my regard. I am more & more persuaded that a monk's perfection is expressed in the words of St. Francis de Sales *ne rien désirer, ne rien demander, ne rien refuser*.[1] I would even think it a certain presumption on my part to *ask* to be sent, as I am more & more conscious that there is so much weakness in me, both physical and moral, that I should very probably be more of a burden than a help to you.

We are doing very nicely here. Our novitiate is filled with fervent novices, full of talent & zeal for perfection; & the theological studies under the guidance of D. Urban [2] are really very complete & quite up to the mark. The house at Louvain [3] is going up. I think it is Father Abbot's intention, when the present wing is finished, to send our theological students there;[4] & thus separate our scholastics from the novices, which I consider a measure of the very highest importance. Please tell F. Prior that I was at Braine-le-Comte again this year, & that *M. le Chanoine* & I spoke a great deal about him. He never speaks of D. Prior but with the greatest affection & veneration. Tell him I have become quite a missionary now, & preach sometimes four times in one day. I remain with profound respect, yrs sincerely & affectionately in J.C.

f. Columba O.S.B.

III.

✠ Benedicite                    Maredsous. Nov. 11, 1897
Right Rev. & Very dear Father Abbot,

Please excuse my delay in answering your very kind letter. I thought it better to wait till all had been settled, & now I send this by the two Fathers who are leaving us & taking my place.[1] Before receiving your Paternity's letter, I had known that there was question of my going to Olinda; & I immediately went to our Father Prior

---

[1] "Desire nothing, ask for nothing, refuse nothing."

[2] Dom Urbain Baltus.

[3] House belonging to Maredsous at Louvain for graduates of the abbey school who were students at the University.

[4] Early ideas for what actually became the Abbey of Mont-César in 1899.

[1] Dom Maur Desrumaux and Brother Mayeul de Caigny, a novice. Dom Maur is mentioned farther on in this letter. The second was already a priest. He was later to found the Benedictine abbey in Trinidad.

& begged him to tell Father Abbot at Beuron that I placed myself absolutely in his hands to dispose of me as he pleased. Had it been decided that I was to go, I should have been very happy to be with you; but, as you are aware, my superiors judged that I was not fit for such a mission; & that it was better for me to try to serve God modestly here at home. I must confess I am sure that this decision of my superiors is but the expression of God's will in my regard. For, past & present experience make me feel how weak & unprovided I am with the necessary virtue to overcome the difficulties & dangers one meets in such missions.

I feel the greatest interest in your work in Brazil, & I daily pray God to bless you & to console your Paternity in the midst of the crosses & trials with which you have to contend. Dom Maur will be a most useful monk at Olinda: he is so obedient & unpretending that God is sure to bless all he takes in hand; & God's blessing is everything: *Nisi Dominus aedificaverit domum*, etc.[2] I have known the R. Fr. Mayeul, as I was his *zelatur* up to quite lately. I have a very high opinion of him. He is very talented, & has a *great deal* of positive knowledge; besides this he is very virtuous & aims at high perfection. If treated with kindness & confidence, you can do what you please with him.

God is blessing our community in a wonderful manner. We have received quite a number of excellent vocations, & I have never seen a greater spirit of union & fervour in the monastery. I am convinced that this blessing comes from the obedience our superiors have shown to the wishes of the Holy Father in giving up some of our best subjects for the interests of the Church in Brazil & Rome.

I suppose your Paternity is aware that I am no longer *zelator*. Dom Urban has taken my place.[3] There are such a number of young postulants, & I have become almost as stout as Dom Feuillen, so that it was necessary to find someone weighing a few *kilos* less & consequently with more "go" in him.

Respectful & affectionate regards to D. Prior, D. Maur & all the brethren.

Most sincerely & respectfully yours,

f. Columba O.S.B.

[2] "Unless the Lord build the house . . ." (Ps. 126:1).

✝ Benedicite                                    Regina Coeli [January?, 1902]
Right Rev. & dear F. Abbot,

Our dear F. Prior told me that you have just celebrated the 25th anniversary of your ordination.[1] As you have always had the goodness to treat me with great kindness, I thought that a line from me to testify my respectful & very sincere friendship for your Paternity might give you pleasure. I shall pray fervently, & obtain the prayers of the dear Carmelite sisters,[2] whose spiritual father I am, for your Paternity, that God may fill you more & more with the gifts of His grace; & bless all you are doing for His glory. I take, as you know, a most lively interest in all that concerns you & your labours.

Here, D.G., God is blessing us *most abundantly*. We live in the *most perfect peace*, & the greatest joy & union. Having said that, I have said all; for you know that if God is with us, all the rest shall be added. We live quietly amongst ourselves, very rarely going out, & yet although here for so short a time, our little community is respected, & has already begun to exercise its influence.

D. Wandrille paid us a visit.[3] I had a long talk with him. He made a good impression; for the life he is leading has done a great work in his soul, has taught him the reality of life. I believe he will be a useful instrument for God's glory.

I sincerely hope you are satisfied with the state in which you found your dear community, particularly the studies. It is so very important for our mission in Brazil that our Fathers should be known as *holy* & *learned* men.

With great respect & sincere affection,

your unworthy
fr. Columba O.S.B.

[1] This undated letter must have been written shortly after the Jubilee in question. Dom Gerald van Caloen was ordained priest on December 23, 1876.

[2] Dom Marmion was at the time chaplain to the Carmelite nuns of Louvain.

[3] Dom Wandrille Herpierre, monk of Maredsous, was sent to Brazil in 1899.

# XIII. TO DOM ANSCHAR HOECKELMANN,
## ABBOT OF ERDINGTON

### SEVEN LETTERS

*This strange mélange of German and English names may be explained by the fact that Erdington Abbey (near Birmingham) was founded by Beuron Abbey in 1876 following Bismarck's May Laws, which suppressed the mother abbey and scattered its community. On several scores the history of Erdington had close links with that of Maredsous. Among the first group coming to this foundation from Volders in Austria (where the Beuron community exiled by the* Kulturkampf *had found refuge) was Dom Hildebrand de Hemptinne, who was prior at Erdington from 1879 to 1881, or until he was recalled to Maredsous as prior and then elected abbot in 1890.*

*Furthermore, Maredsous sent to the aid of Erdington three professed English-speaking monks — the two convert Anglican priests, Dom Bede Camm and Dom John Chapman of England, and Dom Patrick Nolan, an Irishman.*

*During the first years of his assignment to Louvain as prior of Mont-César, Dom Marmion went several times to Erdington to preach the annual retreat: in 1899 (the first retreat he gave in English), in 1902, 1907, and 1915; and he often visited the monastery on other trips to England.*

*The Erdington community returned to the Continent in 1922, and exists today as Weingarten Abbey in Germany.*

### I.

✠ Benedicite                           Regina Coeli. 1 Sept. 1899

Rt. Rev. and Very dear F. Abbot,

Allow me to unite with our Rt. Rev. F. Abbot in wishing you from my inmost heart every benediction and joy on this day of your mystic expousals with the Community which God has destined to be yours from all eternity.[1]

I am exceedingly grateful to you for your very kind invitation to

---

[1] This refers to the Blessing of the first abbot of Erdington.

86

assist at the ceremony of your benediction; but circumstances render it quite impossible for F. Abbot to allow me to absent myself at present. I must be at Maredsous next week,[2] and it would scarcely be worth while to travel so far and remain but a day. I hope that one day I may be able to visit my dear brethren at Erdington. Although absent in body, I shall be with you in spirit; and offer my best prayers to God that He may give your Paternity the grace to make the Community of Erdington a real paradise of delights for Our Dear Lord.

I am so sorry dear little W [. . .] had to leave. I am sure it is for the best. He wrote me a very beautiful letter by which I saw that there has been no resistance to grace on his part; but that God calls him to another life.

Please present my affectionate and fraternal love to the Community.

Begging your Paternal benediction, believe me with profound respect,

Your most humbly devoted in J.C.

fr. Columba, Prior O.S.B.

II.

✠ Benedicite        Abbaye Regina Coeli, Louvain. Oct. 22. 1899.
Very Rd. and dear Father Abbot,

Father Abbot has just told me I am to give the retreat this year at Erdington. This news was a very agreeable surprise for me; for not only it is a great joy for me that God should deign to employ me for His glory, but it will be a very sincere pleasure for me to see again my brothers who are so dear to me in J.C.

I must not conceal from you that I foresee considerable difficulty, at least at the beginning; for it is now so many years that I have been away from my native land, that I find very considerable difficulty in expressing myself in English. However, I have very great confidence in work undertaken through Obedience, and with the blessing of Superiors. May I ask your Paternity to recommend me to God in

---

[2] For the Blessing of Dom Robert de Kerckhove, first abbot of Mont-César.

87

holy prayers that I may receive the light to know and to say what will be most for His glory.

I propose travelling in the habit,[1] (kneebreeches and all, just as we are over here); with, of course, a long over-coat. I expect there is nothing during the journey, nor at Erdington, which would require any change. Is it better to go by Harwich, or by Dover? The journey by Harwich is cheaper; but at this period of the equinoctial-gales not very agreeable; besides I fear I should have to omit H. Mass. However, I shall let myself be guided in that matter by your experience and advice. I am a good sailor, and am seldom ill on sea. I shall ask F. Abbot to allow me to arrive at Erdington a day before the retreat begins, in order to take a little rest after the sea-trip; and pick up my English a bit. I suppose the retreat begins Friday evening (Dec. 1), and ends Friday morning (8th). So I could leave the same evening, and be back here at Louvain for Sunday.

If you have any suggestion to make, or remark to offer, I should be most grateful to receive it.

I remain, dear F. Abbot, with profound respect,

Your unworthy, but sincerely devoted in J.C.

fr. Columba, Pr. O.S.B.

III.

✠ Benedicite                                  Regina Coeli. Dec. 23. [1899]

Rt. Rd. and Very dear F. Abbot,

Please accept my most sincere thanks for your letter and Xmas greetings. May the Divine Infant pour out His most abundant graces on your Paternity, and on the monastic family He has committed to your care. Since my visit to Erdington, I never fail to recommend all my dear brothers there in my prayers, and more especially your Paternity as I promised. May God one day unite us all around His Throne, never to be separated.

As I said in my letter to dom Bede,[1] I got back all right; and have been at work ever since.

---

[1] In his monastic habit, a rare sight in Ireland and in England, where priests and religious appear publicly in a clerical suit; in Belgium, however, the cassock and religious habit are worn on the streets.

[1] Dom Bede Camm, monk of Maredsous, lived at Erdington at the time. See Section XIV for letters to Dom Bede Camm from Dom Marmion.

The more I think of Erdington, the more I am convinced that it is necessary to enlarge the buildings; if you are not content to remain at a standstill for the future. You should have a Chapter-room; and more room in choir. I will pray that God may give you light to solve the problem; as I have very much at heart the development of our dear Congregation in England.[2] I have written to Father Abbot-Primate, and to F. Archabbot telling them of all the charity and edification I received during my visit to S. Thomas.'[3]

Would you be good enough to thank D. Subprior [4] for his letter; and wish him for me a very happy feast. Tell him I will remember him, and his little flock, specially at the Altar on that day.

Begging your paternal blessing, and recommending myself to your prayers,

I remain, with profound respect,

Your unworthy servant in J.C.

fr. Columba, Pr. O.S.B.

IV.

✠ Benedicite          Abbaye Regina Coeli, Mont-César. 2. 1. 1900.
Right Rd. and Very dear F. Abbot,

Please accept my respectful and most sincere wishes for a joyous and holy feast. Since I had the happiness of passing a few days with your Paternity at Erdington, I have been faithful to my promise of recommending you and your intentions to God in my most unworthy prayers; but on your feast I shall be specially earnest in my petitions that the "Father of Lights from whom all good gifts descend," [1] may pour out abundant benedictions on you and on your dear Community.

Here, D.G., all are well; and God is blessing us, not in temporal goods, but in great peace and in holy union in Charity, and, as we seek this in the first place *coetera adjicientur nobis*.[2] Our studies are

[2] Beuronese Congregation.

[3] St. Thomas of Canterbury was patron saint of Erdington Abbey.

[4] Dom John Chapman, whose feast was celebrated on December 27. He was also a Maredsous monk who had been loaned to the Erdington community, as noted in the Introduction to this section.

[1] Jas. 1:17.

[2] "And all these things shall be added unto you" (Matt. 6:33).

progressing in every way. There is a great deal of "go"; the results are very satisfactory.

The Anglo-Boer war is most dreadful: such sacrifices of life! My sister writes to me from Dublin that the whole city is in mourning; so many fine young fellows are missing. May God give them peace! It is a terrible humiliation for England; and I must say, I am beginning to think that God is fighting on the other side. It seems difficult to explain such a series of disasters in any other way.

I am sorry to see that Dr. St. George Mivart [3] is going adrift. I admire some of his works greatly; and always looked on him, up to this, as a most loyal searcher after the truth. Wounded self-love is a sad thing, and makes even clever men do very foolish things.

I hope I shall have the happiness of meeting your Paternity at the General Chapter. [4] I think it is the tradition that the Priors go as well as the Abbots. I have heard nothing on that subject as yet; but it would be a great happiness for me, if God so wills it, to see Rome once again, to gain the Jubilee [5] and, though last, not least, to meet your Paternity.

Please present my affectionate and fraternal regards to all your dear Community, and believe me, with profound respect,

Your unworthy in J.C.

fr. Columba, O.S.B. Pr.

v.

✠ Benedicite                                        Louvain. [about 1901].
Right Rd. and Very dear F. Abbot,
    Please accept my respectful and most grateful thanks for your kind

[3] St. George J. Mivart (1827–1900), learned English convert, biologist and philosopher, and a Protestant convert to the Church. For a long time he opposed Darwinism most vigorously, then partially changed his mind in its favor. Toward the end of his life he adopted a modernist position on religious questions, and "was buried without ecclesiastical rights," according to the *Catholic Encyclopedia* account, although Cardinal Gasquet wrote on January 16, 1900, "I got him to see a priest and receive Extreme Unction." When Cardinal Bourne succeeded Cardinal Vaughan his case was reopened, and his body was reinterred in consecrated ground. See Sir Shane Leslie, *Cardinal Gasquet. A Memoir* (New York, Kenedy, 1953), p. 198; also article in *Catholic Encyclopedia* (New York, 1911), X, 407.
[4] General Chapter of the Beuronese Congregation, to which Erdington and Mont-César belonged at that time.
[5] Holy Year indulgence.

remembrance of me. For my part, I don't forget your Paternity and the little flock committed to your care. I am sorry you are not getting vocations. Perhaps St. Joseph will help you, as he has done at Maredsous, if you invoke him. We are not doing much in that line either. We have but one vocation, a Dutchman; and he has not yet arrived. But new foundations must pass through many tribulations. I am not surprised that the English Bishops have begun to move in the question of *Pontificalia*.[1] It will be a consolation to have something *certain*; and also that our *Ceremoniale* [2] has not been printed till this question had been settled once for all.

I am sorry you had not a retreat to your satisfaction. It is so necessary for most of us to be wound up once a year. I think a Benedictine is always best for Benedictines. We had a retreat some years ago from a Dominican, who had a great reputation for learning and sanctity, but many of his conferences were beside the question for us, and didn't tell. F. Thomas [3] of Maredsous would give you an excellent retreat. Our studies are getting on well, D.G., though I have not all the time I should require to prepare for my class.[4]

God is chastising Portugal.[5] Our work there, to human eyes must seem a failure; but we know that no effort, no prayer offered to God is lost. And so the prayers and fatigues of our fathers there, shall bear their fruit later on. Recommending myself most humbly to your prayers, and begging your benediction, I remain with great respect and affection

Your humble servant in J.C.

fr. Columba, O.S.B. Pr.

[1] The use of pontifical insignia which abbots enjoy by privilege. The suppression of the monasteries by Henry VIII had interrupted this tradition.

[2] The book of ceremonies in use in the Beuronese Congregation. It was published in 1908.

[3] Dom Thomas Elsaesser was a pious monk of Maredsous and a distinguished latinist who published *Nos in schola latine loquamur* (1906 and 1909), and *Linguam discito lingua* (1910), two handbooks of conversational Latin.

[4] At that time Dom Marmion was teaching theology to the young monks from Maredsous who were at Mont-César for their studies.

[5] Antireligious laws inspired by the Masons had closed the monasteries in Portugal. Beuronese monks sent there in 1894 to help their brethren had been forced to leave and return home. This news was sure to cause special distress to Dom Anschar Höckelmann, for in 1895 he had been sent to the Portuguese monastery of Cucujaes as prior. He remained there till 1899 when he was elected abbot of Erdington.

✠ Benedicite                    Mont-César, Louvain. 21 Oct. 1902.

Right Rev. and dear F. Abbot,

Please excuse my delay in writing. Since my return from Metz, where I have been giving a retreat, I have been ill, and am only just beginning to get into form again. I am delighted at the prospect of seeing your Paternity again, and of spending a few days with my brethren at Erdington, who are very dear to me, though I so seldom write.

As I have been ill, and am still weak, Father Abbot wishes me to say that I may not give the retreat to the Oblates, but only the retreat for the Community; that is, two instructions a day. I shall arrive at Birmingham from London, Sunday, 30 Nov. at 1.43. And I suppose we can commence the retreat the same evening. I have permission to remain Saturday — Nov. 29 — at London, where I have a matter to arrange with some friends.

It is a great consolation for me to know that Dom X [. . .] is doing so well; and that Br. Y [. . .] is giving satisfaction. However from what I know of both, I am convinced that it is important that they should, at least for some years, remain as much as possible in the Monastery, and be employed seldom in exterior work. The Irish character is so impulsive, that unless a man has been rendered stable and mature by long years of discipline and fidelity, you can never be quite sure that they won't pass all at once from one extreme to another.

Please give me your blessing, and remember me at the altar, that Our Lord may deign to speak words of life through my mouth; for without Him all our efforts are sterile, even though people may admire and praise us.

My fraternal love to all.

With profound respect,

Your unworthy servant in J.C.

fr. Columba, O.S.B. Pr.

✠ Benedicite　　　　　　　　　　　　　Louvain. 12 Jan. 1903.

Right Rev. and dear F. Abbot,

Please forgive my delay in answering your most welcome letter. I had been hoping to announce that [. . .] was about seeking admission into your dear Community, and was waiting till I had a definite answer. Hence my delay. I have just received a letter stating that there are obstacles, and that it does not seem to be God's Will, at least at present.

Please accept my most sincere wishes and prayers for your Paternity, and for your dear Community; that we may all advance in God's love, and in the spirit of our H. Father St. Benedict.

I was very ill on my way back,[1] as the sea was rough; but in the end it rather did me good, and I have been much better since my return.

All here are doing well, and God is blessing us both as regards our health; and as regards the union and good spirit of our clerics.

The theological Commentary which I recommended was that by Billot, S.J. It is an excellent synthesis and luminous explanation of the text of S. Thomas' *Summa*. It is published at the Propaganda, but any book-seller will have it sent to you. His volumes on *De Deo Uno et Trino. De Verbo Incarnato. De Sacramentis*, are the best. He treats the B. Eucharist in a most masterly way; and certainly follows St. Thomas step by step.

The commentary of *a Piconio* on St. Paul's Epist. is profound, and full of piety and doctrine.

Most humbly recommending myself to your prayers, and thanking you *ex immo corde*[2] for all the kindness and charity you showed me during my last visit, I remain

Most humbly devoted in J.C.

fr. Columba O.S.B.

---

[1] I.e., on his return from Erdington, where he had preached a retreat at the end of December, 1902.

[2] "From the bottom of my heart."

## XIV. TO DOM BEDE CAMM

NINE LETTERS

*As with several of Dom Marmion's correspondents, Dom Bede Camm was a literary man as well as a leading character in at least two spiritual dramas — his own and that of the reconciliation of Caldey Abbey to the Holy See — in both of which Dom Marmion played a most providential role. According to a brief account of Dom Bede's life,*

> *Dom Bede Camm was, like so many distinguished English Catholics, a convert to the Faith. He was born (in 1864) at Sudbury-on-Thames. . . . After two years at Oxford . . . he studied for the Anglican ministry for which he was ordained at Rochester (England), in 1888, at the age of twenty-four. . . . Two years later, however, he was received into the Church at the Benedictine Abbey of Maredsous in Belgium.*[1]

*In a lively narrative, Dom Bede himself relates the steps toward his conversion. It so happened that the decisive moment occurred at Maredsous, where he had come to allay the serious doubts that had been torturing him concerning his situation as an Anglican clergyman. Being unable to open his heart completely to the abbot, Dom Placid Wolter, he had decided to leave on June 6, 1890, when during high Mass he was struck by the words of the Credo*: Et unam, sanctam, catholicam et apostolicam Ecclesiam. *He suddenly understood that he had not believed until then that the word* one *meant* one *Church, and nothing else.*[2] *We shall now let him speak for himself:*

> *It was possible, I thought, that this was a diabolical illusion; at least it might be so. I asked for a sign. I said, "If Father Abbot sends for me to speak to me before dinner, or if he sends someone else to speak to me about my soul, I will open all my heart to him — if not, I will go away*

---

[1] Matthew Hoehn, O.S.B. (ed.), *Catholic Authors* (Newark, N.J., St. Mary's Abbey, 1948), I (1930–47), 100.

[2] *Memoirs of a Benedictine Monk*, published in a collection of seven narratives of conversions entitled *The City of Peace, by those who have entered it* (Dublin, Catholic Truth Society of Ireland, 1903), p. 46.

this evening and say nothing." The Mass ended, the Blessed Sacrament was exposed, and I knelt there in the Church. No one came to me. I stayed there till just before dinner. Then I went upstairs to wash my hands, and felt almost relieved that it was all over; and I determined to go away that afternoon. On going into the Refectory, however, Dom Columba, an Irish monk, whose acquaintance I had made the evening before, touched me on the arm, and said — "Will you come with me for a walk after Vespers?"

I said, "Very gladly, if there will be time before I leave." So after Vespers we went out; and we had not gone far before he began asking me about the Bishop of Lincoln's case. "Now," I thought, "I am in for it." However, I answered; and he began to attack the Anglican position very hardily, I defending it as best I could. We went into a wood, and all of a sudden I turned round to him, and said, "Dom C—, tell me, did the Abbot send you to talk to me about this?" "Yes," he replied, after a moment's hesitation. "And when did he tell you to speak to me — before dinner?" "Yes, after the High Mass, he sent for me and told me I must speak to you about your soul. I did not like to do it, but I have done it by obedience."

I said no more, but it came upon me with overwhelming force that my sign had been granted me when I least expected it. . . . I think, that though I still continued feebly to defend myself, all was over. Before we returned to the Monastery I had promised to speak to the Abbot. Next morning I was with him from 9 to 11 in the forenoon. That afternoon, Dom Columba took me to see Mr. Edmund Bishop, an English Catholic gentleman, and a most learned man, who was staying in the Abbey.[3] He was very kind, and helped me more than anyone. Of course he best understood my position and my difficulties.[4]

[3] Edmund Bishop (1846–1917), convert, civil servant, lay apostle, and the liturgical scholar and historian of whom David Knowles (foremost authority on English monasticism) states that "among those most competent to speak he would be reckoned . . . among the few English scholars of original genius at the turn of the last century." Self-trained, self-effacing, and altogether unselfish, Bishop furnished basic research and priceless leads in the fin-de-siècle development of Catholic scholarship on pre-Reformation liturgical history, exploited spectacularly in the works of Cardinal Gasquet. See Nigel Abercrombie, *The Life and Work of Edmund Bishop* (London, Longmans, 1959), and Leslie, *op. cit.*, Chap. IV and *passim*. Bishop spent five months at Maredsous as a lay pensionnaire in 1891. (MEE)

[4] Bede Camm, *op. cit.*, pp. 46–48. Curiously, the thorough, objective Abercrombie manages to tell the same story without once adverting to Don Marmion or his role of catalyst in the Camm-Bishop encounter. (MEE)

*This encounter with Dom Marmion had thus been for him a clear sign of Divine Providence. He was received into the Church by Abbot Placid Wolter, who had instructed him. Three months later he entered Maredsous Abbey as a postulant. He made his monastic profession in 1891; was ordained priest in Rome in 1895, "and then was stationed at Erdington Abbey, near Birmingham, until 1912" (the while remaining attached to Maredsous). "In 1913, he was appointed to prepare the Anglican Benedictine monks at Caldey, and the nuns of St. Bride's, Milford Haven, for their reception into the Church as communities."* [5]

*The letters published here show first of all the friendly relations uniting the two monks; then the problems one of them had to face after he became Abbot of Maredsous, when the other had reached a new turn in his life.*

*Besides these letters, the archives of Maredsous Abbey contain numerous unpublished documents relating to the history of Caldey, especially letters of the Bishop of Menevia, of Dom John Chapman, who had been named superior, and particularly of Dom Aelred Carlyle, almost all of them sent from Caldey itself to Dom Columba Marmion. Unfortunately, except for two letters written to Dom Bede Camm when he was at Caldey, all the letters of Dom Marmion himself have been lost.*

I.

✠ Pax            Abbaye Regina Coeli Louvain [1899]
My dear Father Bede

Accept my best thanks for your new book.[1] I am so glad you thought of sending it to me, not only because the stories of those "Brave days of old" are for me most delicious reading, but also as a proof that our friendship in J.C. is still as fresh & as true as of yore. Although we are separated by space, we remain united in affection & in prayer.

---

[5] Hoehn, *loc. cit.* Peter Anson gives a racy account of the Caldey episode in his memoir of Aelred Carlyle. *Abbot Extraordinary* (New York, Sheed & Ward, 1958). (MEE)

[1] *In the Brave Days of Old. Historical Sketches of the Elizabethan Persecution* (London, Art and Book Company, 1899).

I was delighted to read your beautiful letter in the *Catholic Times*. It is the real spirit of the S. Heart of Jesus, & of the Holy Father who says *diligat fratres, oderit vitia*.[2] Yes, let us *hate* heresy in all its forms, but let us love our brothers, even when in error.

Here, D.G., we are living in a real paradise. A wonderful spirit of union & charity reigns, & with it God's joy in our hearts *ubi amor ibi Deus est*.[3] May God long preserve us in this holy peace. We are getting on nicely. We are poor, but God provides for all necessities; & then it is so sweet to repose on Him & allow Him to carry us in His arms. We are entering little by little into the scholastic & university life which surrounds us here; for although our students are not to frequent the university classes, still they assist at the public theses; & the *Recteur Magnifique*[4] came to invite the professors to take part in the theological & philosophical discussions.[5] This is not much to my taste, but it cannot be avoided as we form with the Jesuits & Dominicans the third house of studies, & must accept the consequences of our situation. A *report* reached us from Maredsous that we are shortly to have a mitre here.[6] This report has as yet received no official confirmation, so that I give it for what it is worth.

What about Erdington? We heard some months ago that the Archabbot had promised you an Abbot, & in the course of this year.[7] Since then we hear nothing. I hope God may soon arrange that matter, as it would add immensely to the importance, the prosperity & the utility of St. Thomas's.[8]

I hope your dear Father is well & happy. Dom. Subprior told me, he is extremely generous to your abbey. May God bless him & recom-

[2] "He should love the brethren, and hate vice." Rule of St. Benedict, chap. 64, The election of the abbot.

[3] "Where is love, God is there." Ninth anthem for the Mandatum of Maundy Thursday.

[4] Official title of the rector of the university.

[5] At the end of the scholastic year when the candidates for University degrees in theology were required to defend their theses in public, Dom Marmion was often invited to perform the office of official objector.

[6] I.e., a mitred abbot.

[7] In effect, Anschar Höckelmann was elected abbot on July 16, 1899, and received the abbatial blessing on September 3. See above several letters written to him by Dom Marmion.

[8] St. Thomas of Canterbury was the patron saint of Erdington.

pense him for his charity here & hereafter. Please present him my very affectionate remembrances, as also to your Mother etc.

I hope D. Patrick [9] is well, & doing great things for God, & his country by his prayers. Tell him I should be grateful to him, if he would tell me the meaning of the Irish phrase written on his ordination-card, as people ask me & I am ashamed to confess my utter ignorance of my native tongue. You may add that his brother Tomey S.J. is in the same Celtic darkness as myself. Talking of languages, I am pounding the Flemish, as it is *necessary* here. One of my penitents at the Carmelite Convent [10] speaks only Flemish, & as I think it highly probable *now* that I am destined to live & die in this dear Country of my adoption, I must know its tongue.

Please present my respectful & affectionate greetings to the R. F. Prior, & S. Prior, & all my dear brothers, & believe me ever

Your truly devoted & affectionate brother in J. C.

fr. Columba O.S.B.

II.

✠ Pax                    Mont César Louvain 30 March 1903
My dearest F. Bede

Please accept my sincere sympathy in your great sorrow.[1] *Christi amor nos conjunxit,*[2] & I feel that your parents are in some sort mine, & their loss affects me as though it were one of my own. I know that this is a great blow for you, for you were so united with your dear parents in love & affection; but I feel most keenly for your poor father, for whom this loss will be a terrible sorrow which will scarcely quit him here below. However, it is an immense happiness that her death was so holy & so full of hope. I feel *no doubt* for the future. Surely what she did at that solemn moment, and after such terrific suffering,

[9] Dom Patrick Nolan, Dom Marmion's fellow countryman, who knew him at Maredsous during his novitiate. An ardent nationalist, he devoted himself at that time to propaganda in favor of the Gaelic language. He was ordained priest February 25 of this same year, 1899.

[10] The Louvain Carmel where Father Marmion was the devoted chaplain for ten years.

[1] His mother's death.

[2] "The love of Christ united us."

98

must have been the true expression of sincere conviction, & in that case sacramental grace was sure & efficacious. I have begged the prayers of the Community for her, & shall not forget her myself. It seems as though our dear Lord had chosen you to lead to Himself those souls so dear to His S. Heart. You were the first link in that chain of predestined souls, & it is so sweet to have been the instrument in His hands of the greatest blessings you could have obtained for your dear parents. As one by one the dear ones precede us, we ought to detach our hearts more & more from every human tie; give ourselves more resolutely to our dear Lord for the few years which remain *ut ibi fixa sint corda ubi vera sunt gaudia*.[3]

Here everything is going on as usual. The Rt. Rev. D. Gérard Ab. of Olinda [4] obtained permission to take our Dom Léon to his Abbey of S. Andrew at Bruges for a year.[5] This is a great sacrifice for us as we are very short of priests here, & D. Léon was our cellarer, instructor of the lay-brothers, & preached in Flemish, besides being a most charming confrère. However, we could scarcely refuse as the R. A. Primate wished it, & poor D. Gérard was in a most impossible position. He has at Bruges an abbey with a number of young clerics, & practically no one to look after them; as his prior & another priest had been so overworked that — well, they must change their monastery, & rest for a *whole year* at least. The prior is gone to Maria Laach & the other to Beuron. D. Gérard *must* leave for Brazil for important business in a few days. D. Simon is ordained, & quite a number will be turned out this year: frs. Pius, Bruno, Adelin, Autbert, Omer, Achaire, Barnabé, Gérard.[6] I am still at the same work, & find it hard to make ends meet. However, I find that our dear Lord helps most wonderfully, & that if we try to be just a little generous with Him, He takes most of the work on Himself. Please give my most affec-

---

[3] "There only may our hearts abide, where alone true joys are to be found." From the Collect of the Fourth Sunday after Easter.

[4] Dom Gerald van Caloen. See above several letters addressed to him.

[5] In 1899 Father Gerald had restored the ancient Abbey of Saint André; he wished to make it a center of formation for the monks destined for Brazil.

[6] Young monks from Maredsous, living at Mont-César for their theological studies. The first named is Brother Pius de Hemptinne, the second is Brother Bruno Destrée, a minor poet, the fourth is Brother Bede Lebbe, a brother of Father Vincent Lebbe, the well-known Vincentian missionary to China. Dom Bede became the second prior of Glenstal (Ireland).

tionate love to father, & enclosed card. Most respectful regards to
F. Abbot,
     Yours most affectionately in J. C.

                                                  fr. Columba O.S.B.

                                III.

+ Pax                                    Maredsous 5. Jan. [1912]
My dear Dom. Bede [1]
     You will find enclosed the papers you sent me to Laach. I shall be
as short & as *straight* as possible.
     1) Whatever be D. Archabbot's decision, I don't think it would be
prudent to stir before our elections here in May, as a Libero-Socialist
majority would *surely* begin by expelling all Foreign religious.
     2) Our *Seniorat* [2] has decided that it would be wise for us to buy
a property (landed-property) in England, Ireland, or Canada: 1st. as
an investment, which could not be come at by a confiscating government; 2) As a place of possible refuge in case of persecution (F. Archabbot is very keen on this); 3) As a probable nucleus of foundation.
     I have received a number of offers from Ireland, properties just
suiting, & in good condition. Yet, I am rather in favour of England,
for *many* reasons, one being the hostility of Irish bishops & priests to
all monastic foundations. Many here wish that we should buy rather
in Canada, in order to be able to get into contact with the people at
once as they speak French, & are a good honest race. Please show F.
Abbot this letter & ask him to look out for a list of suitable properties
in England. I should prefer the North, p.e. Northumberland, Dur-
ham. We would be prepared to *buy* say for £4000. Except for F.
Abbot & D. Prior please keep this secret for present.
     In great haste, Yours in J. C.

                                                         + Columba

     [1] Since September of 1909, Dom Marmion, confrère and friend of Dom Bede, had
become as Abbot of Maredsous his religious and spiritual father.
     This letter shows the anxiety of the Belgian Catholics at this time: they were ex-
pecting a persecution similar to that in France. As it developed, these elections gave
a slight majority to the Catholic party.
     [2] Our Council.

✠ Pax                                    Maredsous 28 March. [1912]
My dear F. Bede

As you may see by the letter which I have just written to F. Prior the Primate, Archabbot & Assistants are of opinion that it's best for you both [1] to come home to Maredsous for the present at least. When you arrive here, I will let you know what the future seems to reserve for us. I should like you to leave Erdington as soon as F. Abbot can spare you. As you require a rest, you might go from Erdington for a rest with your brother, or other friend, until your retreat at Tyburn.[2] It is my *desire* that during those few weeks you should speak as little as possible of the affairs of Erdington, or of an eventual foundation. Having ceased your connection with Erdington, it is best to allow them to do things in their own way. I shall let you know on your arrival, the views of the Congregation as regards our subsequent action.

Try & profit by your rest to get strong in body & soul, so as to be in a fit state to carry out God's views whatever they be.

Ever Yours affectionately,

✠ Columba
Abb.

V.

✠ Pax                                    Maredsous. 2 Feb. 1913.
My dear F. Bede,

I received your letter and enclosure this morning, and I do feel very

[1] Dom Bede Camm and his fellow countryman Dom John Chapman had just decided to ask to leave Erdington. Canonically they remained professed monks of Maredsous Abbey.

[2] Tyburn, a convent of the Adorers of the Sacred Heart of Jesus, founded by Mother Mary of St. Peter Garnier, which was to be affiliated to the Benedictine Order in January, 1914. Abbot Marmion occupied himself a great deal with this house; he visited it frequently, and kept up a lively and regular correspondence with the foundress. (See Section XXIV for some of this correspondence.) Dom Bede Camm also preached there often, and wrote the life of Mother Garnier (published by Burns and Oates, London, first as a pamphlet in 1924, then as a book in 1934).

It is well-known that the forbidden gallows had formerly stood a few hundred yards from the site of the convent. The lively interest that Dom Bede took in the English martyrs of the Reformation drew him toward this privileged spot where so many Christian heroes gave their lives after terrible torture for their Catholic faith.

strongly on the matter, but not in the way you imagine.[1] I have prayed and reflected a good deal all to-day before writing. . . .

Our whole Monastic life is a *supernatural* undertaking. We promise obedience to an abbot X, because we believe he holds the place of J. C. There is always a certain risk in thus binding ourselves for life. For the abbot may not please us, or not act according to our views. (I knew something of it during 10 years at Louvain.)[2] As long as we continue to look on the abbot *in Faith* as really holding His place, nothing can hinder us from attaining *the one object for which we entered the Monastery*, but when we commence to reason about his manner of governing his abbey, to blame him because he does not adopt our views, we lose the spirit of our vocation, and the monastic life becomes a burden. Once a monk has made his *vow* of stability for his Monastery, and for his Community, nothing but the greatest reasons can dispense him from being faithful to his vows. (These reasons do exist in your case), and I should look on it as a real crime to say a word which could unsettle a professed monk in his vocation, or in his allegiance to his abbot. . . .

For what the monk promises at profession is not to make foundations, or to be successful before men, but to observe his vows. Ever in J. C.

P.S. I shall be delighted to see you on the 8th. I have written the above *sub oculo Dei*,[3] and for the discharge of a duty of conscience.

✠ C.

## VI.

✠ Pax                                           Maredsous 11 April [1913]
Abbaye de Saint-Benoit de Maredsous
My dear F. Bede
Many thanks for your very welcome letters. I had no doubt that

[1] To be properly understood, this letter should be placed in its historical context. Abbot Marmion gives here his first views concerning the change of stability desired by Dom Bede. Later he will in effect admit the validity of the reasons advanced by Dom Bede.

[2] The exemplary obedience practiced by Dom Marmion during his ten years as prior at Mont-César cost him dear; but the abbot himself paid him this eloquent compliment: "I never had a more obedient monk than he." Cf. Thibaut, *op. cit.*, pp. 116–21.

[3] "Beneath the eye of God."

God would preserve the life of the dear R. Mother of Tyburn.[1] It was *really* our Holy Father who cured her. I hope they may tell you the circumstances.

It is impossible to be in charge[2] in a monastery without having care & anxiety at times. It is part of the debt we pay to God for His protection & grace. Novices are always tempted in one way or another, but especially by false suggestions of the devil *sub specie boni*.[3] The

[1] Mother Garnier. See Note 2 to Letter 4 above. Shortly before this she had very nearly died, but in a letter to his sister Rosie Dom Marmion attributed her cure to "the Infant Jesus" Himself, not the Holy Father (See Letter 4, Section VIII). (MEE)

[2] Father Bede had been appointed novice master of the Benedictine community of Caldey Island which had just made its submission to Rome. Abbot Marmion had been invited by Dom Bede, and he came in March to preach a retreat to the newly converted. He devoted himself to them with great zeal, and received from Pope Pius X himself a precious reward in the form of a letter of thanks, written entirely by the Pope's own hand, in his fine and elegant writing. We give here the Latin text and translation of this hitherto unpublished letter.

Reverendissime et Dilecte Fili,

Ob eximiam caritatem erga recenter ab haeresi conversum dilectum Aelredum Carlyle exercitam, gratias tibi ago perquam plurimas et de opere feliciter adimpleto gratulor ex animo. Dum vero una tecum Deum Omnipotentem ad precor ut Monachi universi de Caldey ad fidem conversi pietate ceterisque virtutibus praeluceant in Dioecesi Menevensi non solum sed in Anglia tota, ut quae vere insula sanctorum fuit nuncupata, ad fidei unitatem redeat, tibi tuisque fratribus grati et benevolentis animi testem, Apostolicam Benedictionem peramanter impertio.

Ex Aedibus Vaticanis, die 16 Julii 1914.
Pius Pp. X.
Reverendissimo Domino
Domino Columbae Marmion
Abbati Marctiolensi — Maredsous (Namur).

Right Reverend and very dear Son,

I send you the most sincere thanks for the outstanding charity shown to our beloved Aelred Carlyle recently converted from heresy, and I congratulate you from the bottom of my heart for the task which you have carried out so diligently. Therefore, while praying along with you to Almighty God, that the piety and the other virtues of the monks of Caldey, converted to the Faith, may shine not only in the diocese of Menevia but in the whole of England, so that the land which was called "The Island of Saints" may return to the unity of the Faith, in token of my favor and benevolence, most lovingly I grant you and your brethren the Apostolic Blessing.

From the Vatican Palace, July 16, 1914.
Pius PP. X
To the Right Reverend
Dom Columba Marmion
Abbot of Maredsous-Maredsous (Namur)

[3] "Under a false appearance of good."

desire to become a Carthusian, Trappist, or worse, is quite classical as a novice's temptation. Please tell them from me that it would be most unwise, after the miraculous way in which God has been leading them, to form plans etc. They should just pray "Lead, kindly light," & wait till God manifests His Will. I feel convinced He wants them to keep together, & that those who leave will find themselves *stranded*, & no longer borne on the bosom of God's grace. If you think it expedient, I could come for a few days on my return from Rome, & *tell* them what Rome wants,[4] & what they ought to do.

Br. Aelred [5] has as yet said nothing about B. Aidan accompanying him. I should have been absolutely opposed for many reasons. Yours add to mine.

I have given orders to have the block of the view of Maredsous sent on to you. You have a difficult task, but many are praying for you. Try & keep your eye fixed *semper ad Dominum. Sicut oculi ancillae in manibus dominae suae.*[6]

Give my love to D. Jean, & thank B. Paul, & Whitings for their letters.

> I bless you,
> Tuissimus in Xto
> ✠ Columba, Abb.

P.S. Please tell R. Mother at Tyburn that the abbess O.S.B. at Liège takes a great interest in her, & will visit her in September.

---

[4] In fact he came in June to be present at the canonical erection of the community into a Benedictine abbey.

[5] Father Aelred Carlyle was the superior of this community. He became its first abbot.

[6] "Always towards the Lord" (Ps. 24:15). "As the eyes of the handmaid are on the hands of her mistress" (Ps. 122:2).

## VII

✠ Pax

Abbaye de Saint-Benoit
de Maredsous
My dear Fr. Bede

I beg to acknowledge receipt of your letter & cheque. I am very grateful, as it enables me to pay for my journey to Rome without having recourse to the Cellarer. I have told F. Thomas you are saying the 72 Masses.

Your letters have not *offended* me. I like candid dealing, & that you should say just what you think; but it pained me *intensely*, as I have always had the profound conviction, which a rather long & large experience of our own & other abbeys has but confirmed, that the Constitutions of our Congregation of Beuron, are the most perfect adaptation of the rule & spirit of St. Benedict to the wants & aspirations of our time.[1] There is not a word in the Constitutions which intensifies — were it possible — the power & prestige which St. Benedict assigns to the abbot.

However, I will not discuss the matter with you, you judge of the whole, & of the principle from one or two *cases* of bungling, which occurred from difficulties of nationality. I shall only make two remarks. 1) Putting aside certain exterior marks of deference, the abbot in the English Congr. is just as autocratic, & has a much better time of it than we have. 2) The R. Mother of Tyburn,[2] who is *full* of God's light, & who has studied with greatest care the various constitutions at present in existence, wrote to me lately *De toutes les Constitutions de Bénédictins, celles de Beuron sont celles dont nous sentons devoir nous inspirer davantage. Il nous semble que Dom Wolter a jeté à travers les pages de D. Guéranger comme un souffle plus puissant encore de largeur et d'esprit intérieur, et c'est cela dont nous avons besoin, une constitution expansive, dilatée, apostolique, et en même temps solide*

---

[1] During his whole monastic life, Dom Marmion always showed the greatest admiration for the Beuronese Constitutions, also a sincere love for the Alma Mater from which Maredsous had been founded.

[2] Mother Garnier, foundress of Tyburn, mentioned above. Abbot Marmion knew that Father Bede had great veneration for her, and great confidence in her judgment.

*et vigoureusement préservatrice de la vie contemplative.*[3] She is a Frenchwoman writing of a German, but she is just & true. Of course I admit that changes should be made to suit climate & temperament, but the Constitutions are *excellent.* It appears that Br. Aelred is going to place Caldey under D. Gasquet & the E.B.C.[4] Be it so. In which case the best would be for you to pass at once to the E.B.C.; that Br. Aelred make his novitiate at Belmont; & D. John come back to us. I have not yet seen D. Aelred. He comes here on Thursday. I was not invited to the benediction of F. Augustin.[5]

Ev Yrs in J. C.

✠ Columba, Abb.

[3] "Of all the Benedictine Constitutions, those of Beuron, we feel, should inspire us most. It seems to us that Dom Wolter has infused into the pages of Dom Guéranger a greater broadness of outlook and interior spirit; and that is what we need: Constitutions that are open-hearted, apostolic, and yet which are at the same time solid, and vigorously safeguard the contemplative life."

[4] The English Benedictine Congregation.

[5] These words betray an uncertainty as to what would be the best orientation to give to the converts of Caldey. In fact, Father Aelred was to go to Maredsous for his novitiate. There he made his solemn profession, and received the priesthood in the course of the summer of 1914. A few days after writing this letter, Abbot Marmion had the great honor and joy of taking the Abbot of Caldey to Rome to present him to Pope St. Pius X. The audience took place on May 16. Dom Marmion has left an account of this audience among his private notes. The following lines have been taken from them.

I had the happiness of seeing the Holy Father this morning. The audience began at about 10 ¾, and lasted about 20 minutes. After having given us his foot and hand to kiss, He began by speaking in latin of the great favour and grace received by the abbot and monks of Caldey. I remarked that this simultaneous conversion was due to their liturgical training. The H. Father said it was so, but added that it was miraculous. I then told the H. Father that Br. Aelred was coming to Maredsous for his novitiate, and that after his profession, we proposed having him ordained, when I should know and find him fit. The H. Father then added (repeating the same thing several times with emphasis): We accord the most ample faculties, and all, all dispensations, in order that he may be ordained immediately after his novitiate, and not only for him, but also for those of Caldey. "For they have no need to be very learned, in order to praise God." He then blessed Br. Aelred, and his Community, and promised to pray for him; and all this with the greatest kindness and loving tenderness, and spontaneity. . . .

Then I told him I suffered greatly from drowsiness, which rendered prayer difficult. I added: "Tu es Petrus, cure me." He told me to kneel; He placed his hand on my head and said: "I beg God to cure you, and to give you strength and health to govern your Community for long years." He then blessed all my objects of piety; gave me leave to give the apostolic blessing to Maredsous, Caldey and 3 other Communities (with plenary indulgence).

✠ Pax                                    Maredsous, 24 Sep. 1913
Abbaye de Saint-Benoit
de Maredsous
My dear Fr. Bede

Abbot Butler [1] wrote to me some days ago to say that you had been accepted with practical unanimity by the Chapter.[2] I am glad for your sake, as I do think it is best; but it is a great wrench for us, & particularly for me. It is particularly painful, as I know you are leaving to a great extent owing to your conviction that our Congregation of Beuron does not represent truly the spirit & rule of St. Benedict. I have no intention now of discussing that question, but I shall merely add, that did I share that opinion, nothing could induce me to remain an O.S.B.

The formalities required for joining another Congregation are 1) Leave of Primate. 2) Archabbot's leave.[3] 3) Mine. 4) Acceptance by English Congr. I have given my permission, & I know that the Archabbot *will* give his if asked. I don't think the Primate will make any difficulties. But *they must be asked*.

As regards the books & other objects, many which you have, or have received, since you left Maredsous, we most willingly allow you to take them all with you. So be quite at your ease. The librarian wishes just to know the names of the books you are keeping for our library-list.

As I said in the beginning, I feel your leaving more than I can say; but I feel it is for the best. I shall ever remain your faithful friend, & if ever you need my help or counsel you may *count on me*.

Br. Aelred & I shall be delighted if you can do anything for Caldey or Tyburn in America.

May God bless & protect you. Yrs in J.C.

✠ Columba, Abb.

[1] Dom Cuthbert Butler, abbot of Downside.

[2] Chapter of the professed monks of Downside.

[3] The archabbot of Beuron, superior of the Benedictine Congregation of the same name. The Benedictine monasteries are largely autonomous, but grouped in different congregations. These are independent of each other, although united since the reign of Leo XIII in a confederation under the presidency of the abbot-primate. Dom Bede Camm, who wished to change from the Beuronese Congregation to the English, to which Downside belongs, had to receive these various permissions.

Abbaye de Maredsous                          15 Nov. [1913]
My dear Fr. Bede

Thanks for your letter. I am so glad you like Downside & are happy there.[1] I seek but one thing, your happiness & God's Will. Under the circumstances, I think you would do well to remain on for the year, if the Abbot thinks well of it. Perhaps it might be well if you could get back for a few days at Xmas, & Holy Week; but I don't insist if you can't get it conveniently in.

Everything is as usual here. D. Augustin is rather better, but still suffering a lot.

Fraternal greetings to F. Abbot & all friends.

Ever Yrs in J. C.<br>✠ Columba, Abb.

P.S. If F. Abbot thinks well of it, I don't object to your going to Ireland, as I think it necessary for Oliver Plunket's life. Cardinal Moran's *Spicilegium Ossoriense* contains a lot of original information.

## XV. TO A PRIEST FRIEND OF DUBLIN

### TWO LETTERS

#### I.

✠ Pax                              Mont César, Louvain. 10 July 1904
My dear Jem [1]

I was delighted to get your letter. It proves that true friendship

---

[1] This is a letter bidding good-bye, and without any shadow of resentment. Moreover, Dom Bede Camm did not leave Maredsous for Downside through loss of affection, for this same year he wrote an enthusiastic account of Maredsous in which we find this sentence: "To him [himself] Maredsous is full of holy and happy memories; it was here that he received the priceless gift of Faith, and here, too, that he was clothed with the holy habit of St. Benedict, in the year 1890." This description ends with seven stanzas of lyric poetry on Maredsous. In 1923, when Father Bede published his *Pilgrim Paths in Latin Lands* (London, MacDonald and Evans), he included this description of the Belgian abbey (pp. 245–52).

[1] James Dunne, who later became vicar general of Dublin, was a very close friend of Joseph Marmion when they were together at Clonliffe. See references to him in Section III.

founded on God's love never changes, but becomes deeper and truer as years roll on. I was so very busy with the theological Theses [2] here at the University, that I could only find time for a card, but I have been now five times objecting; that is enough as it fatigues me very much. As you say, I am *very, very* happy & enjoy profound peace. It was my real vocation. I could never have been happy, nor in safety, elsewhere. I have a deal to do as prin. director of several religious communities. I have also a number of priests who come to me,[3] and then I must look after the studies here.[4] I say this to show you that I can't spend all my time in contemplation; though I see more and more that it is *optima pars.*[5]

I am sure you will do much for our Lord's glory as president of *dear old Clonliffe.* When Our Lord asked St. Peter if he loved Him more than all the others, & received his assurance that it was so, He confided to him what was dearest to His S. Heart; and so it is with you. He confides to you what is dearest to Him: His priests. You may be sure I shall not forget you in my daily prayers. I spoke of you yesterday to our community, of our early friendship, which for over thirty years has never been for a moment clouded, & I asked them to pray for you & obtain for you God's benediction.

I am starting for Woolhampton in Berkshire on the 23rd. The English Benedictines expelled from Douai [6] have an abbey & college there at present & I am going over to give them their annual retreat. I shall be back by the 2nd. August. If you pass by this way, I should be delighted to put you up; & as Diest is quite near, we could go together (with permission of my Abbot) & visit the house where St. John Berchmans was born. Montaigu, the great pilgrimage of Brabant, which St. John went to visit every Saturday is only 3 miles — a beautiful walk from Diest. I hope some day His Lordship of Maitland,[7] you & I may be able to spend a day together & make that pilgrimage. I had a very nice letter from him lately. He is a most zealous bishop; but up to his neck in financial difficulties.

[2] See Note 5 of the first letter to Dom Bede Camm (Section XIV).
[3] For confession and to ask advice.
[4] Dom Marmion was prefect of studies for the young monks studying theology.
[5] "The better part" (Luke 10:42).
[6] In 1903.
[7] Bishop Vincent Patrick Dwyer. See Section III.

I hope your dear sisters are well & happy. Tell them I was asking for them, & don't forget them before God.

As ever,

your affectionate brother in J.C.

Dom. Columba Marmion, O.S.B.

## II.

✠ Pax                            Mont César, Louvain. 23 Nov. 1904

My dear Jem

I am most grateful to you for the intentions, may God bless you, & give you all I desire & pray Him to give you, in return.

Nothing is eternal but God, & all that is founded on Him; & as our friendship had Him as its sole link & foundation, it is as fresh now, though we do not often write, as when we tried side by side in dear old Clonliffe, to prepare ourselves for the great grace of the priesthood. The vocation to which God has called you, that of forming young hearts for the grace of the priesthood, is perhaps that which is dearest to our Lord's heart. I am proud of Clonliffe, & each new success is a new joy for me. This year God's blessing has been evident & abundant.

As for me, I am *very very* happy in my vocation. I have no doubt that I am where God wills me to be, & he has so arranged things that besides the choir, which I love & *value* more & more daily, I have much congenial work. Many of the professors, presidents of colleges & young priests come to me; & I try to make them supernatural in their work, & careful in their studies, so as not to be drawn too far by modern rashness. Besides that I have the direction of many convents; & the formation of our young scholastics, so that I get an opportunity of practising what our Lord recommended to His Apostles. *Quod dico vobis in tenebris, predicate super tecta.*[1] I feel, my dear Jem, more & more that the *predicate super tecta* is almost sterile, if it be not preceded by union with our Lord in the *tenebrae* or silence of prayer.

[1] "That which I tell you in the dark . . . , preach ye upon the housetops" (Matt. 10:27).

I hope we may meet again. In any case let us remain closely united in our Lord's love, & in the union of prayer.

Ever yrs most fraternally in J.C.

Dom Columba Marmion<br>OSB

## XVI. TO DOM PLACID WOLTER, ARCHABBOT OF BEURON

### FOUR LETTERS

*Dom Placid, founder of Beuron Abbey with his brother Dom Maurus, was the first abbot of Maredsous. As such he had received in 1886 the young Irish priest who came to ask for admission to the monastery. (See above, Section VI, the letter Father Marmion wrote to his future Abbot shortly before his entry into religion.)*

*It seems that Dom Placid, a very well-intentioned but austere monk, did not fully understand the character of this Irishman, so full of ardor, exuberance, and good humor; and Dom Marmion suffered from being misunderstood, but bravely faced this trial. (See Thibaut, op. cit., p. 44, and particularly p. 67.)*

*In 1890, as Archabbot of Beuron, Dom Placid exercised a paternal authority over the whole Beuronese Congregation, and consequently over Mont-César, which was part of it. With an admirable spirit of faith and a remarkable humility, Dom Columba accounts to him, with great simplicity and frankness, for his occupations and the state of his soul.*

*Archabbot Placid Wolter was at this time aged and ill. He died at Beuron in 1908.*

I.

✠ Benedicite                Mont-César, Louvain. 8 Feb. 1905.

Right Rev. and very dear F. Archabbot,

I know that we must not fatigue you with unnecessary letters, and

III

so I scarcely ever write, as my life is very quiet, and I never have any difficulty with anyone. Yet I feel that you have always retained a very sincere and paternal affection for me, since the day that Our Lord inspired you to accept me as your son in spite of my great unworthiness; and on my side, I have ever guarded a profound veneration for your person, and a childlike affection for your Paternity. You have told me that it is a joy to get a line from me, and so I will just tell you how I am getting on.

For some time past, my soul is in great peace. My temptations have greatly diminished, in fact, almost ceased. God has given me the grace of detachment from creatures; and at the same time I see more and more clearly how weak and unworthy I am in myself, though I have a very great confidence in the merits and in the Blood of J.C. I may be mistaken, but I feel I have but a short time to live; and I try to live in God's presence, and in the preparation for the account I have to render. This does not make me sad, or prevent me from working, but prevents dissipation.

For the last few weeks I give retreats from time to time; and although I am by no means a preacher, Our Lord blesses my words. I like very much to give a retreat at Jupille; their spirit is so simple, so beautiful, and they are at the same time so simple, and so religiously reserved. I go there, and also to their foundation at Lede, as extraordinary confessor. I was at Woolhampton — the monastery of the English Benedictines of Douai — last August. I was greatly edified by their charity. . . . The Nuns at Princethorpe have begged F. Abbot to allow me to give their annual retreat, and he has consented; so that I shall have an opportunity of judging of the life of Benedictine nuns in England.

Here, at Mont-César, God is visibly blessing us. The holy life, and continual devotion of our dear F. Abbot, could not fail to call down a special protection.

Humbly begging your blessing and prayers, I remain most humbly devoted in J.C.

fr. Columba, O.S.B.

Abbot Marmion in 1913.

Maredsous Abbey in 1961. View from the air.

✠ Benedicite             Louvain. Mont-César, 18 June 1906.

Right Rev. and dear F. Archabbot,

On the occasion of my jubilee,[1] I received many congratulations and testimonies of affection; but I can say in all sincerity that none were so dear as that which came from you. As years roll on, I see that I have seldom in life found friendship so sincere and so paternal as yours; and on my part there are few whom I love more tenderly, and to whom I am so grateful as to you. God has been so good to me! *In die malorum protexit me in abscondito tabernaculi sui.*[2] I had been so wicked, so ungrateful, and He brought me to His own tabernacle; and it was you, dear Father, who opened the door, and bore with my weakness and imperfect beginnings. *Protexit me* yes, despite my passions. He has, I hope, preserved me by His grace from all grievous sin, for the last 20 years, i.e. since my entry. I feel a great desire to consecrate my remaining years wholly to His service, and through *love.*

I am very busy here at Louvain. God blesses my work, because I do all in obedience, and in absolute dependence on His Will and grace. I am giving the annual retreat at Ampleforth in September. I will not have the consolation of seeing you at the general Chapter, as the F. Abbot does not think we could both be absent under present circumstances. I seldom have the opportunity of knowing any of our Monasteries; but I leave that in God's keeping. In any case, it would be a great consolation for me to see you again, before we separate for eternity.

I remain with profound gratitude and filial affection, your respectfully devoted son in J. C.

f. Columba, O.S.B.

[1] The 25th anniversary of his ordination.

[2] "In the day of evils, he hath protected me in the secret place of his tabernacle" (Ps. 26:5).

✠ Benedicite                    Louvain. Mont-César, 7 Jan. 1907.
Right Rev. and very dear F. Archabbot,

I have the habit of sending you a line every year at this epoch to thank you for all you have done for me, and to give you an account of myself. You are good enough to tell me that this annual letter gives you pleasure; and for me, it is a consolation to send you at least a line, as I have seldom, or never, the pleasure of seeing you, or in fact, any of our abbots. As since my entry, I have been in Beuron but once, and never in any other of our German monasteries. Next Sunday, 10 Feb., I celebrate the 20th anniversary of my clothing as a novice; and God alone knows all the graces I have received since then. His mercies are above all His works. In return for much sin and ingratitude, He gave me a sublime vocation. And despite my many infidelities and faults, He has, I hope, preserved me from all mortal sin since my entry; and given me the grace of holy perseverance. I am extremely happy in my vocation, and appreciate it daily more and more.

I can do very little for the advancement of our Community, but I feel that humble obedience and observance of my rule may bring down blessings on us. Our numbers are still very limited, but the spirit is good. We have before our eyes daily a model of regularity and generous forgetfulness of self in the person of our Abbot.

The classes are given with zeal; and in our last examinations I was greatly pleased at the great progress of our students. . . . The death of Dom Pius de Hemptinne [1] was a great trial for me. He has been here my pupil and spiritual child for years; and I had a great admiration for that beautiful, virgin-soul. He had such splendid qualities of head and heart that he would have been a great Monk later on; and God knows best, and took him to Himself.

I should be most grateful if you would give me the faculty of anticipating Matins, Lauds at 2 o'clock, as I have from time to time to give retreats, and it is there a great convenience.

[1] January 27, 1907. See *A Disciple of Dom Marmion, Dom Pius de Hemptinne*, by John de Hemptinne (London, Sands, 1935).

Humbly asking your blessing, I remain with humble affection, your grateful and devoted child in J.C.

f. Columba Marmion, O.S.B.

IV.

✠ Benedicite                 Mont-César, Louvain. 19 Feb. 1908.
Right Rev. and dear Father Archabbot,

I write every year at this epoch to ask paternal blessing, and to thank you for all you have done for me. I am a little late, as I have had rather a heavy attack of influenza; and I am only just recovering. I humbly beg you to pray for me; and to offer me and the work which I try to do, to God, in order that through your hands He may accept it.

I am very happy in my vocation, though I am able to do very little. I try to do it in the spirit of obedience, and hope God will accept it, and show me mercy. Our Community here is very united, and I am sure very pleasing to God; as they observe their rule and live in peace, and are all fully occupied. We have no vocations at present; but if we are faithful, God will serve them in His good time.

As regards my occupations, I have a good many little things to do. Then I try to help Father Abbot, though very inefficiently, as I am often told; but I try to do my best, and I hope God will be satisfied.

Father Abbot-Primate kindly gave me an opportunity of seeing Fort-Augustus, by getting me invited to give their annual retreat. It is a most beautiful place, and if well governed, ought to be a centre of light and grace for the whole of Scotland. I got a line of introduction from the Marchioness of Bute to the Bishop of Argyll and the Isles.

His Lordship was most kind, giving me hospitality in his residence at Oban for three days. I had, during that time, the opportunity of seeing Iona, the former home of St. Columba. . . .

I shall be 50 next April, and I feel I have not very long to live; and so I recommend myself very humbly to your prayers, as I never forget you in mine.

I remain, with profound respect, your humbly devoted child in J.C.

fr. Columba, O.S.B.

# XVII. TO A NUN.

✠ Pax                  Mont-César, Louvain. 11 July 1906.

My dear child,

I should like to write you a long letter, but that is impossible at present, as I am overwhelmed with work. I have read your little autobiography with great interest, and quite understand your soul. I shall try to say in a few words what Our Lord inspires to write, reserving for my visit next month what remains to be said.

It is evident that Our Lord has destined your soul to a very close union with Him; and that thus united with Him, you were to have been His instrument for doing much for souls. There are in you excellent natural qualities, which, being elevated and supernaturalized by grace, would render you capable of very high sanctity. But you are a "child of impression"; and having taken the habit of allowing yourself to be guided and led by your impressions, there are in your life most astonishing contrasts. You must begin at the foundation of your soul, and try to accustom yourself to *follow reason enlightened by faith,* and no longer be the slave of your impressions. What distinguishes man from the animal is, that the animal, having no higher principle of action than sense, follows his impressions alone; whereas man has a spiritual principle which he should alone follow, using his senses, his impressions; but without being swept along by them. If you could once succeed in that, all that is good, and unselfish, and noble in you, would come into play; Jesus would become the absolute Master of your heart, and you would do great things for Him.

There is a book I am most anxious you should read and study. It will help you greatly to follow the direction I am giving you. I enclose the name and editor. You must read and weigh every word, for it is profound; but very specially suited for you. It is a very great grace for you to have such a prudent and holy Superioress. I have *very great confidence* in her; and am delighted God gives you the grace to be so open and simple with her. As I said, I hope to see you on my way to [. . .], or on my way back, following the circumstances. Till then, I shall pray for you with all my heart.

Please give my respects to the Community, and believe me your truly devoted father in J.C.

Dom Columba Marmion, O.S.B.

P.S. You *cannot* have too much confidence in the holy sacraments. They are the triumph of the merits of Jesus, and of God's mercy. Both are *infinite*. Provided you receive them with a sincere intention to return to God, they always produce their effects. *Le nom du livre est: La vie intérieure simplifiée et ramenée à son fondement, par le R. P. Tissot. Dernière édition, chez Amat, Paris, ou chez Brunet, 5, rue Saint-Aubert, Arras.*


## XVIII. TO A SUPERIORESS

FIVE LETTERS


I.

✠ Pax                                    Mont-César, Louvain. 2 April 1906.
My dear Rev. Mother,

Let me first thank you again for your great kindness and *extreme* generosity. I have seldom been so happy as during the days I spent at [. . .]. It was like being *at home*. I now daily place all your dear children, and your intentions, in my heart when going to choir and the altar.

I saw His Grace, the Archbishop, yesterday. He begs me to treat a very delicate and confidential matter with you. He has always taken a great interest in poor F. Tyrrell, S.J.,[1] and his large, loving

---

[1] George Tyrrell (1861-1909), whose expulsion from the Jesuits had occurred this year. An Irish Anglican convert to Catholicism in 1879, and a Stonyhurst Jesuit from 1880, he came to deny the validity of Revelation as "a direct communication from God to man" (*Catholic Encyclopedia*), and in general espoused Modernist principles. His attack on Leo XIII's decree *Lamentabili* and encyclical *Pascendi Gregis* in 1907 resulted in his "virtual excommunication," although many Catholics befriended him in charity, and "Cardinal Bourne courageously refused to condemn [him], as he considered he was suffering from disease" (Leslie, *op. cit.*, p. 188); and, upon becoming suddenly fatally ill, he received the last sacraments from a Southwark priest and absolution from his dear friend Abbé Brémond. Concerning relations between Mercier and Tyrrell, see Thibaut, *op. cit.*, pp. 286–90. (MEE)

heart suffers at the thought that that rich nature and brilliant intellect should be in danger of being lost; and also at the thought of his being deprived of happiness and *grace* of daily Mass. His Grace's first thought was to offer him a place in his archdiocese, on the condition that he would neither preach, nor hear confessions, nor publish anything without permission. However, after chatting the matter over with me, he came to the conclusion for *several grave* reasons, that it would not be prudent to do so. His Grace could have him accepted in some other diocese, (Liège or Namur), on the above conditions; but he wishes to be assured of his orthodoxy and actual dispositions, and for this he has recourse to you. Please try and find out his actual dispositions, and, if you are satisfied, you could let him know, — without speaking of the Archbishop, — that there could be found in Belgium an *"Episcopus benevolus"* [2] who would be willing to give him an opportunity of celebrating Mass and of living in retirement. His Grace thinks also of putting him in relation with me, which might be useful for both.

Please let me have your opinion as soon as possible, as I am to see His Grace towards the end of the week.

Pray for me, as I do for you; and believe me with sincere respect, yours devotedly in J.C.

Dom Columba Marmion.

II.

✠ Pax                    Mont César, Louvain. 6 April 1906

Confidential

Dear Rev. Mother,

I have just received the Archbishop's reply. I transcribe the part which regards our case. *Le point important est de savoir si T. a conservé la foi à la présence réelle. Qu'entend-il par "absolute secularisation"? S'il est disposé à vivre dans la retraite, à s'interdire des initiatives, et à seconder seulement celles que je prendrais, ou lui suggérerais, je ferai mon possible pour l'aider. Je ne verrais pas de difficulté à recevoir sa visite. Je lui ferais savoir par avance que le fait de le*

---

[2] "A kindly bishop."

*recevoir ne m'engage, ni ne l'engage, à rien. Ce serait uniquement un moyen de se connaître, et à chercher à s'entendre. Dans un mois par exemple.*[1]

It appears to me that you would do well to acquaint him *very confidentially* with the benevolent dispositions of His Grace, & the conditions which he insists on. He should however keep this strictly secret for the present.

Recommending myself to your prayers, I remain yours most devotedly in J.C.

Dom Columba Marmion, O.S.B.

P.S. His Grace says that having been asked by a religious community permission to expose the B. Sacrament for several hours the 1st Fridays of the month, he has accorded the permission, but on condition that one hour's adoration should be made for His Grace's intention, which is "d'obtenir lumière, force et humilité pour F.T."[2]

III.

Postcard R. Mother Prioress General.

Pax.                                        Louvain Sep. 28 [1909][1]

Pray for newly elected abbot of Maredsous. *Devise:*[2] *non praeesse, sed prodesse*[3] taken from Rule of S. Benedict.

✠ Columba O.S.B.

---

[1] "The important point is to know if T. has kept his faith in the Real Presence. What does he mean by 'absolute secularization'? If he will agree to live in retirement, to initiate nothing, and to support only such enterprises as I might undertake or suggest to him, I will do all that I can to help him. I see no difficulty in receiving a visit from him. I will make him understand in advance that the fact of receiving him commits neither me, nor him in any way. It would be solely an occasion to get to know each other better, and try to come to an understanding: perhaps in a month's time, for instance."

[2] "To obtain light, strength and humility for Father T."

[1] Postcard written the day of his election as abbot.

[2] Motto.

[3] "Not to command, but to be useful." Rule, chap. 64: of the appointment of the abbot.

✠ Pax                                    Maredsous. 27 Oct. [1909]

My dear Mother Prioress,

You can easily understand that every moment of my time has been more than taken up since my election. The administration of this monastery, with its very numerous community (130), its College, its school of art, its farm, & St. Scholastica would take up the time of an abbot at any ordinary time, especially if, as I try to do, he is present at all the divine office; but during these first few weeks, I have had such correspondence, & so many long standing questions to settle, that you can understand why you have heard so little from me. I know you do not attribute it to want of interest or love for your two communities.

Let me thank you, *ex immo corde*, for your kind present: this chain[1] will recall the golden links of affection which our dear Lord has deigned to establish between me & your dear communities.

Our Lord has helped me *wonderfully* up to this; my health is excellent, & all hearts are inclined towards me, so that I meet nothing but docility & good will. In fact, I am astonished & edified at the humility & reverential affection of all, especially of the older members. I attribute this in great part to all the fervent prayers offered for me; & also to the fact that I only accepted the charge when imposed *"in virtute sanctae obedientiae."* [2]

Please tell [. . .] that I shall soon write, & remain ever most intimately united in prayer & holy delectation with all.

Most devotedly yours in J.C.
✠ Columba Abb.

v.

Pax.                                      Maredsous. 14 Dec. [1909]

My dear Mother Prioress,

I have just received your beautiful gift.[1] It is just what I like. As I am obliged to wear gold, I like it pure, simple & solid. Pure, to

---

[1] The chain of his abbatial pectoral cross.
[2] In virtue of Holy Obedience. See Thibaut, *op. cit.*, pp. 172 f.
[1] The chain mentioned in the preceding letter.

symbolise the purity & sincerity of the affection I bear to your two communities. Simple, to symbolise the desire I retain to be humble & poor in spirit beneath the symbols of the dignity which has been placed on my shoulders. Solid, to symbolise the fidelity & strength of that attachment which our Lord has given me for my dear sisters of [. . .].

I do feel it was He who drew us together, & placed in my heart that strong desire of your perfection & prosperity, which forms daily the object of my prayer before God.

Allow me to thank you again for this *too* rich present, & to assure you of my unchanging attachment & devotion to you & to your two communities.

I hope to be able soon to come & pass a few hours with you all, & say all that my heart would say, but finds not words.

Ever in J.C., yours devotedly<br>✠ Columba Abb.

## XIX. TO AN ENGLISH SUPERIORESS

### FORTY-SIX LETTERS

*A nun belonging to a community to which Dom Marmion was preaching the annual retreat attracted his attention. She was a woman of lively intelligence and wide culture. Dom Marmion found her docile to his guidance and capable of progress in the spiritual life to a very high degree; and he undertook the direction of her soul. Hence the importance of the letters to follow, which reveal to us the spiritual master in action. Dom Marmion makes known here what he means by direction. In fulfilling a task that he feels he has received from Christ, he shows a sure authority and a paternal solicitude. We are brought to recognize here a true spiritual friendship at a high level, one in which the director himself is enriched by the soul he is leading with the help of God's enlightenment. "I regard you as one of my fastest and sincerest friends, and on my side this is quite mutual"*

*(December 12, 1909). What a pity that the answers from the mysterious correspondent have not survived!*

*The sisters in religion of this deceased nun have been good enough to lend us these letters for publication, but on the express condition that no allusion be made which could identify the nun herself, or her house. Thus there are many omissions in the text we are going to read — too numerous, even, for us to indicate them each time by ellipsis marks; but we can assure the reader that none of the essential doctrine has been omitted — and this, after all, is the important point.*

*Dom Marmion preaches total surrender to God, placing one's soul without reserve in His hands: the self-effacement of the soul before Christ, in whom it should live, according to St. Paul, who is constantly quoted by him. He had a particular love for this saying of the Apostle: "Gladly will I glory in my infirmities, that the power of Christ may dwell in me" (II Cor. 12:9). If he had taken a too human interest in this soul, he would have given a different reply to her repeated protestations of wretchedness and unworthiness.*

*We have thought it important to throw as much light as possible on the story of this spiritual correspondence by publishing for the first time an English translation of the account this religious wrote in French on January 6, 1938, for Dom Raymond Thibaut.*

*Feast of the Epiphany, 1938.*
*You have asked me, Reverend Father, for my impressions concerning dear Dom Columba of holy memory. I have written them in French, hoping thereby you may be able to make out better my bad writing.*

*He came to us for the first time in 1906. He was then Prior at Louvain. I had had some difficulty in arranging for him to preach us a retreat before our Renewal of Vows. I remember the first interview with him in the parlor. What struck me specially in him was his kindness, a simplicity that immediately put one at ease with him, combined with a sympathetic understanding that greatly helped one to open one's heart. In the course of our conversation, so spontaneous on his side, I was impressed by the breadth of his views; more than anything else, I felt myself really in the presence of a man of God who was filled with supernatural life. It seemed so easy for him to give himself to those souls who approached him with sincerity; and he made them feel the interest he took in them. The frankness that characterized him inspired others with a great confidence to be equally frank with him. He was very Irish in the quickness of his answers and full of the spontaneous humor that marks his race.*

*I remember that during this first interview I ventured to tell him that one of our older nuns, who was very devoted to the Jesuit Order to which a dearly loved brother belonged, had been somewhat hurt by certain criticisms of the "Method of St. Ignatius," coming as they did from a religious, and I asked him to avoid anything similar. I feared that this request was somewhat daring, but I was immediately reassured by his answer: "Well, Mother, I shall be as Jesuit as a Benedictine can be"; and he talked to me about his great respect for the Society of Jesus. I saw for myself later how groundless had been my fears and how unnecessary my remark. There was no narrow-mindedness in Dom Columba. He was far removed from those "who have only their own interests in view." He had a special, fatherly love for those who seek to further God's Kingdom, quite understanding that each religious order is born of a thought from God.*

*The conferences that he gave three times a day during this triduum were for me and for many others a real revelation. He gave us all his beautiful doctrine and we felt as if raised toward God by some tidal wave. For the rest of my life I shall never forget his conferences on the Divinity of Jesus Christ. It seemed to me that, although I had believed it as an article of faith, I had never realized it before to such a degree. I went to make my Way of the Cross and at each station I was seized by the thought: "And He who suffers so, who was thus treated . . . is God." It was a new revelation to me. Father Columba's lively faith had a power of imparting itself to others which one finds only in the saints.*

*This triduum was the beginning of a relationship between him and our community which was to last until his death. His visits were always occasions of grace for our souls and strengthened our appreciation of his doctrine as well as our veneration for him. His humility was remarkable. This theologian, whose writings are comparable to those of the Doctors of the Church, which have been admired and praised by popes, this monk who is rightly called "A Master of the Spiritual Life," humbly sought the opinion of others, and, what is more, followed it even when experience had shown that the criticisms so humbly accepted by him were entirely unfounded. It seems to me that there was a great affinity between him and St. Teresa of Jesus.*

*Dom Columba admitted quite openly that he was very sensitive, an inborn characteristic of the Celts. But he offered the suffering which re-*

*sulted from this sensitiveness wholeheartedly to God and never allowed it to degenerate into resentment. There was never an interval between the pain his sensitive nature suffered and the forgiveness that sprang from his loving heart. His forgiveness was complete, as is that of God himself.*

*We recently received a visit from a father of his Order who had known Dom Columba well, and he spoke of him with enthusiasm. "I have never," he said, "met a man with a more remarkable spirit of obedience; — he was steeped in it. I knew him as prior at Louvain, and I was struck by the manner in which he loved to bring out that he owed obedience in all things and at all times to his Abbot: If Father Abbot approves — If Father Abbot permits — I will ask permission of Father Abbot. One might have thought him a novice in his attitude of dependence, and he had gloried in this state of subjection. It was to obey that he entered religion, and in obedience that he found his happiness."*

*He once told me with great simplicity about an occasion when obedience was really hard to accept, since it concerned a soul whom he had promised to help. To succeed in obeying he made an act of humility as the saints do, and went off full of confidence in God and entirely submissive to his superior who represented Him. A few minutes later he received the permission that had been previously refused.*

*Dom Columba had certainly received magnificent natural gifts; but such gifts are not virtues, and those so noteworthy in him were not acquired without effort. In July of 1916 he wrote to me: "You know, sensitiveness is an Irish fault; I had to combat it for many years." Thus imperfect souls, tempted and discouraged, found in him a compassionate kindness, a tenderness that reflected the kindness and tenderness of the Heart of Jesus. To a soul greatly tried he wrote: "I suffer with you, for you are very dear to me; but I offer you to Him since He wishes it. You are dearer to me than ever in your time of suffering, but I offer you to Him, since this suffering is willed by Him. Unless you embrace not only His Cross, but also His humiliations, you will never be entirely His, and you will never taste either His joy or His peace. He plumbed the depth of tribulation; He suffered more than any man ever suffered; but He embraced it, He loved humiliation because it was His Father's will. That is what I want for you; that is what He asks of you." We have here the combination of kindness and firmness which supposed complete generosity on his part. He spoke to souls, as he said himself, directly, straightforwardly.*

*I have sent you, Reverend Father, the letters I received from him. All that he taught, he lived; and this is also the impression of those who, having known him, read the outstanding spiritual teaching contained in his works. One feels that it is not all the result of study or speculation, but that it has been dictated by his heart and has sprung from a living source. Dom Columba's writings make him known better than anything that could be written about him.*

I.

✝ Pax                                            Mont-César, Louvain.
                                                 19 April 1906.

My dear Rev. Mother,

Since my return from A . . . I have not had a moment free, or I should have written you a line ere this. I was *very happy* at A. . . . I think Our Lord means me to take a very special interest in your Houses. I love the spirit of your Rule; and feel that when perfectly understood and lived up to, it can lead to the highest sanctity.

As for yourself, I have prayed for you daily since I left. Believe me, my dear child, Our Lord wishes to be *everything* for you and in you; that is why He allows you to be so *little in yourself*. Try and assimilate St. Paul's magnificent theology. It is just what your soul wants. You are a capacity, at present almost empty, and Our Lord wants to fill it. I should advise you to read the beautiful little commentary on St. Paul's Epistles by "a Piconio." It is translated into French, (Pichini), and perhaps into English. I should like you to read the life of the holy Martyr "St. John Perboyre" Lazariste, by a member of the same Congregation. His whole spiritual life is just what yours should be.

You will say: "What impertinence to take the direction of my soul without being asked!" I am quite sure Our Lord wishes it. So there is really nothing left for you but to accept the arrangement.

I don't know what answer F. Abbot gave to your letter, as he hasn't said a word to me. So let us leave that to Our Lord.

Assure all the Sisters of my prayer and remembrance before Our Lord.

                                    Your devoted Father in J.C.
                                    Dom Columba Marmion. O.S.B. P.[1]

[1] Prior.

✝ Pax                                                    Mont-César, Louvain.
                                                          1 May 1906.
My dear Child,
    Your letter was a great pleasure, for I see we have the same ideas.
I am the mortal enemy of what is called "direction." The Holy Ghost
alone can form souls; and the director has only to point out to his
spiritual child the road by which God is leading her; give her some
general rules for her conduct, and control her progress; answer her
difficulties, if any, at *distant intervals.* Thus, if I see you during the
Retreat, two, or at most three, letters a year would suffice. This is
specially true of Religious whose interior life is based on the liturgy;
for the source in which they find the food of their souls is so pure,
that their souls are much less liable to error and hallucination, than
those who elaborate their whole spiritual life out of their own inner
consciousness. During the coming Retreat, give me a *humble story
of your past,* and I will tell you, with God's help, what He wants
from you.
    For the moment, I shall give you one or two principles which
ought to be the key-note of *your* spiritual life. 1. God does all things
for the glory of His Son Jesus. Now, Jesus is especially glorified by
those souls who, convinced of their utter incapacity, lean on Him,
look to Him for light, for help, for all. 2. You should try to realise
most vividly that, being a member of Jesus Xt. by your baptism, and
more and more so by every Communion, your needs, your infirmities,
your faults, are in a true sense the needs, the infirmities, the faults of
Jesus: *Vere languores nostros ipse tulit, et infirmitates nostras ipse
portavit. Posuit in eo Dominus iniquitatem omnium nostrum. Factus
est pro nobis peccatum.*[1] 3. When you feel your weakness and misery,
present yourself without fear before the eyes of your Heavenly
Father, in the name and person of His Divine Son. *Libenter gloriabor
in infirmitatibus meis ut inhabitet in me virtus Christi.*[2] The weaker

----

[1] "Surely He hath borne our infirmities and carried our sorrows. . . . The Lord
hath laid on him the iniquity of us all" (Isa. 53:4, 6). "[He, who knew no sin], he
hath [been] made sin for us" (literally: "He is made sin for us") (II Cor. 5:21).

[2] "Gladly therefore will I glory in my infirmities, that the power of Christ may
dwell in me" (II Cor. 12:9). This text will be like a theme throughout these letters.
See Introduction to this Section.

you are, the more Our Lord wishes to be your all. *Laeva ejus sub capite meo, et dextera illius amplexabitur me.*[3]

I am so busy I can't say more for the present; and I reserve the rest for August. I am looking forward with great pleasure to the Retreat. I am so peaceful, and at home, at N [. . .], it is a real rest.

Pray for me, my dear child, as I do *daily* for you, and Believe me

Your devoted in J.C.

Dom Columba Marmion, O.S.B. P.

### III.

✠ Pax                                    Mont-César. 5 Oct. 1906.

My dear Child,

I have been *so* busy since my return. I know you will understand my delay in answering. I am so pleased to hear that Our Lord has blessed the Retreat, and poured out His grace on a Community which is becoming more and more dear to me. I shall first answer your questions, and then add what Our Lord may inspire for yourself:

1. You should insist on having another copy of the *Vie de la Mère Deleloë*[1] as yours is incomplete. The parts I considered unfit for publishing were retrenched when reading the proof sheets.

2. The notes of Retreat I sent, were taken down almost word for word. The Abbess[2] was almost scrupulously careful to reproduce *exactly* what I said. I don't think there is an expression, or a thought, which I had not communicated.

As regards yourself: I am perfectly *certain* that despite your unworthiness and littleness, that God means and wishes to unite you *very closely* to Him. He is Master of His gifts, which He bestows *freely* on whom He wishes. I wish you to give yourself up without fear to the leading of the Holy Spirit. If He unites you *even very closely* with God, don't resist, and don't be afraid. Your misery and

---

[3] "His left hand is under my head, and his right hand shall embrace me" (Cant. 2:6, 8:3).

[1] A Belgian Benedictine mystic. This is probably an allusion to the work of Bruno Destrée, O.S.B., *Une Mystique inconnue du 18° siècle, La Mère Jeanne Deleloë* (Bruges, Desclée, 1904). Author was a monk of Mont-César.

[2] Most likely the abbess of Maredret. This concerns notes of a retreat preached by Dom Marmion in this monastery of Benedictine nuns.

unworthiness, which God has had the goodness to reveal to you, will protect you against illusion, and will but become more and more manifest to the eyes of your soul. God's glory, as derived from us, consists principally in the infinite condescensions of His mercy. The more miserable and unworthy we are, — provided we have a good will and seek Him sincerely, — the more is His mercy exalted in stooping down to our misery. "There is more joy in Heaven before God's Angels for one sinner who does penance, than for the 99 who need not penance"; [3] and there is more glory given to God when He condescends to stoop down to a poor, mean, selfish, ordinary creature, than when He communicates Himself to one of those grand, noble, superior natures which, to our eyes, seem to claim His notice. St. Paul understood this so well: "He hath chosen the weak and despicable things of this world to confound the strong," etc; *ut non glorietur in conspectu ejus omnis caro*," "That man should not glory in His sight.[4]

The triumph of the Passion, and of the merits of Jesus Christ, is attained when they lift up a poor, weak, and miserable creature, and unite it with the Divinity. Therefore, my dear child, fear not to go whither God is certainly calling you. "One soul," says Blosius,[5] "who gives herself up *without reserve* to God, allowing Him to act in her and with her as He pleases, does more for His glory and for souls in one hour, than others in long years of activity." And this is certain.

I am so busy, — we are just arranging classes, studies, etc., — I can't write to you what I intend regarding the H. Spirit. God seeks those who adore Him in *Spirit* and in truth.[6] He is the Spirit of the Father and Son, and those who allow themselves to be led by Him, seek the Father and Son in truth. He is the *Holy* Spirit, because all His inspirations are infinitely holy. He is the same identical Spirit which inspired Jesus in every act and thought; and it is by union with Him that the interior of J.C. is formed in our hearts. He is the *Pater pauperum*,[7] the Father of the poor, and He does not disdain to unite

[3] Luke 15:7.
[4] See I Cor. 1:27-29.
[5] Blosius, (Louis de Blois), O.S.B., *A Book of Spiritual Instructions*, trans. B. A. Wilberforce, O.P. (London, 1900), chap. 1, n°. 4.
[6] John 4:24.
[7] Sequence for Pentecost.

Himself with those who remain in *adoration and spirit of annihilation* in His presence. He is the Spirit of Holy Charity; and being the same in all unites us in holy love.

The new decree [8] about the Pentateuch merely says that the arguments presented up to this have not demonstrated that Moses was not the author of the *greatest part* of the Pent. It leaves us free to believe: 1) that certain portions have been composed by others. 2) It admits the *possibility* of arguments being found which demonstrate that the greater part is not from Moses. My personal opinion is that Moses was the author of the greater part.

Your devoted Father in J.C.

[no signature]

P.S. I enclose card containing names of books for Sister X [. . .]. Please pray for the writer, a young monk, one of my former pupils, one of our holiest and best, *dying*.[9]

(I shall have to undergo an operation for rupture this month. Please pray that all may go well.) [10]

IV.

✚ Pax     Chanoinesses Régulières de Saint Augustin,[1]
Jupille-lez-Liège, 5 Nov. [1906]

My dear Child,

I have just finished my Retreat, which has been greatly blessed by God, and I am worn out; but must send you one line before going to bed. I go to the Institute, Monday 12th. I expect the operation for the 13th or 14th. I shall send you word as soon as I am able. You may be quite sure Our Lord has confided your soul to my keeping; and

[8] Of the Pontifical Biblical Commission. The Fribourg conferences of M.-J. Lagrange, O.P., had dealt with the "Mosaic authenticity of the Pentateuch." See reference to Père Lagrange in Letter 16, Note 2, Section III (to Dr. Dwyer), and Murphy (ed.), *Père Lagrange and the Scriptures*, pp. 185 ff. (MEE).

[9] Dom Pius de Hemptinne, who died on January 27, 1907. See reference in Letter 3, Section XVI.

[10] In those days an operation for hernia seemed more serious than nowadays, and was also much more painful.

[1] Convent where Dom Marmion often preached to the nuns and to the students in their large boarding school for girls.

that you may trust my word. There is *no illusion* in the conviction of intimate union you experience at times; though, when it is past, you may begin to doubt its reality. Our life is a life of faith, and experimental conviction, if continual, *might* diminish the merit of faith. There can never be any illusion in the desire of uniting your will *perfectly* with the Divine Will. You cannot practise this too much. St. Jane Chantal wrote that for years her prayer consisted *"en laissant sa volonté s'enfoncer de plus en plus dans la Divine Volonté."* *C'est là votre voie.*[2]

I pray for you daily, and feel Our Lord will show forth His mercy once more in lifting up your nothingness to His perfect union.

I am to be invited here for the annual Retreat 1907. If A [. . .] has any intention of inviting me, they should write to my Abbot at the beginning of the new year. Otherwise they will be too late.

Tell the sisters I ever pray for all.

Your devoted Father in Christ,
D.C.

v.

✠ Pax                                     Jumet. Institute Dogniaux.
                                          Nov. 29th. [1906]

My dear Child,

I was so pleased with your letter that I must answer it, even though still condemned to lie on my back. All danger, and, I may say, all suffering is now past; and I am to get up tomorrow; and perhaps say H. Mass on Sunday. You will ask me why I was pleased with your letter; well, just because you speak to me just as you think; and that is *so rare.* I can't say how much I value it.

I had had little experience of physical suffering. I always dreaded it; and although I offer myself daily at Holy Mass in union with the Divine Victim, *without reserve* to the love and wisdom of the Heavenly Father, yet I never *asked* for suffering. After the operation you are placed on your back, without a pillow, head down; you are dead sick from the chloroform, and some, like me, have terrible pains in back and loins. You are told that to shift or move is to destroy all; and so there you are all that weary night alone; and the next day and the next

---

[2] " 'Letting her will sink more and more into the Divine Will.' That is your way."

night; a little water to wet your lips. It is like hell. I had no consolation; save the unfelt one of being united to God's Will; and a glance at the Crucifix. Some don't suffer at all so much. After the first 48 hours, things are better. Then you are at your ease. I am *so* glad to have suffered a little. I feel it will do a great work in my soul. I am so unmortified! You need have no more anxiety now, as I am quite convalescent; and stay on here now 10 days, merely to be under the doctor's eye, and rest.

The nuns here are *so* kind to me; and I get Holy Communion every morning; and have long hours alone with God. The more I gaze at Him, the more I see that He is the source of *all* good. It is infinitely better to look at Him than at ourselves.

I can't tell you how pleased I am at your honest (English) way of speaking to me of my notes of retreat. If people only would, or could treat with each other thus, how agreeable life would be! Most people flatter me; either knowingly, or because affection cozens them. What you say is just what I think myself. The notes contain helpful thoughts; but only: 1. for those who know me; 2. or presented in good literary form. I am incapable of writing classical French; and I feel my English wants the ring and flavour which makes things readable.[1]

I have been thinking about your soul. Despite your very real defects and misery, which are doubtless much greater than what we see, God loves you dearly; and wishes to substitute His greatness to your littleness; His generosity to your meanness; His Truth and Wisdom to your silliness. He can do all that, if you only let Him. *Confiteor tibi Pater, Dne caeli et terrae, quia abscondisti haec a sapientibus et prudentibus et revelasti ea* parvulis.[2] You are one of these very little

[1] Here is what his correspondent wrote on June 9, 1923, concerning this remark, in a letter to Dom Raymond Thibaut: "He had sent me several retreat notes taken, I think, by a nun, saying that there was some talk of publishing them and asking my advice. I ventured to write to him that I did not advise it; these notes seemed to me rather poor and it seemed impossible to publish them, at least without working them up. You will see with what admirable humility he thanked me for my advice . . . which was completely unfounded, for his "Retreats" published later were a very great success. I had only known him then for a short time, and I found his spoken word greatly superior to his written."

[2] "I confess to Thee, O Father, Lord of heaven and earth, because Thou hast hid these things from the wise and prudent and hast revealed them to the little ones" (Matt. 2:25).

people whom God deigns to look down on. Try to look much more at God than at yourself; to *glory* in your miseries as being the object and motive of His mercies; to love virtue more than you fear vice; to glorify the *infinite* merits and virtues of Jesus by drawing from them largely to supply your need. When duty permits, don't regard as lost either for you, *or for the Community* the moments you spend in union of love with God. He is the source of *all* the good you will do in yourself, or in others. Now my child, there's a programme for a whole year, yes, for a life.

It would be a great sacrifice if I can't go to A[. . .]. Jupille is asking too. F. Abbot won't allow both. God will decide which he will select. I should be glad to get a reading of F. Tyrrell's *Letter to a Professor*. Poor fellow, I fear he is drifting; God knows whither.

Your very devoted in J.C.

D. Columba Marmion.

VI.

✠ Pax          Tyburn Convent, 6, Hyde Park Place, London, W.
              [no date, 1906 or 1907]
My dear Child,

Just a line to say I am *so* sorry to be unable to pay you a visit. But God wishes it so; and souls united in His love are not separated by distance. I do hope you are very faithful to Our Lord, even in the midst of the darkness through which He so often wishes to lead you. *Etiamsi ambulavero in medio umbrae mortis, non timebo mala, quoniam tu mecum es.*[1] This is a *fervent* peace, and so filled with the evidence of God's very special care.

One case out of many. A young English Protestant lady hears her sister has been converted. She is distracted with sorrow, as she is a *strong* Protestant. She prays: and during the night, Our Lady appears to her and explains all. She becomes a fervent Catholic. She comes here by accident, and feels immediately that she is called by Our Lord. It is discovered after her entry that she is a relation to B. Fenwick, S.J., who was martyred here under Elizabeth. I pray daily for you, and do

---

[1] "For though I should walk in the midst of the shadow of death, I will fear no evils, for *thou* art with me" (Ps. 22:4).

hope you are keeping up your courage, despite the darkness of your
ordinary life. I go to A[. . .] Monday. Can I do anything for you?
Good bye.

> Ever Yours devotedly in J.C.
> D. Columba, O.S.B.

VII.

✠ Pax                                                      Mont-César. 1 Jan. 1907

My dear Child,

Don't be disappointed at my sending you such a scrap, which certainly does represent my desire of having a chat with you. I am
getting much better. The effects of the operation are past, the wound
*quite* healed; and, but for a nasty attack of influenza, I should be all
right again. I begin a short Retreat at the American College [1] tomorrow, which I recommend to your prayers. I suppose it is vain to ask
or desire your going to A[. . .] during the retreat. I should be so glad
to complete what I consider to be God's work in your soul, by deliver-
ing you over completely to Our Dear Lord "Who has looked down
on your lowliness" and wants you *all* to Himself (no accounting for
tastes).

Our Divine Lord inclines me more and more to live in an entire
dependence on Him, and the movements of His Spirit. The Father
has placed all things beneath the feet of His Beloved Son, and I feel
more and more drawn to live in a state of habitual adoration and
annihilation before Jesus in my heart. I tell you this for *yourself,*
because I feel Our lord will lead you also by that path. I pray daily for
you at Holy Mass; and know you do also for me.

I read the *Much abused Letter,* [2] and think it can't be sufficiently
"abused," as it is *pure Protestantism,* and even very low Church. I
did not come across the controversy about Lord Acton; [3] but I was

---

[1] At Louvain.

[2] Tyrrell's communication.

[3] Dom Aidan (later Cardinal) Gasquet, O.S.B., monk of Downside and historian,
whose recently published work *Lord Acton and His Circle* (London, 1906), which
Gasquet's biographer Sir Shane Leslie calls "a stirring of cold embers" was intended
to keep Lord Acton's "memory orthodox." See *Cardinal Gasquet. A Memoir,* pp. 115 f.
(MEE)

133

aware that Dom Gasquet had taken up an extreme position on the question.

Josephine was elected Rev. Mother of Jupille on Holy Innocents, under the name of Mother Columba. She is doing very well indeed. I gave a Retreat to the girls there, which was a great consolation, as God seemed to bless it greatly; despite my unfitness for speaking to young girls, whose *mentalité* is quite a mystery to me.

May God bless you, and take you *all* to Himself. My best wishes *to all* for 1907.

Your Father in J.C.
D. Columba M.

VIII.

✝ Pax            Mont-César, Louvain. 10 Jan. 1907.
My dear Child,

The light and interior movement you received during the Retreat were verily from God, and a grace. When such graces pass, they are often followed by seasons of doubt. S. Theresa, even after moments of highest union, during which she was incapable of doubting of the divine action, frequently fell back into doubt and trouble when the devine contact had ceased. Of course, in your case there is no question of such exalted favours; but I mention the fact in order to show that doubt may succeed to absolute certitude in such cases. Go on quietly living by *pure faith*, without any feeling. Jesus is your supplement in all things; and so in your communications with God, if you find yourself dry and rationalistic, just close the eyes of your soul, and in humble adoration just say one long *Amen* to all that Jesus is doing and saying in your name *in sinu Patris*.[1] This is often my case. The fact that you derive grace from humiliation is an excellent symptom of your soul's health. Our only way of knowing the state of our soul are the fruits. *Ex fructibus eorum cognoscetis eos.*[2] Now be quite at peace. I don't in the least look on you as a saint, or a very spiritual person; but Our Lord has preserved you pure and free from great sin; and I know He wants to have you very intimately united with

---

[1] "In the bosom of the Father" (John 1:18).
[2] "By their fruits you shall know them" (Matt. 7:16).

Him. "I confess to Thee, O Father, . . . because Thou hast hidden these things from the wise and prudent, and Thou hast revealed them to the little ones."[3] You are one of those little ones.

Try and become more motherly and loving.[4] We can govern souls by force and authority; but it is only by meekness and love that we can gain them to God. I *wish* you to read the life of Mme. Jeanne de Chantal by Mgr. Bougaud. She was much tried by temptations against faith for years. There is something in us all in league with evil; and it gives an echo when we come in contact with it. Some time ago, we were reading the life of Luther; and I was distressed at finding in my heart an echo to all his crimes, of which I feel myself perfectly capable. So don't be astonished to feel this at times.

Your devoted Father in J.C.
D. C.

IX.

✠ Pax                         Mont-César, Louvain. March 1907.
My dear Child,

Please excuse my delay in answering. I am overwhelmed with work. I am sure God wishes to lead your soul by the path of *pure* faith; and that is by faith without any of the self-satisfaction which sentiments and perceived certainty give. From time to time, you will receive a ray of light and warmth, and you must live on that; holding on to your faith, without any *reflex* consolation; though ever with a very real, but unfelt joy, in the depth of your soul. Try to love this way of pure faith; it is so sure, so unselfish, so very glorious to God. God never gives virtue in a high degree without our having fought and suffered for it. This is true of faith, which is the "root and foundation of all justice."[1] You will seem to yourself at times, to have lost almost your faith; yet it remains whole and entire in the *fine* point of your soul; all gathered up into so sharp and imperceptible a point that it seems no longer to exist. Close your eyes, and remain united with Jesus, saying a loving *Amen* to all He is gazing at in His Father.

[3] Matt. 11:25.
[4] This nun was superior during most of the time she corresponded with Dom Marmion.
[1] Council of Trent. Session VI on Justification, chap. 8.

135

It is a real sacrifice not to go to see you. A father has sometimes a weakness for the most sickly and less gifted of his children. Yet I am powerless, as I am under obedience; and may do nothing but what I am told. If Our Lord sees that it would be useful He will arrange.

Your devoted Father in Xto.
f. Columba.

## X.

✠ Pax                                   Mont-César. 19 April [1907?]
My dear Child,

I hope you are serving Our Lord in joy and peace. He loves you *so*. I want you to read Blosius. His *Comfort for the Faint-hearted* is just what you want. His spirit is just what I love; it is so true, so like the S. Heart.

It is a real sacrifice not to go to A[. . .] this year. I am always *so* happy and so at home there; and I feel Our Lord did bless my work.

You should try more and more to walk by faith, and not by *impression*. God has given us our reason, and He wishes us to guide ourselves by that faculty enlightened by faith. It is by reason we differ from animals; and God is glorified by our acting according to the nature He has given us. There are so many, especially women, who form for themselves a conscience of impressions which change with every wind.

Yours devotedly in J.C.
D. Columba Marmion, O.S.B.

P.S. You will scold me if I don't tell you I am in first class health, etc.

## XI.

✠ Pax                                   Louvain, 26 April [1907?]
My dear Child,

There is no presumption in following the *attrait* [1] of which you speak. On the contrary it would *displease God* were you to hold back through vain fear. These strong desires are *dans l'ordre de la foi,* [2]

[1] "Inclination."
[2] "In the line of Faith."

136

although very supernatural. Therefore as far as I have any jurisdiction over you — and I understand that you have given me full powers, — I *wish* you to yield without fear to these invitations of grace, and to continue your prayer which disposes you for such union. "A soul that gives herself up completely to God's leading, allowing Him to operate in her just as He pleases, *gives more glory to God,* and does more for souls in one hour, than others in long years." Louis de Blois. God often acts thus with very imperfect, ungrateful souls, *because He likes.* Go to H. Communion every day. I shall pray that Our Lord may arrange things so that you may come to A[. . .]. You are a *pessimistic impressionist,* but have an inordinate fear of *good* impressions. Believe me, *your* discouraging impressions are false; the others generally true.

Yours . . . C.

XII.

✠ Pax                    Mont-César, Louvain, 5 June [1907?]
My dear Child,
    There are two ways of presenting oneself before God. 1) As the Pharisee of the Gospel: leaning on our own works, and asking God to reward us for our justice. "I observe all your law. I fast. I give alms. You ought to be satisfied with me." God detests such self-righteous people, though they may be very correct and irreproachable. 2) As St. Paul: "I regard all my own righteousness as dung (*ut stercora*); my whole confidence is in J.C., who, through His merits, gives to my works all their value." Hence he glories, not in his works, but in his *infirmities. Libenter gloriabor in infirmitatibus meis.*[1] Such people are dear to God, because they glorify His Son; and this is His sole desire. You are rich in infirmities. And were you to lean on Xt. alone, doing all, suffering all, in His name, united with Him, He would render you more and more agreeable to His Father. He would bring you with Him into that sanctuary which He calls *sinus Patris,* His Father's bosom; and there, under God's eye, you would constantly try to please Him by doing what you feel is *most* pleasing to Him. Those

[1] "Gladly therefore will I glory in my infirmities" (II Cor. 12:9). See also Phil. 3:4–11.

137

alone dwell in God's bosom, who have an immense confidence in His Fatherly goodness and mercy, which are *infinite*; and who try their best to please Him in all things. Now there is your programme for the present. I feel Our Lord has given you to me as my child whom I am to present to Him to be one of the triumphs of His mercy. For St. Paul says: "He has chosen the weak, and the feeble, and the things of nothing; that no flesh might glory in His sight." [2] Poor von Hügel.[3] I fear he is *mal entouré*.[4] Tyrrell is, I fear, an evil influence for many.

Ever yours in J.C.
D. C.

XIII.

✠ Pax       Ampleforth College (Oswaldkirk).[1] 9 Sept. [1907]
My dear Child,
    Your last letter was almost a pain, as I see you allow the view of your miseries, which are very *finite* to hide the riches which are yours in J.C., and which are *infinite*. It is a great grace to see our miseries and our littleness, which are really much greater than we imagine; but this knowledge is real poison unless it be coupled with an *immense* faith and confidence in the all-sufficiency of Our dear Lord's merits, riches and virtues, which *are all ours*. *Vos estis corpus Xti et membra de membro*. "You are Xt's body, and the very members of His members." [2] The members really possess *as theirs* all the divinity and the merit of the person whose members they are; and this is what glorifies Jesus: to have such a high appreciation of His merits and of His *love in giving them to us*. (*Et nos credidimus caritati Dei*. 1 John),[3] that our misery and unworthiness do not discourage us. There are two

    [2] I Cor. 1:28–29.
    [3] Baron Friedrich von Hügel (1852–1925), English Catholic philosopher and student of mysticism, who maintained warm ties of friendship with Loisy and Tyrrell without ever leaving the Church himself. (MEE)
    [4] "In bad company."
    [1] Dom Marmion was preaching a retreat at this English Benedictine abbey.
    [2] I Cor. 12:27.
    [3] "We hath believed the charity, which God hath to us" (I John 4:16).

138

classes of persons who give little glory to J.C.: 1) those who do not see or realise their misery and unworthiness, and consequently don't *feel the need* of J.C. 2) Those who do see their misery, but have not that strong faith in the Divinity of J.C., by which they are, as it were, glad to be so weak in order that Jesus may be glorified by them. *Libenter gloriabor in infirmitatibus meis ut inhabitet in me virtus Xti.*[4] How far you are from glorifying in your infirmities.

Try and have a *most pure intention* in all you do. Unite your intentions to those of your Divine Spouse, and don't mind the results. God does not give results (to be) felt. Place yourself daily on the altar with Jesus, to be offered up to God's glory; and to be eaten up by those who surround you.

I did not *promise* to go to see you in December. It is very probable I may not have permission, though I hope to. Just write to me towards the beginning of December, and mention, — which is true —, that my visit will be useful. This will probably determine F. Abbot to allow me.

Ever your gratefully in J.C.<br>D. Columba Marmion, O.S.B.

P.S. The Church, towers, and south wing of our Abbey are yet to be built.

XIV.

✠ Pax St. Thomas' Abbey, Erdington,[1] 11 Dec. [1907]
My dear Child,

Allow me to express my very sincere gratitude for your warm welcome and very generous offering. I pray Our dear Lord to pay you a hundred-fold.

The more I pray for you, the more I see that your *way* is absolute and *unreserved* "abandon." [2] God will care for you just in so far as you cast yourself and all your cares in the bosom of His Paternal love and

---

[4] "Gladly therefore will I glory in my infirmities, that the power of Christ may dwell in me" (II Cor. 12:9).

[1] Benedictine abbey near Birmingham founded by Beuron on the banishment of the Congregation from Germany during the *Kulturkampf*.

[2] "Abandonment," self-surrender.

providence. When in His presence, in the darkness of faith, adore Him in His *ways*, His Providence, His often unfathomable wisdom; then cast yourself on His bosom just as a child *nisi efficiamini sicut parvuli non intrabitis in regnum caelorum.*[3] He will treat you as you treat Him; and give you that "joy and peace in believing" of which St. Paul speaks.[4] Offer Him a daily holocaust of all sensitiveness, leaving yourself and all that concerns you in His loving care. *Jacta super Dominum curam tuam et ipse te nutriet.*[5]

I have been trying to finish this letter for the last few days, and can't. All my moments are taken.

Ever yours in J.C.<br>D. Columba

xv.

✠ Pax             Mont-César, Louvain, 8 Jan. 1908.

My dear Child,

Do forgive me for having left your letter so long without a reply. I have been so overwhelmed with work that I am sure, if you were by me, you would have said: "don't write at present." In any case, were you to measure my interest in your soul by my correspondence, you would be very far from the reality. I do believe God means me to help you; and I pray daily for you. In every soul, three spirits strive for the mastery. The spirit of falsehood and blasphemy, who, from the beginning, ever suggests the contrary of what God whispers. "If you eat of this fruit you shall certainly die," says God. *Nequaquam moriemini*; "you shall not die by any means," [1] was Satan's reply; and all his suggestions are but the echo of this first lie. Then there is the spirit of the world, inclining us to judge things according to the maxims of sense, and of carnal prudence; *prudentia hujus mundi stultitia est apud Deum.* "The prudence of this world is folly with God." [2] Then there

---

[3] "Unless you . . . become as little children, you shall not enter into the Kingdom of Heaven" (Matt. 18:3).

[4] Rom. 15:13.

[5] "Cast thy care upon the Lord, and He shall sustain thee" (Ps. 54:23).

[1] Gen. 3:4.

[2] See I Cor. 3:19.

is the Spirit of God, ever whispering in our ears to raise our hearts above nature *sursum corda*, and to live by faith; *justus meus ex fide vivit*.[3] This spirit always inclines us towards simple, loving faith, "abandon" of self into God's hands. It fills us with "peace and joy in believing"; and produces the *fruits* of which St. Paul speaks.[4]

Now, my dear child, in certain persons the action of these several spirits is more tangible and striking than in others. In you, the influence of these spirits is very marked. You will always know them by their fruits, even though Satan may try to clothe himself as an angel of light. Our Lord says: *Ex fructibus cognoscetis eos*.[5] You will recognize these spirits by the *fruits* they produce in your soul. God's spirit, even when He reproaches us, or inclines us to confusion, or compunction for our sins, *ever* fills the soul with peace, and filial confidence in our Heavenly Father. The other spirits dry up our souls, fill us with naturalistic tendencies; or, if it be the spirit of hell, casts gloom and discouragement into our soul. Now, just as Eve *should* have refused to believe, or even to listen to the infernal spirit when he contradicted God's testimony, just as she ought to have put him to flight by saying, as St. Michael, *Quis ut Deus?* [6] "Do you think I will pay any attention to your hissing lies, when they contradict God's word!" So should we. I recommend you a great fidelity to the movements of the H. Spirit. Your baptism and your confirmation have established Him as a living fountain in your soul. Hear His whisperings, and put the other inspirations to flight *at once*. If you are faithful in this, little by little this Divine Spirit will become your guide, and bear you with Him into God's bosom. The Holy Spirit holds the place for us, that Jesus did for His Apostles during His mortal life. Just as they could have recourse to Him, speak to Him, pray, etc., so He has sent us "another Paraclete to stay with us, and teach us all things which He has told us." [7]

I am on the commission of "Vigilance" for this diocese, which means work, work. Pray for me, for, *in all sooth*, to you, my child, I

---

[3] "My just man liveth by faith" (Heb. 10:38).

[4] Rom. 15:13.

[5] "By their fruits you shall know them'" (Matt. 7:16).

[6] "Who is like God?" — the meaning of the Hebrew name "Michael."

[7] John 14:16 and 26.

say it from my heart, I feel *such* a distance between what I preach and what I practise, that I really tremble lest I become like a sign-post showing the way to others and remaining stationary myself.

I should be very glad to read Maud Petre's work.[8]

Ever yours very devotedly in J.C.

Dom Columba Marmion, O.S.B.

XVI.

✠ Pax                                Downside,[1] 28 April [1908]

My dear Child,

I had been looking forward to the pleasure of seeing you on my way back, but I have just received a letter from the Cardinal of Malines, begging me to come on to Malines on my arrival in Belgium next Tuesday evening, as he wants to see me, and must go away the next morning. I must therefore put off my visit till September. I should have liked so much to have seen you; as I see you want winding up. Your soul is very dear to God, but He wants a more perfect *abandon* into His hands; and allows you to feel all your impotency, as long as you fail to look for all things from Him. Your present state is due in part to physical weakness, and in part it is a trial; when it is past, you will find that you had been getting nearer to God, though it seemed you were drifting from Him.

The sign that your present state is not due *principally* to your infidelities — though of course it is likely that they are not wholly foreign to it — is that you feel deep down in your soul a great want of God, which is a real torment, as you seem so hopelessly estranged from Him. It is He who gives this double, and seemingly contradictory, sentiment. He wants you to *long* for Him, and at the same time to *see*, that of yourself you are quite incapable of finding Him. He will come in the end, *desiderium pauperum exaudivit Dominus*;[2] you are one of those poor ones just now.

This is a most delightful place, in fact too beautiful; and I should

---

[8] A fervent disciple, apologist, and biographer of Tyrrell. The allusion is probably to her work, *Catholicism and Independence* (London, 1907).

[1] Dom Marmion was preaching the annual retreat at the Abbey at this time.

[2] "The Lord hath heard the desire of the poor" (Ps. 9:17).

be very happy, but for the very nasty weather, and the fact that I am feeling rather seedy. This is generally the price I have to pay for God's blessing on a Retreat.

Pray for me, as I do for you, daily, that God may give us the grace to seek Him *alone*. "If your eye be simple, your whole being will be in light." [3]

May God bless you.

Yours very devotedly in J.C.

Dom Columba Marmion, O.S.B.

XVII.

✠ Pax

Mont-César, Louvain, 26 May [1908]

My dear Child in J.C.,

It is really very kind of you to take such an interest in me. It is a joy and an encouragement, because I feel it is so sincere. Well, you may be at peace. It was only a nasty attack of influenza, such as I get every year. The operation I went through two years ago was most successful, and final; and leaves no trace nor weakness. I am getting over the influenza, though still under the spell.

I feel very intensely your bereavement and your suffering. People like you love very strongly and very completely those who are dear to them. And when they lose one of them, they lose part of themselves. Mother Prioress spoke to me of your dear sister, of her beautiful soul and strange career. I believe she was one of Providence's special cared ones; and that all has been for the best. As I know you, I can feel what a void this loss has made in your poor heart. It must bleed for a time; but God Himself wishes to fill up the gap. It is by successive detachments that He ends by becoming *our All*; and at times this separation from all human solace is almost like death. I have gone through it; and know that poor human weakness could not bear it, were it to last. But little by little God becomes *our All*; and in Him we find again what we seem to have lost.

I have been praying much for you. First, I believe God has given you to me to cultivate and prepare for perfect union with Him; and

[3] Matt. 6:22.

143

then again, because I *feel* how you are suffering. Such trials are often for souls like you *le point de départ* of a very perfect life. For souls like yours, God wants to be *All, Deus meus et* omnia;[1] but as long as they could lean on any human aid, how legitimate and holy soever it might be, He could not be their *All*. This is the perfection of the virtue of poverty; it is perfect hope: to have lost all created joy, and lean on God alone.

In Holy *Communion*, you enter into union directly with Jesus Xt., and through Him with the Father and the H. Spirit who are in Him. Again you enter with Him, and through Him, into union with all His members, and especially with those who are perfectly united with Him in glory. This is that *Communion* for which He prayed His Father, *ut omnes unum sint, sicut ego in te et tu in me, ut sint consummati in unum.*[2]

I advise you to go from time to time before the B. Sacrament, and placing yourself at Our Lord's feet, beg Him to be *all* for you.

I shall be delighted to read your sister's biography. I feel she is already in peace and light; but you may depend on my prayers and sacrifices just as if she were my own.

I do hope, on my way back from Woolhampton, that I may be able to spend a day with you. Ask our Lord, and if He sees fit, He will arrange it.

Believe me ever yours very devotedly in J.C.
Dom Columba Marmion, O.S.B.

XVIII.

✠ Pax                             Brussels; 8 July [1908]
My dear Child,

*His qui diligunt Deum, omnia cooperantur in bonum.* "For those who love God, all things cooperate unto good." [1] Of course nature must have its way, and our poor hearts must bleed when those whom we have loved are taken from us. I would not like to think you did

---

[1] St. Francis of Assisi.

[2] "That they may all be one, as thou Father, in men, and I in thee . . . that they may be perfect in one" (John 17:21–23).

[1] Rom. 8:28.

The Abbot's Irish cross and ring.

With Queen Elizabeth of the Belgians
at Maredsous in 1920.

not feel this trial; for Jesus wept over Lazarus; and He has given us human hearts; but yet we must lift our thoughts to God's bosom, and see those we love, there waiting for us, and loving Him in our place. As you say, my dear child, I feel Our Lord has given you to me to fit you for Himself. I do not write much, but I bring you *daily* with me on the altar; and there I offer you, and all your needs and pleadings, to God through J.C.

It seems to me that you are now more than ever my child; and as such I shall say Holy Mass for *our* mother with all the affection and fervour I would have for my own.

I have just given the monthly conference at the Institut Saint-Louis, Brussels [where] I am writing this. . . .[2]

May God bless you and sanctify you.

Ever your devoted Father in J.C.
Dom Columba Marmion, O.S.B.

XIX.

✠ Pax

Mont-César, Louvain, 15 Nov. [1908]

My dear Child in J.C.,

You must have a little word for your jubilee. It is the 22nd anniversary of my entrance into the Religious life,[1] so I shall thank God at H. Mass next Saturday for all the graces given us both; and ask for grace to make a new start. I am very *glad indeed* you were inspired to take up St. Gertrude. Her spirit is just the antidote for your spiritual ills. Her views of our faults is absolutely true. Faults arising from weakness, and really detested in our hearts, do not prevent God from loving us. They excite His compassion. *Quomodo miseretur pater filiorum misertus est Dominus timentibus se*, quoniam ipse cognovit figmentum nostrum.[2] This was St. Paul's great devotion: to present himself before his Heavenly Father with all his infirmities; and as he looks always on himself as a member of J.C., these infirmities

---

[2] Cardinal Mercier had asked Dom Marmion to give a spiritual conference each month for the clergy of Brussels.

[1] November 21, 1886.

[2] "As a father hath compassion on his children, so hath the Lord compassion on them that fear Him: for He knoweth our frame" (Ps. 102:13–14).

145

were really Christ's. *Libenter gloriabor in infirmitatibus meis, ut inhabitet in me virtus Christi.* Try and fill yourself with that spirit of childlike confidence in God, and it will give you the same attitude towards those who call you "mother." God treats us as we treat others; and the more loving and indulgent we are towards others, the more God bends down to us in our weakness.

It appears to me that the more closely I become united with Our Divine Lord, the more He draws me towards His Father; and the more He wills me to be filled with His filial spirit. You could not do better than follow out that thought. It is the whole spirit of the new law: *non accepistis spiritum servitutis iterum in timore, sed accepistis spiritum adoptionis filiorum, in quo clamamus Abba Pater.*[3] Most of your difficulties come from your not allowing yourself to be guided and inspired by this spirit of love, but listen too often to the other spirit of fear, which paralyses your soul, and prevents God's grace. There is a very good French edition of the works of St. Gertrude: *Le Héraut de l'Amour Divin. Révélations de Ste. Gertrude. Traduites par les R. R. Pères de Solesmes. Chez H. Oudin, Paris. 24 rue Condé. 1907.*

It may interest the Community to hear the account of a very strange experience I had on my way back from Germany. I had leave to spend a day at Aix-la-Chapelle. I lodged at a Sanatorium kept by Franciscan Nuns. I got there Tuesday night; and during supper, the Superioress told me there was a sad case in the house. A lady of a wealthy German family, mother of six children, had left her husband and family on account of his conjugal infidelity. She had become an atheist; and spent her time travelling. She had joined a masonic society in Italy, undertaking never to call a priest, and to die without Religion. She had taken an apartment in the Sanatorium, just to study anatomy, and while away her time. She was utterly without religion.

The Superioress asked me to try to bring her back to God. As I had to leave next day at 3 o'clock, I had very little hope. However, after my Mass, I felt I ought to try, and begged Our Lord to act through me. I asked the lady to dine with me. She consented through

---

[3] "For you have not received the spirit of bondage again in fear: but you have received the spirit of adoption of sons, whereby we cry: Abba: Father" (Rom. 8:15).

146

curiosity. A very charming person, 37 years of age, speaking fluently French, English, Italian, etc., and very clever. God gave me the grace to touch her heart. She consented to confess *to me*; but I had no faculties to confess there; and I had to leave at 3.

Most unexpectedly a materialistic doctor turned up at 2 o'clock, and offered to bring her and me for a drive in his motor-car. He brought us across the Frontier to Moresnet, in the diocese of Liège, in which I have full faculties. Just as we got there, his machine broke down; and he was obliged to spend an hour mending it. During that time, I prepared the lady, and heard her confession in a Church close by. She was most beautifully disposed; and I had the happiness of giving her H. Communion next morning. Such experiences confirm our faith.

I am going to Bruges in January to give a retreat at St. André.

I daily pray for all.

Yours in J.C.

Dom Columba Marmion, O.S.B.

## xx.

✠ Pax

Chanoinesses Régulières de St. Augustin,

Jupille-lez-Liège, 7 March [1909].

My dear Child in J.C.,

I was so pleased to receive your letter, and to see that Our Dear Lord has lifted the veil a moment; just as He did for the disciples. Of course we must walk, not by vision, but by *faith*. Yet He condescends to our weakness, and, from time to time, allows the light of His divine mercy and beauty to pierce the clouds and darkness in which He habitually envelopes Himself. *Nubes et caligo in circuitu ejus.*[1] You have come down from the mountain on which you would have dwelt forever. *Domine, bonum est nos hic esse.* You now see "only Jesus" *neminem viderunt nisi solum Jesum.*[2]

My dear child, *you* must never forget that in the present order of

---

[1] "Clouds and darkness are round about him" (Ps. 96:2).

[2] Allusion to the Transfiguration of our Lord, an episode frequently referred to by Dom Marmion in his conferences: "Lord, it is good for us to be here. . . . And they lifting up their eyes saw no one but only Jesus" (Matt. 17:4–8).

Providence, God is glorified by our *faith. Sine fide impossibile est placere Deo.*[3] He, from time to time, gives us to *feel* that He is sweet, and that He loves us; but that is the exception. He expects us to believe, and confide in His love without any feeling of it. *Nos credidimus caritati Dei;*[4] "we, says St. John, we have believed in God's love for us." In the Psalm *Attendite,*[5] God is ever complaining that, despite the repeated *proof* of His ever-loving providence, the Jews were ever falling back into distrust: *non fuerunt memores multitudinis misericordiae suae.* "They were not mindful of the multitude of His mercies," and so He complains of them *semper errant corde.*[6]

Now, my dear child, I have studied your soul in prayer, and I *know* that God wants you to serve Him by pure faith in spite of all sorts of repugnance; and so you must be satisfied to go in faith without consolation, nor feeling, trusting in Him, and in the words of His minister, who speaks in His name. He will often leave you in your weakness, and seem to deprive you of every help; yet He is ever in the centre of your heart, guiding and protecting you. You must have a great faith, not only in His *love*, but also in the *wisdom* of His guidance. It is *impossible* that Our Lord should command you by the voice of obedience to undertake anything which would be detrimental to your soul. It will seem to you at times, that the task imposed is above your strength; but God is *bound* to give you all the light and grace necessary to fill an office in which He Himself places you. You know I bring you *daily* in my heart to the altar; and place all your wants and intentions in Our Lord's hands.

I daily get marks of His loving care. I had a great desire to make a good retreat; but have been prevented for some years to make my annual retreat. And even when I can make it, I am so often interrupted I cannot fully recollect myself. I also longed for years to visit Paray-le-Monial. And now the Cardinal has just obtained permission from my Lord Abbot for me to accompany him to Paray-le-Monial during his retreat, which he will make there this year on returning

---

[3] "But without faith, it is impossible to please God" (Heb. 11:6).
[4] I John 4:16.
[5] Ps. 77.
[6] "These always err in heart" (Ps. 94:10).

148

from Rome. I shall let you know the date in order that you may accompany me by your prayers.

I must now leave you; but you may ever count on my prayers; and my sincere attachment in J.C.

Dom Columba Marmion, O.S.B.

XXI.

✠ Pax  Douai Abbey, Woolhampton,[1] R.S.O.,<br>Berks., 2 August [1909].

My dear Child,

I had been looking forward with such pleasure to spending a few hours with you; but Our Dear Lord asks a sacrifice this time. F. Abbot and our Subprior are leaving for the Congress at Cologne[2] tomorrow; and as the Monastery will be thus almost without any Superior, I have received a formal order to go back *directly*, as soon as my work here is finished. It is a real sacrifice for me not to see you, and I know it is also for you. Let us offer it up for your sanctification. I *do* so desire and pray that God may give you the grace to throw yourself without reserve into His arms, and *find all in Him*. I want your very special prayers for myself, for the next *few* weeks. I can't say by letter what I should otherwise confide to you; but I have reason to fear that the general chapter, at which I have just assisted, may be the occasion of very important changes in my life and responsibilities.[3] Please don't say anything of this, as nothing is certain yet. I am giving a retreat at Ramsgate, 3–11 Sep.; and at Maredsous, 12–19 Sep. This latter retreat is very important at present. I shall of course write as soon as I have anything definite to tell you.

God bless you, my child,

Yrs. in J.C.<br>D. Columba, O.S.B.

[1] Dom Marmion was preaching the annual retreat here at the time.

[2] International Eucharistic Congress.

[3] This concerned the probable resignation of the abbacy of Maredsous by Dom Hildebrand de Hemptinne, who had been appointed Primate of the Benedictine Order. The monks of Maredsous therefore had to elect a new abbot, and Dom Marmion knew that the choice might fall on him. See the letter to follow; also Section X, Introduction.

✠ Pax

St. Augustine's College, Ramsgate [1]
7 Sep. [1909]

My dear Child,

Just one word to say I am praying for you. I do *so* yearn to see you give yourself without reserve to God, and find *all* in Him. The glorious Communion of Saints appeals to me more and more. We are really so *"one"* in J.C. The more closely we are united with Jesus, the more closely the bonds of holy love embrace and envelope us. It is in Jesus, and in Him *alone*, that you will find those who are so dear to you *in truth*. He is Truth, and the more closely we abide in Him, the *truer* is our union with those we love. If we *only* find them in ourselves, in our own poor human hearts, in our feelings and remembrance, our union is fruitless for them; — for us, it only makes the void deeper and more hopeless. But when we unite ourselves to them in Jesus, our union is a joy for them, and peace for us. Now, my dear child, *do* meditate on those lines. I feel Our Lord inspires me to write them for you.

As regards myself, I give the retreat at Maredsous from Sep. 12–19. (I leave here Saturday morning.) After the retreat, there is a canonical visit, beginning the 20th. This will *most likely* be followed by the election of a new Abbot for Maredsous. There *was* some probability of my being selected; but my own Abbot (Louvain) has the right of veto, and he means using it; as he told me he is convinced that my place is at Louvain. I am at perfect peace, as I wish only for God's will; and I am sincerely convinced that the position — for many reasons — was far beyond my strength. Of course, the other Superiors can override the veto; but this is scarcely likely. Of course you will look on this as *very confidential*; but I may not hide anything from my dear child.

Ever yrs.
D. Columba, O.S.B.

[1] At the time Dom Marmion was preaching the annual retreat at this English abbey.

✝ Pax

Maredsous, 12 Dec. [1909].

My dear Child,

It is really too bad of me to keep you so long without any news. You *know* it is not from any want of interest or affection. I regard you as one of my fastest and sincerest friends; and on my side this is quite mutual. My charge here is so vast, so engrossing; the large Abbey, the college, the school of arts, the convent, the wide relations with all sorts of people, so take up, so eat up my day that I find no time for recollection or reading. However, God is very good to me. And I beg Jesus every morning to govern the Monastery through me; and He does so most wonderfully, despite my infidelities and mistakes. My Monks are wonderfully docile; and do their best to help and sustain me. Yet of course there are many crosses, and heavy responsibilities. My health is good, though I am often tired and weary. But I must confess that, up to this, things have been much easier than I had anticipated. I see more and more that the great point is to sink our personality, and let Xt. act in us and through us. How I long to see you, my dear child, place *all* your consolation in God; not in the sense that you should reject all other joy, but that no human consolation should be *necessary* for your peace.

I never forget my dear children at [. . .]. I *daily* bring them in my heart to the altar, that united with our dear Lord they may be accepted by the Father.

Ever yours most faithfully,
✝ Columba, Abb.

XXIV.

✝ Pax

Maredsous, 16 June [1910]

My dear Child,

It is a long time since I heard from you, or you from me. Friendship founded on God is independent of time or distance, for it partakes somehow of God's own Eternity; and so I have no fears that your friendship for me has, in any way, changed or diminished.

Mine has not in any case. . . . For that place which I have given you in my heart is ever yours; and you accompany me daily to the altar where we meet in that *Communion* of which Jesus is the centre and the bond.

I am getting on well, D.G. The Community is most docile and devoted. And the difficulties — some of them very considerable — which I found on my arrival, are, by God's grace, gradually melting away. I should so like to see you, but am not certain that I can. I have promised Stanbrook for years to give them a retreat, & am going in August. I start on the 16th & must be back in Brussels on the 27th. The Abbot of Erdington wants to see me & has made me promise to pay them a visit. I may be going to Farnborough in November.

Ever yrs. in J.C.

✠ Columba, Abb.

XXV.

✠ Pax

The Abbey, Farnborough [1] Hants., 19 Nov. [1910]

My dear Child,

I had been looking forward with a *real longing* to see you. It was on that account that I had put off answering your very welcome letter. I have just received a wire from Belgium calling me back as quickly as possible. I must leave here *immediately* after the retreat, and go home directly. This is a real trial for me, for I am most devoted to you; and it would have been a real joy to have spent a day or more with you. Had I seen you, I should have spoken to you nearly as follows: God has poured forth all "the treasures of His Wisdom and of His Science" [2] on the Sacred Humanity of J.C. because of its union with the Word. And *the measure of His gifts to us, is the degree of our union with this same Word.* Now, this union with the Word is effected by the power and efficiency of the Sacred Humanity, especially in H. Communion. What we have to do is to maintain ourselves, through the Sacred Humanity, in an habitual state of absolute adoration and *submission* to the Word, Who resides within us. Our life must be an "Amen" ever echoing the wishes and the designs of

[1] Dom (Abbot) Marmion was preaching the annual retreat at this English abbey.
[2] Col. 2:3.

that Word on us. A soul, once arrived at that state, becomes the object of the outpouring of God's best gifts. Monday, my 24th anniversary of entry, I shall say H. Mass for *us two*, that Our Lord may do for you all that I should have wished and more.

In great haste,

Ever yrs. in J.C.
✠ Columba, Abb.

XXVI.

✠ Pax

Abbaye de Maredsous, 6 Dec. [1911]

My dear Child,

I was so glad to get a word, for I never forget, though I don't write. It is a great happiness for me to know that God is taking possession of His Kingdom in your soul. All your trials were intended to prepare and purify your interior for Him. As I promised you, I take you daily in my heart to the H. Altar, and make all your intentions and your interests *mine* in Our Lord's heart. I feel this manner of praying for those we love is most efficacious. As regards the retreat, I am fully determined to go, and prefer August; though as yet I can't fix the date, as I must be present in mitre and crosier at the Marial Congress at Maastricht, which takes place some time in August, somewhere about the 15th.

I have most weighty matters on hand at present. The Abbey and College are going on well, D.G., and God is helping me wonderfully; but I have a lot of relations and official matters outside of my ordinary work, which take up all my moments. Then I have no secretary, nor personal helper. Pray for me.

Ever yrs. in J.C.
✠ Columba, Abb.

XXVII.

✠ Pax

Abbaye de Maredsous, 6 Feb. [1912]

My dear Child,

Just a word to ask you to fix the date of your retreat, as I have such a number of arrangements to make. I am giving the retreat to the clergy of Westminster from Sep. 2-6. I should be glad to go to you, so as to have finished a couple of days before beginning at Westminster. I am often very worn out after a retreat, & I shall need all my strength for that of Westminster. . . . All the month of August up to the 25th is taken up in various ways, & our own retreat here begins Sep. 24.

I have seldom been so busy as I have been this year. I hope next year to be able to breathe more freely; and not *seem* to forget those whom I really love so dearly in J.C. It is especially at H. Mass that I find myself united in J.C. with those I love; and beg Him to be *my all* for them, as He is more and more every day for myself.

I must say good bye. I start for Rome on the 25th with the Cardinal. I shall ask St. Peter to give you a stronger faith.

Ever yrs. in J.C.

✠ Columba, Abb.

XXVIII.

✠ Pax                            Rome, 22 Sep. [1912]

Just a word to say I had a long audience from the Pope to-day (25 minutes). He was *most kind*. He wrote the enclosed for you, and I send it as a token. His words are those of J.C., who really intends to fill you with every grace and benediction. He wrote on the card you gave me the following words: *In cunctis rerum angustiis vere cogita 'Dominus est.' Et Deus erit tibi adjutor fortis.*[1] *die 22 Sep. 1912. Pius PP.X.* I send you this as a mark of my profound and very true affection in J.C.                      ✠ Columba, Abb.

On your card Pius X has written with his own hand *Deus repleat te omni benedictione.*[2] *Pius PP.X.*

XXIX.

✠ Pax                           Maredsous, 5 Dec. 1912.

My dear Child,

I have been waiting to see if I should have any news, which might

---

[1] "In all trials think truly: It is the Lord. And God will be for thee a powerful help."

[2] "God fill thee with all blessing."

154

interest you. Up to this, nothing. For me, I am in God's hands for *all*, — have no desire but to be His very humble instrument in all things. I would not like to move a finger in any direction, lest I might get out of His keeping.

I read some accounts of Maud Petre's Life of F. Tyrrell.[1] It is sad, sad reading. When fundamental sincerity and straight forwardness are wanting, a man, particularly a priest, may do *anything*. Baron von Hügel would consult better for his reputation by silence. There is not a particle of likeness between F. Tyrrell's life and St. Augustine's Confessions. The one is a humble confession of sin with efficacious resolution of amendment. The other is a vain boasting of ill-doing; and the open avowal of systematic disloyalty towards the Church.

I often think of our walk in the convent park; and of how perfectly our souls agree. If I am the guide Our Lord means for you, you are for me the soul who understands me best, and who could best counsel and encourage me. It may be that you are to have that role later.

Ever Yrs. in Xto,

✠ Columba, Abb.

xxx.

✠ Pax

Jermyn Court Hotel, Piccadilly Circus,

[London]. 7 Jan. (1913).

My dear Child,

I have just got to London, and must get on to Erdington in the morning. . . . I am in very good health; and very happy trying to live *only* in J.C. hidden in God. I feel you are getting very near His S. Heart, and will help me to *live* only by Him, and in His Spirit. *Qui spiritu Dei aguntur, hi sunt filii Dei.*[1] . . . I shall be at Erdington till the 16. Send me just a line.

Ever Yrs. in amore Xti,

✠ Columba, Abb.

[1] *Autobiography and Life of George Tyrrell* (London, 1912). On Von Hügel see Note 3 to Letter 12 of this Section.

[1] "For whosoever are led by the Spirit of God, they are the sons of God" (Rom. 8:14).

## XXXI

✠ Pax

Tournai, 16 Feb. [1913]

My dear Child,

. . . Your letter was a great consolation on my jubilee day.[1] I do hope that I may henceforth live all for God *alone*. I feel Our Lord wants me to live as He did, *propter Patrem*;[2] and that in two senses. 1. That all my inspiration may come from Him; 2. all my activity be employed for Him.

There is to be an election in May for a coadjutor-Primate O.S.B. with the right of succession. It is of very great importance for us. The Cardinal thinks I may be selected; but I don't think so. I would be much freer during vacation than I am at present; but I leave all that to God.

God bless you and keep you close to His Heart. There I find you every morning.

Yours in J.C.
✠ Columba.

P.S. I am going to buy a pocket Breviary with your *too* generous gift.

✠ Pax

Abbaye de Maredsous, 8 Dec. 1913.

My dear Child,

Just a word to say that since my last visit, I feel more than ever that God has given you to my keeping, to help you to arrive at perfect union, and the perfect accomplishment of His will. It is not that I am any better, or as good as many of those who have come in contact with you, but I feel that I have been *sent*; that Our Lord has said to me when confiding your soul to me: *Ego ero tecum*.[1] I try to answer this call of the Divine Master by *daily* prayer for you. I want, before you leave, to give you a pledge of that union which Our Lord

---

[1] Twenty-fifth anniversary of his monastic profession on February 10, 1888.

[2] "By the Father" (John 6:58).

[1] "I will be with thee" (Exod. 3:12).

has established between our souls. It is a reliquary which I am sending you by this post. It contains two relics; both absolutely authentic. The one of St. Edmund has just been sent me from Pontigny, where the Saint's body is preserved; and it is a piece of his flesh. The other is a bone of St. John Berchmans.

In all your troubles and pains know that you have a friend, who is most sincerely devoted to you; and whose greatest joy will be to help you gain that perfect union with God in Xt., which is His own dearest wish.

I am suffering from a severe attack of influenza.

Ever Yrs. in J.C.

✠ Columba, Abb.

### XXXIII.

✠ Pax                                   Maredsous, 30 Dec. [1913].

My dear Child,

I am *so* busy, but you must not think that when I used to spoil you with long letters we were more, or as, united in J.C., as now. I ever pray for you; and feel Our Lord has given you to me to prepare for union with Him. The little Infant, who is in our heart, is gazing on the Face of His Father, *semper apparet vultui Dei pro nobis.*[1] He *sees* in His Father's Eternal Love the place you occupy; God's plan for you, a plan so minute that "not a hair of your head falls without Him."[2] Give yourself up to Jesus, the Eternal Wisdom, in order that He may lead you and guide you to the fulfilment of that ideal. Now this is enough for you to think about in that till I see you. I should *so* wish to run down to see you; but I fear that is impossible.

May God bless and protect you.

Ever Yrs. in J.C.

✠ Columba, Abb.

---

[1] "That he may appear now in the presence of God for us" (Heb. 9:24).
[2] See Matt. 10:29–30.

✛ Pax                                      Roscrea [1] 6 Jan. 1914.
My dear Child,
   Just a word to say, I have got *all* the letters and am writing. . . .
Were I to listen to my heart of hearts I should certainly go to see
and bless you; but this may not be this time. As I know you will be
pleased to hear it, I shall tell you that God is blessing my retreat
wonderfully. They are in a state of great enthusiasm over it. May
God be blessed who thus employs such poor little creatures to be
His instruments. As regards your question *Secretum meum mihi*; [2]
God does not expect you, nor approve of your opening your heart
often. No one has a right to such communications, but those to whom
God has confided your soul.
   May God bless you and love you as I do in Him,
                                                   ✛ Columba, Abb.

## XXXV

✛ Pax                          Abbaye de Saint-Benoit, Maredsous,
                               par Maredret, le 14 March 1914.
My dear Child,
   The time approaches when you must leave, and go where God
calls you. I very often think of this, and, to be candid, with a certain
sadness. I want you like Abraham to put yourself in God's hands
*absolutely*. Every time that God called Abraham, his invariable answer was: *Adsum*, [1] no explanations, no plans. The *Lord* calls, and
the servant obeys. I want you to choose a day on which you wish to
make your offering of self to God's loving Providence. Let me know
the day, and I shall offer H. Mass for you, and place you on the
paten with Jesus, so that your oblation may be agreeable to the
Father. The more I gaze at God through the eyes of Jesus living in
my heart, the more clearly I see that nothing can be so high, so

---

[1] Cistercian abbey in Ireland where Abbot Marmion was preaching the annual
retreat.
   [2] "My secret to myself" (Isa. 24:16).
   [1] "Here I am" (Gen. 22:1). This was Abram's response when the Lord called him
and instructed him to take his beloved son Isaac, begotten in his old age, and sacrifice
him to the Lord.

*divine*, as to remit oneself totally to God. Surely the Creator has a right to dispose of the creature whom He has drawn from nothing; surely He, in His infinite wisdom, knows what we are suited to accomplish in His plan. Surely His infinite Love is the most secure resting place for our blindness and weakness. What I want to see in you, dear child, is that profound conviction that all our real strength is in the *Virtus Christi*. St. Paul is so anxious that this virtue alone should be the source of all his activity that he rejoices in his weakness and takes glory in it.[2] It is this divine virtue, coming to His members from Christ, which gives all this beauty to our actions. As the Church prays in one of her collects: *in sola spe gratiae celestis innititur*.[3]

I am D.G., well and happy, though daily trials meet me. His Eminence is here at present in retreat. He is a real saint.

May God bless and guard you and lead you to His perfect love.

Ever Yrs. in J.C.

✠ Columba, Abb.

XXXVI.

(Postcard)

London, Tyburn, 23 Sept. 1914.

I have just got through the German lines, and was on the point of being shot. I was looking for a house for a great part of my Community,[1] as we can't hold out any longer.

✠ Columba, Abb.

XXXVII.

✠ Pax                23, Parkhill Rd., Hampstead, [London]
                     15, Dec. [1914].

My dear Child,

I am sending you the photo promised. I am *so much better*. You told me I could have recourse to you in my wants with a brother's freedom. Well, if you could send me a *little* altar-linen, for our new house, it would be most welcome. We shall be six priests, and we

---

[2] II Cor. 12:9.

[3] ". . . [so that thy servants] putting all their trust in the hope of thy heavenly favor." Collect of the Fifth Sunday after Epiphany.

[1] The youngest monks, who had taken refuge in England after the invasion of Belgium. They found shelter at Edermine, Ireland, thanks to a generous benefactress.

159

shall want purificators, etc. *Just a little, s.v.p.*[1] Our address is Edermine House, Enniscorthy, Co. Wexford.

I pray for you all with all *my heart.* Do ask Our Lord to take me back to His Heart during these few days I shall be spending at Edermine. I get there about the 21st.

Ever Yrs. in J.C.
✠ Columba, Abb.

## XXXVIII.

(Postcard)
✠ Pax            Edermine, Enniscorthy.
2 March [1915][1]

I have just received your letter. I could come either the week before, or the week after Laetare Sunday, that is to say between 8–13, or between 15–21. How many a) days? b) conferences?

My voice has come back but is still feeble. I am better since I came here. The solitude is delightful and the community most fervent.

Dom Chapman went to Rome to work with D. Gasquet on the Vulgate.[2]

Yours (in J.C.)
✠ Columba, Abb.

## XXXIX.

✠ Pax          Edermine, Enniscorthy. 28 June [1915]
My dear Child,

Don't be cross with me, but I fear I must modify my plans, *malgré moi.*[1] My retreat at St. Bernard's[2] ends on the 18th. I may get up to

---

[1] *S'il vous plaît* (If you please).

[1] The original of this letter is in French.

[2] Dom Chapman (whose remarkable *Spiritual Letters* were published in 1935) was still at this writing a monk of Maredsous. After the War he transferred to Downside Abbey, where Dom Aidan Gasquet (who had been made a cardinal in 1914), was also a member. These two monks worked in Rome on the revision of the Latin Vulgate text of the Bible, an assignment given them by the Pope himself.

[1] "In spite of myself" — i.e., in spite of my wishes in the matter.

[2] Mt. St. Bernard's, Cistercian abbey in Leicestershire, England, where Abbot Marmion was preaching the annual retreat.

London that night or next day. I must remain at London 2 or 3 days, as 8 of my young Monks have just been convoked for the army; and I must leave no stone unturned to prevent their going out as *soldiers*.[3] Four of my young Monks who arrived at Calais lately were told that they were not wanted, — and are trying to get [assigned] as vicaires[4] in a French diocese; and nevertheless they insist on my sending out 8 more, who are in holy orders and at their studies. I am then *obliged* to go to Ramsgate to settle a delicate matter with two of my monks, who are in that monastery. Then I *must* go to Sheffield the 23, 24–25th on important business regarding our financial position, & on the 26th I begin at Southwark![5] As I finish at Southwark on the 31 . . . I must return to begin a retreat at Dublin the 5th.[6]

In your last letter you told me you were suffering. I have seldom suffered more *in every way*, than for some time past. I feel we have to take out our part in the general expiation, which is being offered to God's justice and sanctity. My soul, my body, my senses, [. . .][7] God Himself, all things seem to combine to make me suffer. May His holy name be blessed. I pray daily, and *name* you daily at Mass. I feel then the Communion of saints, and sinners.

May God bless and protect you all.

Your Father
✠ Columba, Abb.

XL.

✠ Pax

Abbaye de Maredsous, 16.VII.19.

My dear Child,

I have just received your letter. I have been praying for you — as I do daily, for I look on you as that soul whom Our Lord has confined to me above all others; and with whom I am the most united. God has given me lately to *see* that the greatest and highest act of love is

---

[3] Actually they did their military service as medical orderlies.

[4] Literally, "vicar," but equivalent to "curate" or assistant pastor.

[5] A retreat to the clergy.

[6] A retreat to the Dominican nuns.

[7] An erased word.

to offer oneself to Him to bear the burden of souls which He lays on us. It is the highest obedience. It is most like that of Jesus. St. Benedict thus described it: *regere animas et multorum servire moribus* — "to govern souls and become the servant of the characters and whims of many." [1] Let us help each other by our union with Jesus, — in Him by the union of our prayer. My cross at present is *very heavy*. My Community is very numerous; but they are, though *very fervent* and excellent, in many ways affected by the wave of democratic ideas which fill the air. Then I am beginning to feel the effects of age (61), especially since my last grave illness.[2] I am still in good health, but weak, and more and more inclined to drowsiness, which is a *torment* at Office, at prayer, and even at H. Mass.[3] It costs me more to say my *fiat* to this, than to any other divine permission. I should like immensely to see you. . . . Still, God gives me great grace, and I become more and more detached from all creatures; and keep my eyes ever fixed on eternity.

Ever Yrs.

✠ Columba, Abb.

XLI.

✠ Pax

Abbaye de Saint-Benoit, Maredsous, 21.VI.20.

My dear Child,

Please forgive my long silence. It is not forgetfulness, for I pray for you *daily*, and with my whole heart of hearts; but I am crushed with work and worries. On reading your letter, I saw that your soul is passing through the fire of *love in darkness*. St. Francis de Sales paints your state perfectly, while describing his own during the last years of his life. A prince had a musician who was most devoted to him. His joy was to rejoice the heart of his prince by his beauteous

---

[1] Rule of St. Benedict, chap. 2: What sort of man the abbot ought to be.

[2] During a journey to the British Isles in 1919, Abbot Marmion became so seriously ill in Dublin that he thought he was dying.

[3] This almost insurmountable drowsiness was a great trial, and one that lasted until his death. See his private note in which he reveals that he had asked the Holy Father's intercession for relief from this affliction (Section XIV, Letter 7, Note 5).

singing, and the sweet harmony of his music. However, at the same time, he himself took a vast pleasure in listening to his melodies. At last he became absolutely deaf. He could no longer find any pleasure *for himself* in his music and chant; but he continued to play and sing with *all his heart* just to give pleasure to his beloved prince. This is your case. I *know* your heart; and I know that you love God dearly, as He loves you. But just as Jesus on the cross, He alone must see and feel the fragrance of that love. You must be immolated in the darkness of Calvary. Take this as *certain*.

I had a nice visit from the Queen.[1] She was most gracious, and had a long chat with me in my apartments. She also had herself photographed several times standing by my side. She gave me a beautiful chalice all adorned with pearls and rubies. I am very fond of her.

May God bless and love you, and take you *all* to Himself.

Your most devoted in J.C.

✠ Columba, Abb.

### XLII.

✠ Pax

Maredsous, 8.IX.1920.

My dear Child,

I am grateful to God for having heard my prayer for you. That light *did* come from Him. The S. Humanity had no human person; (it is that *human person* that is the object of our self love, and all its consequences: sensitiveness, susceptibility, etc.; we must immolate it to the Divine Spouse the Word, and thus all such barriers are broken down); and so gave itself to the Divine Spouse the Word without *any barrier*. This is your *exemplaire*. If you could dash every child born of self-love against the rock Xt.[1] your union would be perfect. I pray for this for us.

God bless you and love you as I do.

✠ Columba, Abb.

---

[1] Queen Elizabeth of the Belgians. See Section III, Letter 20.
[1] Rule of St. Benedict, Prologue. See also I Cor. 10:4.

XLIII.

✠ Pax

Maredsous. 30-V-21.[1]

My dear Child in Jesus-Christ,

There is some discussion about the meaning of Canon 645. Some have a little doubt that it applies to those who have finished these three years. However, the most probable opinion, and one which agrees perfectly with the spirit of the Canon is that if there has been no deceit or deliberate concealment, an illness which appears after profession is not a legitimate cause for dismissal. I should never dare act on such a motive, but I should try to bring the person to ask for a dispensation, or to leave voluntarily at the expiration of the 3 years.

I shall pray a lot for you these days. I too need prayers to know and carry out God's will. My niece, [Annie], is at the point of death; as also my nephew Jos. Marmion, who was an army doctor during the war, and fell ill at Gallipoli. He never entirely recovered. He was an excellent christian, going to Holy Communion almost every day. He was operated on last Friday, but there is little hope for him.

God bless and love you.

P.S. May I ask you to send me back the note-book, as I need it for reference.

XLIV.

✠ Pax                                    Maredsous, [October, 1922]

My dear Child,

I have been praying for you from my heart of hearts that God and His H. Spirit may give you the light and the strength to draw, from the trial He has sent you, not bitterness, but holy joy in union with that of Jesus in His Passion. It is certain that our Heavenly Father so loves that a hair of our head does not fall without His permission. I am sure that all that has happened to you, in its intimate details, was known and even willed for you by Him. You need have no fear that I should let any one know your sentiment, just as I don't tell

---

[1] This letter is retranslated from the French translation of an English original that has been lost.

you theirs. I *do* want you to unite with Jesus in His acceptance of the humiliations and deceptions He has endured for us: *Saturabitur opprobriis*,[1] Until you can *embrace*, not only His cross but His humiliations, you will never be *entirely* His, nor taste His peace and joy. He touched the very bottom of the abyss; and loved it, because it was His Father's Will. That is what I want from you; what *He* wants from you.

I am *so* rushed at present. I really have not a moment.

May God bless and love you.

✠ Columba, Abb.

## XLV.

(Fragment from a lost letter.)

1. [. . .] full of abandoning of self to His love will come of this. I feel like Mary gazing on Jesus dying on the cross. I suffer because you are very dear to me; but I offer you to Him, because He wishes it so. You may depend on my absolute discretion, as I do on you. [. . .] [. . .] remembrance at the Altar. You are dearer to me now in your hour of suffering than ever, as you are certainly dearer to Him.

May God bless and love you.

✠ Columba, Abb.

## XLVI.

(Fragment from another lost letter.)

2. My dear Child,

I am in retreat, and have besides many cares and preoccupations; but I won't interrupt my retreat to send *you* a few lines. For I do most firmly believe that Our Lord has united us in His love for our mutual help. I never celebrate H. Mass without offering you, and all your wants and infirmities in union with Jesus to His Father. I am glad you so [. . .]

[. . .] I was delighted you had such a beautiful retreat. [. . .]

---

[1] "He shall be filled with reproaches" (Lam. 3:30).

## XX. TO AN ENGLISH BENEDICTINE ABBESS

✠ Pax                         Maredsous 7 Sept. [1910]
My dear Lady Abbess
     I have just received the two notices of the death of our two dear sisters. I shall say H. Mass for them on Friday, though I scarcely think they need it. Dear Filomena had promised me, as soon as she saw the Lord, to speak to Him of me & my miseries. I had been suffering intensely in many ways for some time past, & all at once on the 4th, the clouds lifted; & all at once peace & sunshine came back once more to my heart. Surely it was the fulfillment of a promise. These two souls will be a great blessing for your community. For their love is now pure & perfect in God.

     I have been *very much* occupied indeed, & have passed through many trials since I left you; otherwise I should have written to tell you how very grateful I am for all your kindness to me.

     I have spent very happy hours indeed at S[. . .] &, as I promised, I daily carry its members in my heart to God's altar. I forget names, but many of those I met are very distinctly before me. I hope dear Rosalie is trying to love God as He loves her. Then there is Sr. Paula, & others, in whom I take a special interest. Please tell Sr. Laurentia I was so sorry to have missed Miss S.[. . .], but I shall be passing through London in November on my way to Farnborough, & shall try to meet her. Tell Sr. Gertrude I have just met a charming young American girl from Florida. She is a Protestant but, in her heart, a Catholic. Do pray for her. With my heart's best wishes,

Yrs. in J.C.
✠ Columba, Abb.


## XXI. TO A YOUNG GIRL

### TWENTY-ONE LETTERS

*In these letters to a young girl who had confided to Dom Marmion
her desire for perfection, we shall see her attempting in vain two
forms of the religious life and unable to adapt herself to either.*
     *Dom Marmion shares these trials with infinite delicacy, anxious to*

*prevent discouragement or disobedience; teaching serenity in the seeking of God's will, which is not to be founded in any one external form of life, but in our inner sanctification. The efforts, often apparently futile, which we make in the pursuit of our true and definite goal, namely, perfect union with Christ, mark, nevertheless, a progress according to the designs of Divine Providence.*

*To this soul eager for God, Dom Marmion teaches the prayer of contemplation in the darkness of faith, and the interior life centered on the person of Christ. In her trouble, he shows her how to suffer as a Christian should.*

*These letters reveal all the human sensitiveness of Dom Marmion; without any attempt to hide it or to force it, he places it at the service of his spiritual fatherhood. The letter of May 15, 1915, illustrates this very well.*

I.

Maredsous, 27, Dec. 1913.

My dear Child,

Let me call you so. Although I am fearfully busy, I must write to you, for I see you are passing through one of these terrible trials through which every soul called to close union with Jesus (& you are one of these) must pass. "Because you were pleasing to God," said the Angel of Tobias, "it was necessary that temptation should try you." [1] My child, we cannot go to God but through union with Jesus. "I am the way. *No one* goeth to my Father but through me." [2] Now Jesus went to His Father by passing through Gethsemani & Calvary, & every soul united to Him must pass by the same way. These temptations against Faith are a real crucifixion; & yet you really do believe, but unconsciously, & that is why your love subsists, & seems to go ahead of your Faith.

The devil is doing his best to cast you into despair, for he sees that you will one day be very, very closely united with Him whom he hates. Hence he casts darkness & trouble into your soul, & revolt perhaps in your senses, but this is the path by which all interior souls *must* pass, if they are to reach perfect union. "Blessed is the man who suffers

---

[1] Tob. 12:13.
[2] John 14:6.

temptation, says St. James, for when he has been tried, he will receive the crown of life." [3] The greatest saints passed by that path. St. Hughes, bishop of Grenoble, was tempted to blasphemy *for years.* St. Jean de Chantal was tempted for long years against Faith, & had to be constantly upheld & reassured by her director St. Francis de Sales. St. Vincent de Paul had such *terrible* temptations against Faith that he was on the point of falling into despair, but wrote out an act of Faith, placed it in a little bag over his heart, & when tempted just pressed it as a sign that he adhered to all it contained. I am *quite sure* you don't offend Our Lord in all these temptations. St. Catherine of Sienna having been fearfully beset with foul temptations, felt as if she was abandoned, & on the point of falling. When the combat was won she said to Jesus, "Lord, where were you?" & He answered "My daughter I was in the centre of your heart sustaining you all the time." And so it is with you, dear child, Jesus *is* in the centre of your heart; it is He who causes you to long for Him. So be in peace. I am praying for you.

I get to London Charing Cross, Jan. 2 at 5. (Dover boat train.) From there, I go to Tyburn.[4] Do come & see me a moment. I must leave next morning for Ireland, but shall be back in Tyburn for the 16th. I leave here on the 1st Jan.

May God bless & strengthen you. He surely calls you to union with him.

Yrs. devotedly in J.C.<br>✠ Columba Abb

II.

**Pax**

Abbaye de Saint-Benoit
de Maredsous.

10. Feb. 1914.[1]

I am really ashamed of myself to have kept you so long waiting; yet I want you to feel that our dear Lord gives me a great interest in

---

[3] Jas. 1:12.

[4] Benedictine Convent in London where Abbot Marmion was known and welcome. See Section XXIV, Introduction.

[1] The original of this letter is lost. The text published here was taken from a copy made by the addressee herself.

you, and I wish to help you till you are at home in His own home. As regards your fears of selfishness, you know that God is "The Lord," and that He has the first call on us. "He who loves Father or Mother more than me, is not worthy of me." [2] Ordinarily, on entering religion, our greatest pain is the pain we cause others. The whole question is: *does* God call you; and I must say, unless you wait for a revelation, it would be hard to have greater evidence. You are not *necessary* for Mother, and so if Jesus calls you to "leave Father and Mother and sisters and brothers, etc., and Follow Him" [3] He has a right to be obeyed, and your happiness, and that of those you love, may in great measure depend on your fidelity in this matter.

I don't think you are called to Carmel; and practically *you* will find in a Benedictine Abbey as much austerity and contemplation as you are called to. Perhaps you might do better to enter one at home than on the Continent — in giving you this advice I am writing against my personal inclination, as I should like to have my little child near me to guide and help her — but it will certainly be easier, and less heart-rending for Mother. Now there is an *excellent* Benedictine Abbey at [. . .]. I have given a retreat there and they have everything you could desire.

As regards your questions —

1) You would be allowed to write often, particularly in the beginning, say once or twice a month.

2) Your Mother, or friends, could see you alone; but there would be a grill — not a double one like in Carmel, but just a grill; you could shake hands, etc.

There is nothing selfish in seeking high perfection; as it gives such glory to God. "In this is my Father glorified that you bear *much* fruit" [4] so — "Be ye *perfect*, as also your heavenly Father is perfect." [5] Jesus did not die merely to save us, but above all to sanctify His Church. Our sanctification is the triumph of His precious blood, — a glory for *all eternity*.

Please tell Mother I pray for her, as I do for you *daily*. Of course

[2] Matt. 10:37.
[3] See Mark 10:29.
[4] John 15:8.
[5] Matt. 5:48.

169

it is perfectly allowable to offer your entry into religion for a special intention: the conversion of your family.

Don't forget to go visit Tyburn sometimes. M[. . .] and G[. . .] would be *delighted* to help you, and they are very enlightened souls.

Now, my dear little child, good night, may God bless and love you.

✠ Columba, Abb.

## III.

✠ Pax

Edermine,[1] Enniscorthy. 15 May 1915

My dear M[. . .] —

I was delighted to get your letter, & see that our Lord continues to draw you nearer & nearer to Himself. It is impossible to get near God, without feeling the thorn and the Cross, and even at times the agony of that S. Heart. We can't be Spouses of a Crucified, without being crucified ourselves. St. Paul says "Those who are Christ's have crucified their flesh with its sins & lusts."[2] The Saint whose life I wanted you to read was, I think, *St. Jean Perboire*, Lazarist & Martyr. His life & spirit are so like those of Xt. I am so glad that you got the little vacation in that very Catholic house at 23 Park Hill. I hope dear M[. . .] is well. A[. . .] I expect. Is[. . .] forgets me. School-girls are like that. I am very fond of her. She is so good & so affectionate. Poor I[. . .], I often thought of her, since I heard she was ill. How fleeting & unstable is all human beauty. I[. . .] is so pretty & so lovable, & yet how easily death could wrench her from those who love her. I do so wish never to get attached to anyone. (I am not at present) I am of a very loving nature, & yet I would not allow a fibre of my heart to go to anyone but through our dear Lord's hands. I am so perfectly at home with you; for though I am very fond of you, I never felt the slightest inclination to be attached, but only to help you to follow our Lord Perfectly. You may be sure, if you give yourself to Him, He will let you know His will in His own good time. I don't think, now that I know her & all circumstances, that you could leave Mother at present. Would it be too much to ask you, when you have a little spare money, to buy me a book

[1] Sojourn in exile during World War I.

[2] Gal. 5:24.

called, *Enchiridion*, by Denzinger.[3] You will get it at Burns & Oates, or at Washburn Paternoster Row.

Love to M[. . .], & A[. . .], also to I[. . .]. Give my affectionate respects to Mother, Father, & also to Is[. . .].

Yr very sincere Friend & Father,

✠ Columba, Abb.

P.S. My health is better. Nothing yet settled about my return to Maredsous. Don't be afraid to write. Your letters are a pleasure.

IV.

✠

Edermine, Enniscorthy. 29. May. 1915

My dear Child,

As you write to me with such simplicity, I shall write you simply; sure not to be misunderstood. I believe that your director is *excellent*; & that for all that regards the ordering of your life, your time, your vocation, you could not be in better hands; but I am sure he would not understand your prayer; it is so different from what has been taught to be the only prayer. God is calling you to interior union, which is more useful to you, & more fruitful for the Church & souls than all your activity. "A soul that gives herself up unreservedly to God, allowing Him to act & operate in her & with her as He wills, does more for His glory & for souls in one hour, than others with all their activity in years." (Blosius, one of the greatest mystics & theologians of our Order.)[1]

You see, my child, God has created us for Himself & we can do nothing greater than to give ourselves up to Him to carry out His wishes. To allow God to act on us in prayer is neither laziness or inactivity. At such moments, down deep in the imperceptible depths of our soul there is passing a *divine* activity more precious than all our own human activity. As the soul gets nearer to God, she becomes simpler; & no words, no forms can express, nor formulate, what she

---

[3] Collection of dogmatic definitions of ecclesiastical authority.

[1] Blosius. *A Book of Spiritual Instructions*, trans. B. A. Wilberforce, O.P. (London, 1900), chap. 1, No. 4. An important text that Abbot Marmion quotes several times in these letters, and often in others.

would say; but as the Church prays in her liturgy "Oh God to whom every heart is open, & to whom every *will speaks*, & for whom there is nothing hidden, purify our hearts by the infusion of the H. Spirit that we may perfectly love thee, & worthily praise thee." [2]

When you feel invited to remain in silence at our Lord's feet like Magdalene, just *looking at Him* with *your heart*, without saying anything, don't cast about for any thoughts or reasonings, but just remain in loving adoration. Follow the whisperings of the H. Ghost. If He invites you to beg, beg; if to be silent, remain silent, if to show your misery to God, just do so. Let Him play on the fibres of your heart like a harpist, & draw forth the melody He wishes for the Divine Spouse. Souls like yours, called to interior prayer, are often greatly tempted, in all ways, by the senses; to blasphemy, pride, etc. Don't be afraid. You can't do anything more glorious to God, or more useful for souls than to give yourself to Him. If you can find *Spiritual Doctrine of Blosius*, by Wilberforce it will greatly help you at present. The Word is ever in your heart "if anyone love me, my Father will love him, & *We* will come & take up *our abode in* him." [3] Yet after H. Communion, & when near the tabernacle, the S. Humanity of J.C. (which is the link between us & the Word) brings us nearer to Him, & more efficaciously.

Some nuns (O.S.B.) are opening a house just near us, under my direction, in a beautiful solitude. Come some day & see.

Write soon & say if you have understood.

Dear little M[. . .], Ever yours in J.C.

✠ Columba, Abb.

v.

✠ Pax

Edermine, Enniscorthy. 1 July 1915

My dear Child,

I am *so* busy, & yet it rests my head & heart to write to you, just because our Lord leads you along the same path as myself. I shall be very brief. 1st, want of time. 2nd, I shall be in London (41 Elm Park Gardens Chelsea S.W.) from the 19–22, & later on for longer; & I hope

[2] Roman Missal. Collect to ask for the grace of the Holy Spirit.
[3] John 14:23.

to see you. 1) Your passive giving up of yourself to God's action is the *most pleasing* thing you can do for Him, & most useful for the Church. In such prayer there is often little *explicit* light, or feeling, but the soul is really filled with light, & the heart with love. It is not selfish, as God created you *for Himself*, & you can do nothing greater than give yourself up to His will. 2) The more one approaches God, the simpler his prayer becomes, till it ends in one long *sigh* after God: "God heareth the *desire* of the poor." [1] St. Francis of Assisi passed a whole night in one prayer "my God & my all"; & St. Jeanne Chantal tells St. Francis de Sales that for years her only prayer, at all times, at Communion, Mass, Meditation was *de s'enfoncer de plus en plus dans la Volonté divine* to bury herself deeper in the Divine Will. Don't trouble the unity of your prayer by thinking of *distinct & special* intentions. God knows them all; & it suffices to remember them from time to time. While given up to God's action in prayer, you are doing more for God's glory & souls, than all human activity could do. God has no need of our activity. If He wants it, He will point it out to us.

*Vere languores nostras ipse tulit, & dolores nostros ipse portavit.* [2] Truly hath He borne our infirmities, etc. has a very deep meaning. 1) It means that He took all actual, deliberate sin on Himself, & expiated it in His person. *Posuit in eo Dominus iniquitatem omnium nostrum* "The Lord hath placed on Him the iniquity of us all." [3] 2) It also means that, as Head of the Church, He accepted in our name (His members) all our miseries, our meanness, our infidelities, our sufferings, & suffered from them in our name, & sanctified & deified them in His person. No pain or suffering or weakness of His members was hidden from Him, & He took them *willingly* on Himself. 3) It also means that by thus taking them on Him — He took the sting out of them, & helped us to bear them. Yes, try & love Him *alone*, & all others in & for Him.

May God bless & sanctify my dear little M[. . .].

☩ Columba, Abb.

P.S. You kindly said you would willingly send me a book if possible. I badly want a "Pontifical Canon," a book used by prelates when cele-

---

[1] Ps. 10:17.

[2] "Surely he hath borne our infirmities and carried our sorrows" (Isa. 54:4).

[3] Isa. 53:6.

brating Mass. I am too poor to buy one. You will find a cheap one at Burns & Oates. Love to M[. . .], respects to Mother & I[. . .].

VI.

✠ Pax

Edermine, 29. Sep. 1915

My dear Child,

I can only send you just a line, as I am overwhelmed at present. Your letters are *ever welcome* as yourself. So don't be afraid. You are just going through what *all* souls called to close union with the "Crucified" must suffer. God sometimes allows sufferings of all sorts — health, weariness, temptation, difficulties, etc. to swoop down at once on the soul to purify her. She must *feel* her utter *dependence* on Him. Souls united as yours is with our Lord, whose whole life comes from Him, suffer more than others when He leaves them. This winter is only to prepare for a more fruitful summer. All you can do is to bow your head, & accept the trial, & bear with the Lord till He comes back. Jesus gives us the example. In the Garden of Olives it is said "He began to fear, & to be weary, to be heavy, & sad." [1]

I pray for you with all my heart.

I shall be at Tyburn in Nov. & hope to see my little M[. . .].

Yrs. ✠ Columba Abb.

VII.

Pax

Edermine,[1] Enniscorthy. 2. November. 1915

I am laid up with the influenza, and a Doctor, who examined me lately, says my heart is very weak; so you must pray for me. I shall be at Tyburn from 10–20 Nov. and shall be delighted to see you any time. I am busy and can only just say the things which I think our Lord wants me to say. 1) No amount of exterior work is as pleasing to God, or as useful to the Church and souls, as that loving contemplation, in which the soul allows God to act as He pleases in her. It is for that He has created her. "Mary has chosen the better part which shall not be

[1] See Mark 14:33–34.
[1] See Note 1 to the Letter 2 (Feb. 10, 1914).

taken away from her." ² 2) When given up thus to God in prayer, it is a mistake to attend to *detailed intentions*. One glance at them in the beginning of prayer is enough. 3) Our activity is pleasing to God just in so far as it is the *trop plein* ³ of our union with Him. 4) Your desire for union is most pleasing to Him and *comes from Him*. 5) People whom God leads thus suffer terribly when He leaves them to themselves. He is *all* to them and without Him they feel their poverty more than others.

I have a thought regarding your vocation, which I will tell you about when I see you — till then pray.

The *director* is God's organ for communicating His will to you. Pray and consult; but be sure it will be by him you will finally come to know God's will.

VIII.

✠ Pax        Benedictine Priory of the S. H. Ventnor, I. Wight ¹

24. 3. 16

My dear M[. . .]

Your letter has just reached me here. I have been very ill with bronchial asthma & heart fatigue. I have suffered a lot, & hope it will be for the good of my dear Community. I was just on the point of starting for Belgium, & had taken my ticket when God intervened. I still hope to get to dear Maredsous for Easter.² I have gone through such trials out in this cold, weary world. Pray for me as I *do* desire to get back to my abbey-home. I shall say H. Mass tomorrow — Feast of the Annunciation — for your dear Mother, & beg the Word to fill her with His light. I feel He will hear our prayers, especially your aunt M[. . .]'s, for she is a most holy soul.

You must not pay too much attention to the fluctuations, which are ever passing over the *surface* of your soul. Like the sea, it is constantly

² Luke 10:42.

³ Overflow.

¹ Before leaving Ireland to return to Belgium, then occupied by the Germans, Abbot Marmion fell seriously ill in London at the end of February. Not fully recovered, he went to take several days' rest at this priory of Benedictine nuns, which had been founded by the Abbey of Liège.

² As it turned out, he could not return until May 19.

ruffled, but in its depths it is all God's. Ask the H. Ghost to give you abundance of His gift of *Fortitude*. Nothing so honours God as to lean on Him in full confidence, just when we feel weak & incapable. "When I am weak, it is then that I am strong. . . . I glory in my infirmities that *Xt's Strength dwell in me"* St. Paul.[3] May you be filled with Xt's Strength. The spouse is never so pleasing to her beloved as when she leans all her weight on the strong arm of her beloved. I pray for you daily as you are very dear to me in J.C.

I am here with the Benedictine nuns from Liège. They have a darling little Monastery & chapel looking down on the sea. The climate is delicious & I hope soon to get better. When I come back to London before starting for Belgium, I hope to see you at my address (41 Elm Park Gardens, Chelsea)

Love to M[. . .]. Ever Yrs in J.C.

✠ Columba Marmion Abb.

P.S. Once for all, your letters are never too long. I have the greatest pleasure in reading them, in helping you to respond to God's great love for you. How is Is[. . .]? Get Mgr. Hedley's little book on contemplation.[4]

IX.

✠ Pax
Abbaye de Saint-Benoit.

Maredsous, le 27. X. 1919

Poor little M[. . .],

I do feel so much for you, & beg our dear Lord to console you. Your entering at Carmel was most pleasing to Him, for it *showed* Him that as far as your heart goes, you are *all* His. It was not His will that you should stay; & we must love His Father's will above all. "He who doeth the will of my Father is brother, sister & mother to Me." [1] I fear you have a false American view about doing good. You seem to feel that you can't show your love, or be useful unless, by some form of *external* activity; & yet the absolute donation of self to Xt, so that He may dispose of us as *He pleases*, is above every other form of love

[3] II Cor. 12:10.
[4] Bishop Hedley, O.S.B., *Prayer and Contemplation* (London, 1916).
[1] Matt. 12:50.

176

& more useful to the Church than any form of human activity. Our Lady is the brightest saint in heaven, & yet what was her life? For 30 years she lead the life of a poor artisan's wife. Her ordinary actions were insignificant, yet what holiness? Jesus also, lived as a workman, for 30 years; & it was during His 3 hours of absolute immobility on the Cross that He did most for His Father's Glory & our redemption. If you wish peace, & joy, & absolute perfection here below, give yourself up to God's good pleasure. Let Him dispose of you according to His divine plan. Louis de Blois (Blosius) says that a soul that gives himself up without reserve to God, allowing Him to act in her as He pleases, will do more for His glory & souls than others with all their activity in years.[2]

Read the life of St. Thérèse de l'Enfant Jésus. She was quite little but full of grace, & thus glorifying [five words illegible].

Yrs devotedly
✠ Columba Abb.

P.S. I am going to London the 4th Nov. & giving a retreat at Westminster Cathedral to Canons 6-11. I shall go see you. Or come to see me.

x.

4-XII-19.[1]

[. . .] God expects each creature to serve and love Him according to its nature. The Angels must love God *angelically*, that is without heart, sentiments, affections, for they have none of these things. But He expects man to love Him *humanly* that is with all his heart, soul, strength and mind, and *his neighbour in the same way*. We are neither spirits nor ghosts, but human beings; and we cannot go higher than perfect humanity elevated by grace. Now Jesus is perfect humanity, perfect Deity. He loved His Mother as a child should love, not only with His head, but with His heart. He kissed her and was fondled by her, and liked it. He loved all men: a) for their souls, in view of eternity; b) for their *entire persons*, humanly; c) He loved some with

---

[2] *A Book of Spiritual Instructions*, chap 1; No. 4.

[1] The original of this letter is lost. The text published here was taken from *Union with God, according to the letters of direction of Dom Marmion*, pp. 166-68.

177

a special human love. He wept when Lazarus died. Where did these tears come from? not from His soul, but from His Heart. He did not love angelically, because He was not an angel but the Son of Man; no one was ever so human as Jesus. His Father found all His delights in Him. Amongst the creatures which God has given us to lead us to Him, and to *render our exile here possible*, are the love and affection of those who surround us. Who implanted in the mother's heart her love of her child? It was He; and how could He be displeased at our accepting this great gift! We must be on our guard not to let the devil deceive us by presenting something above human strength, and contrary to God's intentions. He has said "My yoke is light and My burden easy," [2] it would be unbearable if we were obliged to act as *souls without bodies*, being at the same time enveloped in sense, affections and human ties despite our will. Let us be content to be as perfect as the *Man*-God. Jesus loved Mary: 1) Because He saw in her the image of His own perfection; 2) because she was His Mother. He loved her with a child's love raised to infinite heights by the hypostatic union, but still remaining human. 3) He loved her because of all the virtues and gifts He had placed in her; and so of others.

Now, my deal child, don't go sublimizing too much; just act *simply*, and ask Jesus to give you the gift of loving with detachment; that is, so that no human affection should *be necessary*. "One thing is is necessary." [3] Use affections as you do other creatures. You will not *rest* in creatures, if you desire to use them according to God's Will. See St. Teresa keeping her niece in the convent with her; St. Francis de Sales and St. Chantal; St. Augustine weeping for his mother . . . without a scrap of attachment. [. . .]

XI.

✠ Abbaye de Saint-Benoit.

Maredsous, le 31 XII. 1919

My dear Child,

I have read your letter attentively in the presence of God, & am quite convinced that you are called by God to a high union with Him.

[2] Matt. 11:30.
[3] Luke 10:42.

178

Your present state of soul bears all the marks of one of those interior trials, or passive purifications, through which the soul *must* pass before attaining to union with *Infinite Purity*. The H. Ghost says "Blessed is the man who is tempted," [1] & St. James adds "Beloved, be filled with great joy when you pass through various temptations." [2] Those against faith & hope are the most distressing, a real agony, but *most* salutary. The secret *subconscious* longing for God is a *sure sign* of the presence of the H. Ghost in your soul. It is a vision of God's beauty in the darkness of faith; but just as the beatific vision, which the soul of Jesus *always* enjoyed, did not diminish His agony, nor prevent His soul being sad even unto death, so with yours. It is your purgatory; & our Lord is holding your soul in those flames until all selfishness & self-seeking are burned out. Then you will enter into the *ineffable grandeur* of God. The *very nature* of the trial through which you are passing is the terrible uncertainty it leaves in the soul as to her state. She *seems* to herself to have lost faith & love, for she *feels* nothing. It is pure naked faith. This longing for God is a most powerful & constant prayer; for God reads the inmost thoughts of our hearts; & this thirst of Him is a cry to His Father's heart *desiderium pauperum audivit auris tua.* "Thy ear hath heard the *desire of the poor,*" [3] & no one is poorer than those who are serving God in the trials of pure faith.

So now courage, M[. . .]! You are on the right road, & all you require is *great* patience & absolute confidence in our Lord's loving care. You are very dear to Him, though you may imagine the contrary. He wants you to see for yourself how really miserable & unworthy you are, & that it is His sheer mercy which thus clasps you to His heart. During all Eternity God will give Himself to you in the full & unremitting blaze of His beauty. Here below, His glory requires that He be served *in faith*. Let us try & serve Him in faith, just as if we gazed on Him in vision. Blosius says that a soul who delivers herself up to God without reserve, to suffer, or do just as He pleases in her, gives Him more glory, & does more for souls in one hour than others in years. St. Chantal was tormented all her life by temptations against faith, & yet received a special gift of faith & contemplation

[1] Jas. 1:12.
[2] Jas. 1:2.
[3] Ps. 10:17.

from God. In practice Adore God profoundly; then tell Him you accept *all* He has revealed *on His word alone*; & as the Church speaks in His name you accept her voice & teaching as His. Make then acts of love, even though you feel nothing. My little child Violet, who gave me my ring,[4] & was converted from being a Jewess, has passed through all these trials, & could help you greatly if you went to see her. (35 Brompton Square) Pray for me. God bless & guide you.

✟ Columba, Abb.

XII.

✟ Pax
Abbaye de Saint-Benoit.

Maredsous, le 20. 2. 1920.

My dear M[. . .],

As we are in Lent & I am very busy, I must be brief.

I see by your letter that you are very dear to our Lord. He is lending you by the way which is most glorious for His Father, & most advantageous for you: the way of *pure faith*. God intends giving Himself wholly & without reserve, in the full blaze of His light, to you in perfect love *for all eternity*. Here below His glory requires that we love & serve Him in faith. He gives us consolations & lights to help us go on in the darkness, but these are not essential; & when He sees a soul decided to love & serve Him despite all, He tries her by leaving her in darkness without feeling or special lights. In reality there is a deep, but invisible light in the inmost recesses of her soul. It is this invisible light which gives her the longing for God. This *longing* is a most efficacious prayer, & a homage to God's beauty. St. Francis de Sales says we ought to be satisfied with God's way of leading us, & not expect "particularities." God loves to see a soul content to go on in the way He leads her; & you are doing this. I read your daily order. It is quite sensible, & just what suits you. Don't follow it too rigidly but in an elastic way, yet faithfully.

When you feel a sweet calm take possession of your heart & soul, just remain there in silent love, & *let God act*. It is not surprising that what formerly filled you with devotion, as the Passion, etc., does not excite you any longer. It will all come back again, *but in another way*.

[4] Abbot's ring.

Louis de Blois says, "A soul which gives herself up without reserve to God's action, allowing Him to act in her as He wills, does more for His glory, & for souls in an hour, than others by all their activity." Ask H[. . .] to pray for me as I do for you both. How is Is[. . .]? You know I am very fond of the child; but fear she is being spoiled.

St. Monica prayed for 30 years for the conversion of her son, St. Augustine, & what a magnificent answer she had at the end!

Ever Yrs. in J.C.<br>✝ Columba Abb.


XIII.

✝ Pax
Abbaye de Saint-Benoit.

Maredsous, le 10 IV. 1920

Poor little M[. . .],

I do feel intense pity for you, & pray for you with *all my heart*, as I know what you are going through. No, dear, it is not pride — of course there is pride in us all — but that is not the reason of the loneness, of the awful isolation, & want & hunger for God's love. No, dear, it is God's own doing. He is purging your soul in order to prepare it for union with His Divine son. "If anyone bear fruit, my Father will purge him, that he may bear more fruit." [1] Now I want you to have confidence in me & believe my word. It is not our perfection which is to dazzle God, who is surrounded by myriads of angels. No, it is our misery, our wretchedness *avowed* which draws down His mercy. *All* God's dealings with us are a consequence of His *Mercy* (Mercy is Goodness touched by the sight of misery); & that is why the great St. Paul says, let others go to God leaning on the perfection of this life (as the Pharisee, "for me, I take glory in my infirmities that my strength may be Xt's virtue." [2] Look, M[. . .] dear, if you could only once understand that you are never dearer to God, never glorify Him more than when in full realisation of your misery & unworthiness. You gaze at His *infinite* goodness & cast yourself on His bosom, believing in faith, that His mercy is *infinitely greater than* your *misery*.

St. Paul tells us that God has done all *in laudem et gloriam gratiæ*

---

[1] John 15:2.
[2] II Cor. 12:10.

181

*suæ*, for the praise & glory of His Grace.³ Now the *triumph* of His grace is when it raises up the miserable & impure, & renders them worthy of divine union. See Mary Magdalene: She was a *sinner by profession*. She had 7 devils in her, whom Jesus expelled; & yet He now not only allowed her to touch His Divine feet, but it was to her that He appeared first on Easter morning.⁴ He is a Spouse infinitely rich & powerful, & when He chooses a poor little M[. . .] like you to be His bride, His joy is to enrich her poverty, & clothe her with His own beauty. M[. . .] dear, you are now passing through a period of trial, but Jesus loves you *dearly*. He is so happy to see you *want* to be loved by Him. That is not self-love; it is wishing for what God wants you to wish. If I could only get that into your head, & keep your eyes fixed on Him, on His goodness, & not on your little self. "Seek the Lord; seek His face constantly." ⁵

*Thanks* for the book. I shall be in London for the retreat of Westminster clergy about 9–15. August. A book which will quite help you is *Maxims of B. Laurence*, & his other little booklets. May God bless & love you more & more.

Your father ✚ Columba

XIV.

✚ Pax        Abbaye de Saint-Benoit, Maredsous, 22. IV. 1920.
Dear M[. . .],

I have been thinking a lot, and praying for you. Here is the result of my reflections: 1. You *can't* keep on in your present state. It is bad for you, body and soul; and it is too great a suffering for Mother. 2. I am quite clear that God calls you to *deep* and *perfect* union with Him in faith; and that the trials through which you are passing are preparing you for that union. But as regards your entry into Religion, it is not yet clear. The B. Thomas More was for 8 years in the Charter House at London trying to become a Carthusian, after which state he had been sighing for years, and yet he writes that God did not call him to that state, but to another which led him to the crown of martyrdom.

You must decide this once for all. Now, God ordinarily does not

³ Eph. 1:6.
⁴ Mark 16:9; Luke 7:38.
⁵ Ps. 104:4.

manifest His Will by revelation, but by circumstances: health, dispositions, character, etc. It *appears* to me that the state of your health and character, indicates that you *could* not, despite your desire, persevere in the Religious state. I fear your physical and mental strength would not bear the strain. However, let us give it a last trial. I shall be in London, at the beginning of August. I know two convents of our Order. It is possible that one or the other might suit. I propose to take you with me to visit one or other of these convents; and examine your vocation *then* with me and the Superioress.

1. [. . .] It is a *most fervent* little Abbey, in which there reigns *great charity*, a love of prayer and Office; and it is so beautifully situated that you would have ever before your eyes the spectacle of the sea and mountains. I am not sure that the climate would suit you. Then they take a *few* pupils.

2. [. . .] It is a *very fervent* monastery. [. . .] There is an Abbey of Monks just near, so that you would have good direction. If you came up with me, you could stay a few days, and see if God calls you. You *could not* endure the life of a Carmelite, or Clarisse. God does not call you to that. If any Religious Life is possible for you, it is the Benedictine. If we decide *not*; you must then organize your future life *definitely*, and *unchangeably*.

May God bless and love you.

✠ Columba, Abb.

P.S. Just a word to say what you think of my proposition.

XV.

✠ Pax                                      Maredsous. 29. IV. 20.
Dear M[. . .],

It is quite impossible at this distance to make *final* arrangements. But I shall let you know my possibilities at once, in order to leave you free to arrange according to your convenience.

Two possibilities: 1° I could start from London the 3rd or 4th August, so as to pass a couple of days with you at [. . .], and be back in London for the 8th, as I begin my retreat at S. Edmund's Ware [1] the 9th.

---

[1] The Westminster diocesan seminary (near London), where Dom Marmion was to preach the annual clergy retreat at the personal invitation of Cardinal Bourne.

2° possibility. My retreat ends on Friday 13th (not 17th). I could leave for York on Saturday 14th, and get up to [. . .] Monday, with you and Mother. I could stay a few days then; and then get back to London. I should require a few days in London, as I must visit Haywards Heath and Ventnor; and be back about the 20th in Belgium.

Just let me know what you prefer. Then, when we get near August, I shall write to the Abbess to expect me with a wee M[. . .]; and get them to pray for you.

I know the Nuns at Talacre [2] quite well. They are very good; but almost all converts. I think you would be better at . . .

Now, M[. . .] dear, I am not at all sure that you will be able to stay there. I fear that conventual constraint is too much opposed to your physical and mental strength; but you will have done your best to settle the question; and be able henceforth to follow your way, whatever it be, in peace. St. Joseph Benoit Labre tried *several* times to enter an Order; but could not stay, not for want of love or generosity, but because God had other designs on him. So it *may be* for you. Having made trial, you must conclude that you have found your way — God's Will.

It appears to me, you ought to remain on at the [. . .] for a couple of weeks. If you see, and that the Superior see, it is not for you, well, you will know God's Will. If on the contrary, you think you could live there, you can fix the date of your final entrance there.

As you know the hours of trains, etc., I hope you will look it all up for me. I shall be *delighted* to have Mother with us.

Yours,<br>✠ Columba Abb.

XVI.

✠ Pax

Abbaye de Saint-Benoit.

Maredsous, le 7. VII. 1920

Poor little M[. . .],

I can't tell you what pity I feel for you, & this pity comes from *His*

---

[2] Convent of Benedictine nuns, originally the Anglican convent of St. Bride's, Milford Haven, which was reconciled to the Church at the same time as the monks of Caldey. This reconciliation was largely the result of the efforts of Abbot Marmion. See Section XIV, Introduction.

heart, for He sees & knows your love, but wants to keep you on the *cross in faith*. Just as the H. Spirit supported His Sacred Humanity on the cross, giving It strength to bear up in *pure* love, without a scrap of consolation, "My God, my God, why hast thou abandoned me" [1] so it is with you. I know your heart, & I know that you *do* love Jesus, & would die rather than refuse Him anything in your power; but this does not take away the struggle, the awful repugnance, just as it did not take it away from Jesus' heart in Gethsemani, nor from Teresa's heart at the moment she was entering Carmel. I myself had been longing for 10 years to be a monk. It was my dream, my ideal. As soon as I entered, all was dark. I was like one suspended in space, deprived of all I had loved. It is this which gives merit to our "Lord, we have left all things & followed Thee." [2]

Now, M[. . .], I don't know if our Lord really wants you to be His in a *Cloister*. He certainly *does want your whole heart*. It is merely a matter of detail, that you be His *in* or *out* of a convent. Mary was all His, outside a convent, at the foot of the Cross. You must do your *honest best* this time to keep on at [. . .]. If it can't be, then you have shown Jesus that you have done all in your power to be there where He seems to invite you. You will have *all the merit*, as, if you can't stay, it is not your fault. In any case I want you to spend, if it were only a few weeks in contact with our Benedictine ideas. Your thoughts about Jesus are too *narrow*. He isn't a bit like what you imagine. His heart is as large as the ocean, a real *human heart*, He *wept* real salt tears when Lazarus died. "See how He loved him." [3] He does not expect you to be a spectre or a ghost, no, He wants you to be a *thorough* woman wanting love & giving it; & when you leave those you love, He wants you to *feel it deeply*. Don't be ever scrutinizing your poor little heart in fear, but look at Him. He possesses for you His spouse, all that your poverty lacks.

Ever Yrs. in J.C.

✠ Columba, Abb.

P.S. I shall be in London 3rd August (Jermyn Court Hotel, Piccadilly) for a few days. Phone there, & make appointment.

[1] Matt. 27:46.
[2] Matt. 19:27.
[3] John 11:36.

## XVII

✠ Pax                                    Maredsous, 30. VIII. 20
Dear M[. . .],

By entering at [. . .] despite your repugnance, you are giving our Lord the best proof of your desire to do His will at *all costs*. It is quite possible, even probable that it is all He wants, & that you may have the merit of the sacrifice *just* as if accomplished, as Abraham. I shall pray for you with all my heart. If the repugnance, etc., continues, consider the interpretation of it by the Abbess & director as a *most certain manifestation* of God's will. Don't have any scruple in following it, & never look back again. If our Lord wants you a nun He will make it possible & *delightful*, for He has said "My yoke is sweet, & my burden light" [1] He has promised the hundredfold, even here below, to those whom He calls.[2]

He certainly calls you to close union, & perfection, but it is for Him to determine the "how"

Yrs. in great haste,
✠ Columba Abb.

## XVIII

✠ Pax
Abbaye de Maredsous                              15. X. 20
My dear Child,

Your letter was not a surprise for me; nor indeed a real pain. It is so clear that you have been and are doing God's will, & surely He is Master & can do with us as He thinks fit. I am glad you made the two trials. They are most meritorious and very practical proofs to our Lord of your sincere desire to stop at nothing to accomplish His will. That will is perfection. At the first moment of the union (hypo-static) of the S. Humanity with the Word, the first movement, which St. Paul says summed up all sanctity, was the acceptance of the Divine Will. "On the first page of the book it is written of me that I do Thy will. Behold I come to accomplish it" [1] & Mary's whole life

[1] Matt. 11:30.
[2] Mark 10:30.
[1] Heb. 10:7.

is summed up in the word "Behold the handmaid of the Lord, be it done to me *according* to Thy will" [2] & she lived not in a cloister, at least not one built of walls.

Now my dear child you must henceforth consider the question of vocation as *definitely settled*. Don't go back on it. Don't doubt. God could not make it clearer, unless by a vision or revelation, & this we may not wish. Now you must begin & organise your life in the world. For that your friend & director [. . .] is just what you require. I could give you little help in that matter; as it is not in my way. You may however always count on my prayers, & daily remembrance in H. Mass; & of course I shall always be delighted to meet you, if our paths cross each other. May God bless & love you, & lead you to His perfect love by a life of faith & fidelity.

Ever Yrs. in J.C.
Columba Marmion Abb.

P.S. Affectionate regards to Mother, M[. . .], Is[. . .], & friends.

XIX

✛ Pax                                   Maredsous, 6. 2. 21
My dear M[. . .],

How far you are from sounding the depths of our Lord's heart, & of its love for you! There is no question of a want, or a diminution, of love. He loves you dearly & you are His dearly beloved little spouse "His strong arm encircles you, & his hand bears up your hand, as you repose on His heart." [1] The fact of living in a cloister is a mere accident, & cannot affect or diminish your love, if, as in this case, it comes from His wish, from His mysterious designs on your soul. St. Joseph Labre, who is a great Saint, canonized & venerated by the Church, had a most powerful attraction for our Benedictine life. He entered several times (3 times I think) & after doing his best, was obliged to leave. He became a *Saint*, which he most probably would not have been in the cloister, *because* it was not the way Jesus had chosen for Him. A Saint's whole life may be summed up in these words of

[2] Luke 1:38.
[1] Cant. 2:6 and 8:3.

the S. liturgy *Hic vir perfecit omnia quæ dixit illi Deus.*[2] That is *perfection.*

Now M[. . .] dear, I know you *perfectly* now, & I assure you 1) that Jesus loves you *dearly.* 2) That He is quite satisfied with the efforts you made to carry out what you thought to be His will. 3) That you can attain just as high perfection, & just as close union with Him, by performing with *great love*, great *patience with yourself*, & great humility, the task which His will sets you daily. I assure you it is the demon who tries to cast darkness & distrust into your soul. There is nothing our Lord demands so much from His lovers as "hoping against hope"[3] just trusting in His loyalty, His fidelity, His love; & nothing so wounds Him as any distrust or want of confidence.

Abraham is the "Father of our faith."[4] And what faith! When God calls Him, his answer is ever *adsum* here I am![5] At 75 years of age he is told from heaven that he will be father of an immense progeny. *Credidit Abraham Deo.*[6] Years roll on. He arrives at the age of 100 years. Again he is told he is to have a child. Everything seems against it. His body is dried up & "dead" says S. Paul. His wife is sterile.[7] Still *credidit Abraham Deo*; or, as St. Paul puts it *credidit in spem contra spem.*[8] And when Isaac is born, & the object of an *immense love*, God tells him to take the "boy he loves, & immolate him."[9] Abraham does not hesitate. God is so filled with admiration that He swears that he is to be the *father of all believers.*[10] Now dear, that is what Jesus wants from you. St. Paul says of Abraham *non respexit corpus suum emortuum* Abraham did not consider, did not look at his decayed body;[11] no, he looked at God.

Now M[. . .], you look too much at your littleness, at your miseries, at your shortcomings, & too little at Jesus. He is so great, so loving,

[2] "This man has accomplished all that God asked him to do." Responsory from the Office of a Confessor not a Bishop.
[3] Rom. 4:18.
[4] Antiphon of Vespers of the Saturday before Quinquagesima Sunday.
[5] Gen. 22:1.
[6] Gen. 15:6.
[7] Rom. 4:19.
[8] Rom. 4:18.
[9] Gen. 22:2.
[10] Rom. 4:11.
[11] Rom. 4:19.

so *faithful*, so wise, so powerful. Say often "Oh S. Heart of Jesus, I have confidence in You" even though you don't feel it — *feeling makes no matter.*

There is a little leaflet by Mgr. Goodier S.J. Archbishop of Bombay, called "A higher way." It is published by the S. Heart Nuns at Roehampton. The Jesuits could get it for you. It will *just* suit the state of your soul, & say fifty times better than I could what I have been saying.

Pray for me. I want much prayer at present. Affectionate remembrance to Mother, H[. . .], etc., M[. . .].

Your poor devoted,
✠ Columba Abb.

P.S. Neither our Lady, nor many of the holy virgins & spouses of Jesus, — Thecla, Agatha, Agnes, Cecilia lived in a convent, yet they were perfect spouses of Jesus!

xx.

Maredsous. 15. 6. 21.[1]

I am *so* busy — yet I must send you a line to say you are getting on quite well. That hunger for Jesus and for His love is a *continual* prayer; Our Lord keeps you dry and hungry just to excite the longing, which is *so* pleasing to Him. You are all right. *Your* way is *faith*; faith without feeling — faith made strong in the weakness of temptation and doubt. You must accept your *way*. It is He who chose it for you.

I sent my 1st Vol. to Mgr. Goodier at Bombay. He wrote me such a long, lovely letter; we shall be great friends.[2] Could you send me a couple of copies of his "Higher Way." I shall be in London 1st April, and give a retreat to Westminster Clergy at St. Edmund's Old Hall, 1–6 August. Then I may stay a few days in London, and then go on to Ventnor I. of Wight to rest with my brother. I am praying for you daily with *all my heart*, and should be delighted to meet you.

[1] See Note 1 to Letter 2.
[2] Read the letter on this great friendship, sent to Dom Raymond Thibaut on Sept 14, 1933, by Archbishop Goodier, and reproduced as a preface to the book *Union with God* (2nd ed.; London, Sands, 1949).

✠ Pax                                    Maredsous. 21. XI. 22

My dear Child,

If I have not written to you for a considerable time, it is not for want of interest in your soul. Two motives have prevented me. 1) I don't like to interfere with a soul who has a director. For it only complicates the soul, & prevents her from living by faith. 2) I have been crushed by work.

Union with Jesus is *consummated* in *faith*. *Sponsabo te mihi in fide.*[1] The *sense* of union with Him, is His gift, but not Himself. We must leave it to His wisdom & love to give or withhold it. We can do nothing without Him. "Without me you can do nothing."[2] This perfect detachment from creatures, & adhesion to Him must come from His grace, & is the recompense of humble prayer & patience. When Dame Gertrude More (daughter of St. Thomas More)[3] was dying, her director F. Baker, OSB, who had done *so much* for her, came to see her, the abbess told her he was there. She said "I need no man." Jesus was all to her. Of course this is very perfect; & we must not fly till our wings are strong enough. Perfect patience under all that God *permits*, unites us to Xt's Passion. *Passionibus Xti. per patientiam participamus.*[4] Try to *smile lovingly* at every manifestation of God's will.

I must leave you as I am very busy. I pray for you with all my heart. Please give my love to Mother, M[. . .], I[. . .], etc., etc.

Yrs. in J.C.

✠ Columba Abb.

---

[1] "And I will espouse thee to me in faith" (Osee 2:20).

[2] John 15:5.

[3] In reality, this Benedictine mystic was the great-granddaughter of the Chancellor-Martyr. She died very young in 1663. See *The Inner Life and the Writings of Dame Gertrude More*, revised and edited by Dom Benedict Weld-Blundell (2 vols.; London, 1910–11).

[4] "It is by patience we take part in the Passion of Christ." Rule of St. Benedict, end of the Prologue.

## XXII. TO A TEACHING SISTER

(Visiting card: Dom Columba Marmion O.S.B.
Abbé de Maredsous)

16 June [1914]

My dear child.

I have just heard that you have been called to Bruges; and that you are to form souls for our Lord. I never write to you; though I often thought of your soul *coram Domino*.[1] Your "way" is so simple; you need no exterior help. I shall only say: I shall pray for you that you may form souls for Xt, according to the intentions of His wisdom. For that, you must more and more place yourself in His hands; and then *apply yourself actively* to form your children according to the model of your order and Constitutions, according to the interior of Jesus.

[no signature]

## XXIII. TO ONE OF HIS NIECES, A NUN

### FIVE LETTERS

I.

✠ Pax                                    Maredsous. 29 Dec. [1912]

My dear Child,

I was greatly pleased to get your letter. All those who seek God sincerely pass, sooner or later, through a crisis. It is *necessary*, in order to make any real progress. "He who remaineth in Me and I in him beareth much fruit. If anyone bear fruit, my Father will *prune* him in order that he bear more fruit."[1] "Unless the grain of wheat falling on the earth die, it remains alone; but if it die, it bringeth forth much fruit."[2] It is just like nature which, every year, must, as it were, die,

---

[1] In the presence of the Lord.
[1] John 15:5 and 2.
[2] John 12:24.

and remain gripped in the icy grasp of winter. It *seems* to die, but this death is necessary before the spring-time.

I start for England next Monday week (6th), and fear it would be impossible to get to J[. . .] before that; but I shall arrange so as to go see you, at least for a few hours, on my way back. I must be at Maredsous for the 20th, and so will see you before that. I shall pray daily that God may give you *submission* and humble *abandon* of yourself in His hands, in order that He may carry out the designs of His love and wisdom on you.

Yours affect.

✠ Columba, Abb.

II.[1]

✠ Pax                                    Maredsous. 26 march [1913]

My dearest Child,

I cannot tell you what pleasure your letter gave me. I must say that your reserve towards me in the past did make me suffer, as I was very fond of you and I sincerely desired to do you good and form your soul for our Divine Master. The little crisis through which you have passed has ploughed the ground of your soul, has opened it up and already quite transformed it. It is a great thing to be conscious of our weakness and of the necessity of asking Our Lord's help. He said: "Without me you can do nothing." [2] You knew this already, but now it has become a deep conviction. Our miseries are our title to God's mercy. St. Paul was conscious of his weakness, but instead of being discouraged he said: "Gladly will I glory in my infirmities, that the power of Christ may dwell in me." [3] When one has been in the habit unconsciously of leaning on one's own strength, and this fails, it requires a certain time to get accustomed to leaning on God alone. This is the state you are in. You have made much progress in recent months, but you have not yet learned to put your trust in God alone. In your spiritual life, avoid examining yourself

---

[1] This letter was written in French, and translated into English by the recipient herself.

[2] John 15:5.

[3] II Cor. 12:9.

too much. It is enough that God knows you. Lose yourself in him, and you will find yourself in him. It is far more advantageous for you to look at God than to look at yourself. Your union with God who is immutable will give you the stability, the steady line of conduct which you seem to lack more or less at present. . . .

The conversions at Caldey are a great consolation, but also an increase of responsibility, work and correspondence for me; and I have no secretary. They are beautiful souls, very simple, and several of them are very close to God and far advanced in contemplation. I shall have a lot to do to arrange their canonical position in Rome, for there will be great difficulties. Abbot Aelred will accompany me to Rome. We shall be passing through Ancona. . . .[4]

Yours very devoted in J.C.<br>
✠ Columba Abb.

III.

✠ Pax                                          15 Feb. [1917]

My dear Child,

I have but a few minutes to tell you what pleasure your letter gave me. I am *most* anxious to go to J[. . .], but after my long absence in Ireland, I dare not leave here for some time, especially as I am *obliged* to go to Brussels this week for the marriage of Mr. Desclée our founder's son. There is no doubt whatever that your interior sufferings are part of God's merciful plan for the sanctification of your soul. We have all gone through that winter. For "If the grain of wheat falling in the ground *die* not, it alone remains, but if it die, it beareth much fruit."[1] Your soul *needed* to be deepened by suffering, that the sentiment of utter abandonment by God which is the greatest of all sufferings: "My God, my God, why hast Thou abandoned me?"[2] You would never be anything but a weak, superficial being, if you did not pass through such suffering. "Because you were

---

[4] See Peter F. Anson, *Abbot Extraordinary. A Memoir of Aelred Carlyle*, pp. 181–83, for details of this expedition to Rome. (MEE)

[1] John 12:24.

[2] Matt. 27:46.

pleasing to God, it was necessary that temptation should try you."[3]
After the winter will come the Spring and the Summer. . . .
Love to all.

Yours in J.C.

✠ Columba, Abb.

IV.

✠ Pax                                           Maredsous. 8 . IX . 21.
My dear Child,
I assure you, you are not as anxious to see me as I am to see you,
but I really don't see how I can manage. I have just come back from
Holland to see our Primate.[1] I shall be at Brussels Sunday for the
Congrès Marial. Monday, confessions at Liège; 13 Professions; and
then I must leave immediately to be at Philippeville to consecrate the
Church with the Bishop.[2] Our retreat begins 18th and goes on till
26th. Then I have reunions of community [3] for several days, etc., etc.
I can't get away. Pray for me as I have many cares, and I am getting
old and easily worn out. Your Mother is looking splendid; she is
very good; and God is taking good care of her.
I should love to see dear Rev. Mother, but I must suffer this
privation. God bless and love you as I do.

✠ Columba, Abb.

V.

✠ Pax                                           6 . VII . 22.
My dear Child,
I quite understand that you are enraged against me. I deserve it;
but I am so accustomed to be pardoned by my Heavenly Father that
I know you will forgive me. I can assure you that it is not want of
affection or forgetfulness; but my life has been so rushed and so
crushed with work, worry and responsibility, that I gave all my time
to *unavoidable* correspondence, and left the rest. Many of my friends
are just as enraged against me as you. I do think of you and pray

[3] Tob. 12:13.
[1] Dom Fidelis von Stotzingen.
[2] Bishop Heylen of Namur.
[3] Meetings of Chapter and Council.

for you *daily* at my Mass that God may give you the grace, which He gave me so abundantly: that of seeing my misery in His mercy, and of taking my glory and confidence in His aid and love. I had been hoping that some thing would have brought me to Rome and to you this year; but I don't know Pius XI, and I have nothing to treat with him. He sent me a letter to thank me for my vol. of conferences; but it was mere formality; I don't expect he ever read it. I am going to Lourdes this year for the first time. I am to direct the pilgrimage from 12–26 Sep. I shall have to preach and pontificate. It is possible I may be able to take Mother with me. She is very anxious to come. . . .

I have had to go to Paris and London on legal business, just a *run* over, all in 4 days. Our Bishop,[1] when he goes away, looks on me as his auxiliary, and gets me to do all his pontifical offices for him, and as he is the president of the Eucharistic Congresses, this means a lot. So my monks, like you, are often enraged against me because I leave them; but I can't help it. If I were to follow my *attrait*, I would give my resignation as Abbot, and retire for my last years as chaplain to a convent, to pray, write and rest while preparing for the last great voyage.

The dear old Abbess, O.S.B. of Liège [82] was complaining lately to one of our abbots that she had no time to look after her own soul. He answered: "Your soul! Why! a Superior has no soul. It is buried in God; and He takes care of it."

Our poor country is in a pitiful plight. English rule was bad enough; but to be governed by a pack of lunatics is worse. . . .[2]

If I could see you, as I desire ardently, — for I do love you dearly — I would preach a sermon on our solidarity with Jesus. He has so taken our weakness and miseries on Himself, that we can all day long present ourselves to the Father in His Person. Let us look at our Father in faith, and say: "Father, what You do to the least of those who are belonging to Jesus, You do to Him." As Jesus has refused His Father nothing, He can refuse nothing to us.

[1] Bishop Heylen.

[2] This was during the strange interlude of strife between left-wing "republican" Sinn Feiners and the provisional government. See Letter 19, Note 5, and Letter 20, Note 3, of Section III (to Bishop Dwyer). (MEE)

I am giving a retreat to *Gr. Séminaire*[3] of Tournai: 29 July–6 August. Then another to clergy of Nottingham 7–12 August. Pray for me too; for I am getting old [64], and these things tire me.

May God love and bless you, as I do from my heart of hearts.

✝ Columba, Abb.

## XXIV. TO A BENEDICTINE NUN OF TYBURN CONVENT

### THREE LETTERS

*From 1908 onward, Dom Marmion maintained a regular correspondence with the venerable prioress of this convent, a holy nun of French origin, Mother Mary of St. Peter Garnier. She had founded a congregation, the Adorers of the Sacred Heart of Montmartre, of which Tyburn was the first foundation in England. In January, 1914, this congregation was affiliated to the Benedictine Order, and the advice of Dom Marmion had greatly contributed to this development.*

*Dom Marmion had preached the annual retreat there in April, 1909, and when he passed through London he was always welcomed at the convent. When forced to leave occupied Belgium in disguise in September, 1914, Dom Marmion succeeded in reassembling his young refugee-monks in a property that a generous gift had enabled him to acquire at Edermine, in County Wexford in Ireland. But resources were lacking, and Dom Marmion had to go in search of means of subsistence. It was thus that he asked the charity of the Tyburn nuns to obtain clothing.*

*The chief interest of these letters, however, lies in the grave anxiety revealed by the author concerning his difficulty in corresponding with Maredsous in Belgium while it was occupied by the German armies; his ardent desire to return to his monastery; his fear lest this prolonged absence be misunderstood. It was for this reason that he tried to get in touch with his friend Cardinal Mercier, who was the soul and bulwark of Belgian patriotism at that time.*

[3] Major seminary.

✝ Pax            Edermine, Enniscorthy. 3 May [1915].
My dear Sr. H [. . .]

. . . Please tell dear R. Mother I am still suffering greatly from influenza, obliged to remain in bed most of the day. Tell her also, I got as yet no answer from Card. Mercier, but one letter from Count de Grunne [1] tells me it will be practically impossible for me to get back at present; Mgr. de Wachter [2] writes me the same. Nevertheless, if the Cardinal advises me to return, I shall get out in God's name. Of course I shall pass by Tyburn.

May God bless and love you all as I do in J.C.

✝ Columba Marmion, Abb.

✝ Pax            Edermine, Enniscorthy. 7 May [1915].
My dear Sister H [. . .]

Many thanks for your kind offer. May God bless and love you.

I send you a rough estimate of our wardrobe, though of course I know you can't do more than fill up a gap here and there. We are getting on splendidly, and God is very good to us. I have been suffering a *deal* from influenza, but am on the mend. I can't assist at the Office, and speaking at once gets me coughing.

Besides this, I hear I am looked on at Maredsous somewhat as a pastor who has deserted his flock. This is very painful to bear; it is so far from the truth. Most of my letters get stopped, and so I can't explain. I wrote the Cardinal Mercier explaining my position, and asking his advice and help; but I fear my letter never got to him. The Count de Grunne, to whom I wrote, writes that he, and all the persons he has consulted, consider it *impossible* for me to get back to Maredsous at present.

Perhaps you could communicate with his Eminence by Mrs. Mercier. Note the following points: 1) I left Maredsous 14 Sept.,

[1] Count Willy de Grunne, of the Belgian Legation in London, a graduate of Maredsous Abbey school.

[2] Of the Nunciature at The Hague, and a friend of Abbot Marmion.

when all danger had ceased in that part of Belgium.[1] 2) I left on unanimous advice of Seniors, and the Bishop of Namur. 3) As soon as I had assured existence of my monks here, I sought to return, and have received official information from Nunciature at Brussels, and *Légation Belge* at London that my return is impossible. I beg Cardinal Mercier to explain this to my Community; and if he considers I ought to return, to help me to do so; as it would greatly compromise my Community later, were I to seek a passport from the Kaiser by way of our Primate.[2]

Pray for me, as I daily do for you all. These pains of body and heart are bringing me daily nearer to God, and detaching me from the world.

May God bless and love you all.

Your Father,

✠ Columba Marmion, Abb.

P.S. The H. Father Benedict XV has sent a magnificent letter to Cardinal Amette, in which he openly espouses the cause of France.

III.

✠ Pax                Edermine, Enniscorthy. 17 May 1915.
My dear Child,

Your letter was a great joy and consolation to me. I can say with St. John (III Epis. 1,3): *Majorem horum non habeo gratiam, quam ut audiam filios meos in veritate ambulare.* "I have no greater joy than to know that my children walk in truth."

Our life is agreeable to God just in proportion as we are united to the Word by love and resignation. The Sacred Humanity gave a special glory to God during His *weakness* at the hour of the Passion. *Deus qui in assumptae carnis* infirmitate *jacentem mundum erexisti.* "O God, Who didst raise up the fallen world by the *weakness* of this assumed human nature." [1] Our Divine Lord associates each

---

[1] Abbot Marmion wishes to make it clear that it was not from fear that he had left Maredsous, but only in order to find a refuge from the enemy for his young monks.

[2] The Abbot-Primate of the Benedictines was at this writing a German, Dom Fidelis von Stotzinger, former Abbot of Maria-Laach.

[1] Prayer from the Mass of Palm Sunday, quoted with a slight modification.

one of His elect with one of these *states* which He has sanctified and deified in His Divine Person. Some are united to His infancy, others to His hidden life, others to His apostolic life, others to His passion, some few are associated with the *weakness* of His agony, and these give Him the most glory.

In our activity, we are so apt to *substitute* our human natural activity to God's action. But when God strikes us down, despoils us of *our* activity, He takes full possession of that person, and deifies all his activity, which flows from Him. This is what God has done for you. Your prayer should be to sink deeper and deeper every day in that Divine Will. Place your heart in that of Jesus, and let Him will for you. I daily pray that God may give you the grace to bear, and love, the cross He places on you. Blosius says: "A soul which gives herself up without reserve to God, allowing Him to operate in her as He pleases, does more for God and for souls in one hour than others by their activity in long years."

I got a letter from Cardinal Mercier telling me not to go back to Belgium at the present, and promising to explain all at Maredsous. I am now much better. I shall soon write to R. Mother.

Your father in J.C.<br>✠ Columba, Abb.

P.S. I need much prayer and expiation. I daily offer you to God. Do so for me.

## XXV. TO A BENEDICTINE NUN OF VENTNOR

### FOUR LETTERS

*This religious belonged to the Priory of Ventnor in the Isle of Wight,[1] which had been founded by the Benedictine nuns of Liège.*

*Since the originals of these letters have been lost, the text is taken from copies made by the correspondent herself.*

*Abbot Marmion was living at that time at Edermine in Ireland with his community of young monks from Maredsous; moreover, he*

[1] Since 1922 this community has been at Ryde under the name of St. Cecilia's Abbey.

*gave numerous retreats in that country and in England, "preaching Jesus and trying to gain souls to him." In this way he helped at the same time to support his monks in exile.*

I.

✠ Pax                                                    Sept. 1915.[1]

My dear Child,

Thanks for your dear letter. I have been ever so busy since, preaching Jesus and trying to gain souls for Him. I know you are helping me, and that is a very great support and consolation. I saw papa yesterday. He is charming. . . .

I was very happy at Ventnor. I know now why God sent me there. I have felt ever since such help and joy; I feel I am being prayed for. In that way you share in my mission which is to preach Jesus Christ, and make Him known and loved. We go half and half. . . . I shall write again.

I have a big Community here. They are very kind to me; but are not O.S.B.

May God bless and love you.

Your father in J.C.<br>✠ Columba, Abb.

II.

5 Jan. 1916.

My dear Child,

Although I do not write, I never allow a day to pass without thinking of and praying for you; for God has united us in His holy Love, and we are to help each other to keep near Him.

I should *love* to go down to Ventnor, but circumstances have prevented me up to this. If I go back to Belgium, as is probable, I will try to run down for a day.

I have been *very ill*, and in fact in great suffering — in danger. I had offered myself to God to suffer, if He helped me to bring back a poor priest [. . .] who was dying far from God. I received him back on Christmas Eve. I *feel* you are praying for me. What God

---

[1] This letter must have been written from London, where Abbot Marmion was preaching a retreat at the Convent of the Assumption at the time.

200

wants of you is absolute abandon of yourself as a poor little sinner to His Love. . . .

Good-bye, dear Child, may God bless and love you.

Your father,

✝ Columba.

### III.

[. . .] As regards your questions:

Sanctifying grace exists in different degrees in souls according to God's decrees, *secundum donationem Christi*,[1] and their own cooperation. Thus Our Lady was "full of grace," *gratia plena*, sanctifying grace. But as a person in the state of grace *merits* an increase of sanctifying grace (and love) by each good action, it went on in her all her life. Actual grace consists in "illuminations and inspirations" which flow from Sanctifying grace, as from their Source. (People in the state of sin receive also *actual* grace, without which they could not get back to God's grace).

Sanctifying grace, no matter how abundant, is lost by one mortal sin, but *cannot be dismissed*; this is quite certain; but its activity and fecundity are diminished by venial sin. In the case of a person in mortal sin, it is not quite certain from what source the actual graces flow. Theologians dispute about it; but nothing certain is known.

Just as the essence of our soul is the source from which our *natural* powers flow and issue, so Sanctifying grace becomes a kind of second and higher essence from which *supernatural* life, powers, virtues flow. Our degree of glory in heaven depends on the degree of sanctifying grace (Charity) possessed at the moment of death.

A good book on grace is *Le Saint Esprit* par Froget, O.P. Also *La grâce et la gloire* par Terrien, S.J.

### IV.

. . . *Etiam si ambulavero in medio umbrae mortis, non timebo mala quoniam tu mecum es.*[1]

[1] "According to the gift of Christ." See Eph. 4:7.

[1] "For though I should walk in the midst of the shadow of death, I will fear no evils, for thou art with me" (Ps. 22:4).

The bride is never dearer to the Beloved than when she leans in full confidence on His strong arm, fearing nothing because He is there to guard and love her.

My Child, believe me, Jesus loves you dearly, and wants to be served by pure love. Sincere love is the fertile root of all virtue: *Caritas omnia credit, omnia sperat, omnia sustinet.*[2]


## XXVI. TO A DOMINICAN SISTER OF DUBLIN

✠ Pax                    41, Elm Park Gardens, Chelsea, S.W.[1]
                         27. 2. 16.

My dear Child,

It was a real sacrifice for me not to have been able to see you before leaving. I had all arranged for that; but unforeseen circumstances prevented me. I start to-morrow for Holland; and hope to get on to Maredsous. You must pray for me, as I shall run much dangers during these days.

I offer you daily to God at the H. Sacrifice that you may be wholly His. Never forget, dear Child, that that which is not made for God is lost. God alone, and what is done in Him, *opera in Deo facta,*[2] are eternal. Sr. M. of the Angels, Tyburn Convent, is reading my little note-book. She will send it to you, when she has done; and you, please, send it to D. Aubert, Edermine, Co. Wexford, when you have finished.

Keep on the path I have traced for you. Never forget this, that the more you lean on Jesus, the more you glorify Him; and thus enter into the views of the Father. *Libenter gloriabor in infirmitatibus meis.*[3] May God bless and love you, is my sincere prayer.

Yous ever in J.C.

✠ Columba Marmion, Abb.

---

[2] "Charity . . . believeth all things, hopeth all things, endureth all things" (I Cor. 13:7).

[1] Quite a number of letters written at this time were sent by Abbot Marmion from this same London address.

[2] "The works done in God." Council of Trent, Session VI, chap. 16: On Merit.

[3] "Gladly therefore will I glory in my infirmities" (II Cor. 12:9).

# XXVII. TO A NUN

### SEVEN LETTERS

*These letters were written to an Irish sister who was in a convent in Belgium. Before her entry into religion she had lived in the world until her husband's death. She had a son named Charlie, who became a monk at Maredsous. He is mentioned several times in these letters. Abbot Marmion, who received him into the novitiate, gave him his own monastic name of Columba. This monk died some time before his mother.*

*In these letters we can appreciate the way in which Abbot Marmion understands spiritual direction, and the formation to contemplative prayer.*

I.

✠ Pax                       Maredsous. 12 Jan [1911]

My dear Mère Emmanuel,

    I delayed writing until Charlie had finished his retreat, so as to be able to give you my opinion. He is leaving today, or tomorrow, after a very serious retreat. As Dom Paul was obliged to leave the abbey for a few days, I confided Charlie to D. Idesbald, Master of novices, who had helped him on a former occasion. We are both of opinion that Charlie has a true monastic vocation. His motive for wishing to be a monk is, that in the monastic state one loves God more perfectly & consecrates oneself more entirely to Him than in the world. This, of course, is a very high & noble motive. It is better that neither you, nor your Rev. Mother, should make any allusion to his vocation until it is a *fait accompli*.[1] He has an intense repugnance to being *driven* towards the religious state; & is most sensitive on that point. Of course *I know* you do not "drive" him; but he has got it into his head; & this was a real obstacle. I feel he will be a very good monk.

    Please present my respects to your Rev. Mother, & believe me, yours devotedly in J.C.

✠ Columba, Abb.

---

[1] An accomplished fact.

✠ Pax. Abbaye de Saint-Benoit.        Maredsous. le 21. IX 1919
My dear Child,

I have just received your letter. I too believe that our Lord wishes to confide your soul to my care. I am not a great partisan of much direction. I feel that the H. Spirit is the one director who is capable to give the true light & inspiration. Yet it is God's way to direct us by His Ministers; especially as says St. Fr. de Sales, *La femme, quelque intelligente ou sainte qu'elle soit, doit être conduite par le Ministre du Xt.*[1] This is God's way. What is necessary, is that the director know the soul *perfectly*; & that once done, he must indicate the way she is to follow, & then leave her to the H. Spirit. From time to time, at long intervals, he must control her progress; & if anything out of the common way should happen, he must know it. But in my opinion, long & frequent letters of direction do more harm than good.

Charley is doing very well indeed. I must try & have him ordained *here*, about Easter-time, & then you could come & put up at the hospice for the ceremony & the first Mass.

I am really anxious to go and see you, but can't as yet fix the date. It will be soon, please God. I shall let you know some days before-hand, so that you may be prepared.

May God bless & love you, & make you all His own. Yrs. in J.C.
✠ Columba, Abb.

III.

✠ Pax. Abbaye de Maredsous.        2. X. 19
My dear Child,

I hope to get to Binche at 10:19. Monday; & leave on Tuesday at 12:30. I can see you as long as may be necessary; & give a conference to the Community at the hour which suits best. On reading your letter I felt that I understand what God wants from you. 1) The H. Spirit is inviting you to passive prayer, & you must not "extinguish the Spirit"[1] by misplaced activity. Nothing is more glorious

---

[1] "A woman, however intelligent and holy she may be, should be guided by Christ's minister."

[1] I Thess. 5:19.

to God, nor more advantageous for us than to give God a free hand in our souls, once He intimates His desire to have it. Blosius says that a soul which abandons herself to God's action without reserve, allowing Him to operate as He wishes in her, does more for His glory, & for souls in one hour, than others in years.[2]

2) Once you feel the attraction to remain in the silence of adoration in God's presence, you must give yourself entirely to the H. Spirit, & remain there in *pure faith. Desponsabo te mihi in fide.*[3] If God gives you no feeling, no sentiment, no distinct thought, just lie there before Him in silent love. During such moments He operates insensibly on the soul, & does more for her perfection, than she could in a life-time by her own thoughts, etc.

3) If at any moment you feel attracted to petition, or other acts, follow this attraction. It is not necessary to pronounce words, or to form *distinct* thoughts. Just present yourself & your petition in silent prayer before God's face. He sees all that your heart is saying *desiderium pauperum audivit auris tua.*[4]

4) The distractions are only on the surface of your soul. They are a cross, but you must learn to despise them. Your prayer goes on in the hidden depths of your soul, which is, as it were, lying on God's bosom, His Essence, & drinking in vast draughts of love & light.

5) If God ever speaks interior words, be sure to submit them to your director before acting on them. Be very prudent in speaking of your interior, even to priests, many of whom have no experience of such things.

Pray for me. May God bless & love you.

✠ Columba Marmion, Abb.

IV.

✠ Pax                                                      Maredsous. 20.2.20
My dear Child,

As it is Lent, & I am very busy, I may only send a word. Your last letter helped me for what you say of God's Maternity (for all paternity & maternity are united in Him, & derive from His bosom)

---

[2] Blosius, *A Book of Spiritual Instruction*, chap. 1, N° 4.
[3] "I will espouse thee to me in faith" (Osee 2:20).
[4] "The Lord hath heard the desire of the poor" (Ps. 9, 17).

struck me very much. I feel a great longing for heaven. Yet I don't feel as if my work was done. I fear the judgement; & yet I cast myself on God's bosom with all my miseries & my responsibilities, & hope in His mercy. Nothing else can save us, for our poor little works are not fit to be presented, & only His Fatherly affection deigns to accept them. *Non aestimator meriti sed veniae* [1] as we pray at Mass. The little Servants of the H. Sacr. will have a great place in heaven, *vos permansistis mecum in tentationibus meis.* [2]

Columba is doing well, & will be a very holy monk I feel. I know you pray for me, as I do for you. May God bless you, & give you grace to refuse Him nothing.

I *may* see you in March.

Yrs. in J.C.

✝ Columba, Abb.

v.

✝ Pax. Abbaye de Saint-Benoit.     Maredsous. le 27. IX. 1920
My dear Child,

I am glad to hear that your soul is in peace. *Querite pacem et persequere eam.* [1] God would have us do all in our power to be in peace, in order to communicate Himself to our souls. *Non in commotione Dominus.* [2] You must not go back on the past. God does not wish it, except in a general way, just to humble yourself *before Him*, casting yourself at His feet as a poor sinner, & asking His pardon. "Oh God, be merciful to me a sinner." [3] You are called to be united to the *Word* as His S. Humanity is, that is to say, in deep adoration & annihilation of your personality, — His Humanity had no human personality — , & consequently, all its powers belonged *immediately* & *exclusively* to the Word. If you give yourself up without reserve to the *divine* action of the S. Humanity, He will take you with Him in that Divine Current which flows like an impetuous torrent ever into the bosom of the Word. There your little personality will be lost,

---

[1] "Not weighing our merits, but freely pardoning us our sins." From the Canon of the Mass.

[2] "You are they who have continued with me in my temptations" (Luke 22:28).

[1] "Seek after peace and pursue it" (Ps. 33:15).

[2] "The Lord is not in the wind" (III Kings 19:11).

[3] Luke 18:13.

& disappear in deep adoration & perfect love; & so all that comes from that personality, — self-love, susceptibility, sadness, etc., will be destroyed. I must leave you. I commenced this several times, but could not get on. Charlie is as good as gold. Every one loves him. He loves Xt. with all his heart; & is most charitable, joyous, & fervent. God has spoiled you.

My humble respects to your good Superioress.

✛ Columba, Abb.

P.S. I need *great prayers* at present, for a most important matter which regards my person, *entre nous.*[4]

## VI.

✛ Pax                                    Maredsous. 2. I. 22.

My dear Child,

It is certainly very nasty of me to have left your two letters so long unanswered. However, it is neither want of interest, nor forgetfulness: I pray daily at H. Mass for you. It is from sheer exhaustion & overwork. Your soul is all right. Look at God through Jesus' eyes, & don't bother about where your imagination is. We are the members of J.C., & our miseries, assumed by Him, cry out Mercy in His Name to the Father. He is ever before God's face *for us*, & hidden in Him. His prayer, as He gazes on His Father's face, becomes ours. I understand so well St. Paul's *Libenter gloriabor in infirmitatibus meis ut inhabitet in me virtus Xti.*[1] The H. Ghost is the link which unites us to Xt. When before the B. Sacrament, don't think that the B. Sac. is *outside* you. It is *in* you by the H. Ghost; & each *inmost* thought is there *in Him*, more really & surely than if you held His Sacred feet like Magdalen. This is why St. Paul says, "No one can say Dne. Jesu *except in the H. Ghost.*"[2] That is, it is the H. Ghost who introduces us into the interior of Jesus. I shall look to dear D. Columba's studies. He is a most holy monk, & loved by everyone. Pray much for me. Best wishes to R. Mother & all for 1922.

✛ Columba Marmion, Abb.

[4] Between us.
[1] "Gladly therefore will I glory in my infirmities, that the power of Christ may dwell in me" (II Cor. 12:9).
[2] I Cor. 12:3.

207

VII.

✠ Pax. Abbaye de Maredsous.                    18. VIII. 22

My dear Child, I have just got back from London & am *so* busy, yet I *must* send you a line. It is a real crime to preach such doctrine to souls, who have left *all* for Jesus, & to whom He has promised on *His Solemn word, (Amen, Amen dico vobis),*[1] that they will have the hundred fold in this life, & *life eternal*; & mind He says Omnis *qui reliquerit.*[2] Jansenism has done more harm to souls than Protestantism. For it cloaks its venom under the veil of sanctity. The Church teaches that God wishes to show His power *parcendo* maxime *et ignoscendo.*[3] We are to glorify God's mercy. We are so weak, so frail, so deeply wounded, like the man that went down to Jerico, that we touch His Father's heart. Now, my dear Child, just put those thoughts away, & go to Jesus as you always do. He is your strength. St. Paul took glory in his infirmities, in order that *Xt's strength* might dwell in him.[4] There is your path. God loves you, & it would pain His loving heart were you to distrust Him. Say with St. Paul *Scio cui credidi et certus sum.*[5]

I am praying for you.

                                    Yrs. ✠ Columba, Abb.


## XXVIII. TO THE POOR CLARE COLETTINES
## OF CORK

### FIVE LETTERS

*Abbot Marmion had just preached the annual retreat to these religious in November, 1921. This contact had sufficed to create between*

---

[1] "Amen, amen, I say unto you" (John 6:31, 47, 54) — an expression often repeated in the Gospel according to St. John.

[2] "Everyone that hath left . . ." (Matt. 19:29).

[3] ". . . more than in all things else . . . by sparing and by having mercy . . ." Collect for the Tenth Sunday after Pentecost.

[4] II Cor. 12:9.

[5] "For I know whom I have believed" (II Tim. 1:12).

*him and these contemplative nuns a strong link of great spiritual intensity which can be seen in these letters.*

I.

✠ Pax                              Maredsous. 17 – 12 – 21.

My dear Children,

Just a little word in the midst of my work to wish you all, from my heart of hearts, a holy, happy Xmas. May the Infant Jesus, who chose the poverty of a stable, choose your hearts for His palace; and repose in joy on the love of your immolation. I think of you all *each day* at Holy Mass, and offer you to God in union with the Divine Victim. In fact, I *very, very* often think of you, and pray for you; for I feel somehow that it was Jesus who called me to help you, and has in some way confided you to my loving care. I feel, since the retreat, that Our Lord was pleased with me for having gone over to you; for I have received many special graces and marks of His love since I have been with you. I know that you don't forget me; for what God has united, is one for eternity; and neither time nor space can separate hearts united in Jesus Christ. The Holy Scripture tells us that Jacob loved Joseph more than all his other children, because God had given him to him in his old age.[1] It appears to me that I love this child of my old age which God has given, more than all the others. Now, my dear children, my ambition for you is to see you all, as your holy Foundress St. Clare, wholly detached from all by your sublime vow of poverty; and *wholly* given up to Him Who will come to your hearts with such love on Xmas night.

We begin office here at 10½ p.m. At midnight I sing solemn Pontifical High Mass (for my monks); then solemn Lauds, over at 2½. At 8, I say private Mass in my oratory, (for my family and friends; and you are in that Mass). At 10, a second Pontifical High Mass (for my spiritual children), you are this in first place. You see, neither time, nor space, can separate hearts united in Jesus Christ. Jesus is so good. He takes on Him not only our sins, but all our miseries and sufferings, and makes them *His own*; and as such they

---

[1] Gen. 37:3.

209

cry out, as the voice of His Only Begotten Son to the Father, to obtain mercy for all. I am in good health, D.G.

May God bless and love you all, as I do from my heart.

✠ Columba, Abb.

II.

✠ Pax                                Maredsous. le 1 / 5 / 22.

My dear Children,

Please forgive me. I have been longing to write to you, and to each one; but I have been terribly rushed and crushed more than you could think. And often I have to think of what the Abbot of Solesmes said to the saintly Abbess of Liège, (she is 82, and my spiritual child for years); she has a Community of 100 nuns, two other abbeys to govern, schools, etc. One day she said to the Abbot of Solesmes: "My Lord, I don't know what to do. I have not a moment for my own soul." "Your soul?" said the Abbot. "A superior has no soul, it is hidden in Jesus, and He looks after it, while she looks after His lambs." Well, we meet very often in J.C. I rise almost every night at 12, just for a few moments; and then I say, my dear little children at St. Clare's are now going to praise God. Oh, Holy Spirit, give them tongues of fire, and hearts of Seraphim. At Mass, I put you all in my heart every morning; and as I pass through the veil of the Holy of Holies—the Sacred Humanity of Jesus crushed and wounded for us—into the Presence of Our Great God,[1] I take you with me and present you to the Father as brides of His Son, who so love Him that they despise all else, and that in their heart of hearts they ever sing "my God and my *all*."

Easter has been a time of grace and light. I was able to celebrate the great Pontifical Offices and Masses of Holy Week; and ever since the glorious Risen Christ has been coming to see me, and speak of His Kingdom. The great lesson which He taught me is that God's plan for the Redemption and Sanctification of the world is just the opposite of what we would have thought. We should have expected that God would have come into this world in great power and majesty, and, surrounded by a group of learned men, convert the world. But no. He came as a *poor, weak* little infant; He lives in

---

[1] See Heb. 6:19–20; 9:11, 12, 24.

210

obscurity and labours for years; and then is murdered by men who seem to have conquered Him, and defy Him to save Himself and come down from the Cross. His whole work is ruined; and His reputation blasted. And it is then He conquers! It is the triumph of weakness for "what is weak in God is stronger than all men's strength; what is folly in God is greater than all men's wisdom, in order that no flesh may take glory to itself." [2] This is God's way. And on Easter Sunday I *saw* that it was the divine triumph of God's weakness.

Now this is why I love you *so*. I see in you, more than in any other Community, God's weakness, God's poverty, God's helplessness; and all that appeals to God's compassion and goodness. Your strength, as poor Clares, is your poverty and helplessness which cry out for help in *Jesus' Name* to His Father. A community of Poor Clares, if they only understand their greatness, is Jesus crying out in His poverty to His Father: "what You do for them, Father, You do for me." [3] Oh, my darling children, if I could only impress this great lesson on you, you would become *invincible* before God; for the glory would be His.

I have gone through a deal since we parted. I have lost relations; my little sister Peter of Clonakilty was near dying. I have had difficulties; and been laid up. I can't find time to do the half of what I ought. My consolation is to know and *feel* that my little ones at St. Clare's plead for me; and I remain intimately united with them in holy charity and in prayer.

Oh, let us pray for poor Ireland. Over here, people are saying: "Oh, it is evident Ireland is incapable to govern herself. She needs the strong hand of England to keep peace." This pierces my heart. Prayers and immolations alone can help in such a situation. [4]

I often think of each one in my heart; and some day I hope to come and see you; but I can't write to each one. You *know* I do love all, and each one, in J.C.; and would give my heart's blood for her sanctification. May God bless and love you all, as I do from my heart of hearts.

✠ Columba, Abb.

[2] II Cor. 1:27–29.

[3] Adaptation of a saying of Jesus in Matt. 25:40.

[4] For other comments on Ireland, see Section III, Letters 19 and 20, and Section XXIII, Letter 5.

✛ Pax                                                    12 - 7 - 22.

My dear Child A[. . .],

I *often* think in *Jesus*; for you are there in His heart. I unite each night at 12, with your Matins. I do want to see you *all His*; and I daily beg this from His Heart. Tell Sr. F. . . . I pray daily for her. Don't forget that you are with Jesus on the Cross: *Christo confixus sum cruci*,[1] and that the Father sees you thus united as a spouse with His Son. All your crosses, pains, actions become *His*, and as such are the object of supreme complacency to the Father. It gives Him an opportunity of paying back Jesus for all He has done for Him, for He has said "what you do to the least of mine you do to Me." [2]

Pray daily for me, as I do and shall ever do for you.

✛ Columba, Abb.

(*To the same*)                                          [no date]

My dear Child A[. . .],

Don't think I ever forget you. I want you to become a saint, to love Jesus with me and for me. Just give yourself to Him; and let Him act in you. He loves souls who, like His S. Humanity, live and act by Him, just leaning on His and His power. If you fall into any fault, don't be surprised; just go to your Heavenly Father, like a little child who, having soiled his frock, goes to his mother to have it cleaned.

I have now divided my day into two parts: 1. I live on my morning Communion; 2. I prepare for the next. Jesus loves us to profit by our Communion.

I bring you daily in my heart to the Altar, and unite you with Jesus, and through Him to my poor heart. Let us love Him together.

May God bless and love you as I do from my heart of hearts, that is Jesus.

✛ Columba, Abb.

[1] "With Christ I am nailed to the Cross" (Gal. 2:19).
[2] Matt. 25:40.

✚ Pax                                                    30 - XII - 22.

My dear little Children,

The Irish have great faith, and even when God seems to forget them, they cry after Him until He is forced to turn to them, like the Cananean woman.[1] I have often thought lately that you might be tempted to think I have forgotten you. Quite the contrary, I daily think of you and place you in His Heart, which is the centre of mine while I celebrate. I beg Him to take us all together through the mystic veil of the Holy of Holies; which St. Paul tells us, is the mangled body; and then to present us before the Throne of God.[2]

You have no idea of how I am taken up at every moment, while I am ill and suffering; and every body expects me to be ready. Our Lord helps me, for He has taken all our sufferings and weakness on Him. At present, I am *really* crushed with work and anxiety, and suffering from the 'flu. I have a big stack of letters before me, one more important than the other; and I don't feel fit to write them. So, my darling little children, you see it is not want of affection, but over-work and weakness, which keeps me from sending you what my heart would say to you at present.

I will tell you a *great secret*. It is just possible I may have to come over to Ireland (Tuam) in a few weeks. Don't say a word of this to anyone, except to Jesus. If He wants it, I shall come and pass a couple of days at College Rd. on my way back.

I am *most grateful* to you for the two lovely books: *The Irish Progress*, and the *Daughters of Bamba*. May God bless and love you all, as I do from my heart of hearts.

✚ Columba, Abb.

P.S. My special blessing to Sr. F[. . .].

[1] Matt. 15:21–28.
[2] Heb. 9:11–12.

# XXIX. TO A YOUNG GIRL

✠ Pax

21 Elm Park Gardens, Chelsea, London. 6. VIII. 22.

My dear Miss C[. . .],

I am a very busy man, and have been particularly occupied lately. I have just finished a Retreat to Clergy at Tournai, and am passing through London on my way to Nottingham, where I begin another tomorrow. Please pray, as it is an important clergy-retreat.

I quite understand your difficulty, as it used to torment me also, but does no longer.

The S. Humanity is the *way*, the Divinity is the term or end. It is God's wish that we go to Him through the S. Humanity: "I am the way; no one comes to my Father save through me." [1] My Humanity is the way which bridges over the infinite gulf which separates all creatures from the Divinity. His Humanity is the veil of the Holy of Holies, (Hebr. X) through which Jesus, the High Priest, passed at the Ascension, bringing us with Him. We may not enter this Sanctuary, and repose on God's bosom, but through this veil, all steeped in the Blood of Jesus. Once on God's bosom we have reached the goal; there is nothing higher. We must not quit it; but each Communion takes us further and further into the infinite abyss of the Divinity.

We must follow the inspiration of the H. Ghost, and do no violence to our "attrait." When in the presence of the B. Sacrament, or at Communion, the S. Humanity, exercises a most potent influence on our souls. *Virtus ex illo erit*,[2] and for that, we need not go out of ourselves. Distance does not exist for the S. Humanity. If, when in the presence of the B. Sacrament you feel drawn to speak to Jesus, you may do so either by finding Him in your soul and heart through the medium of His Divinity; or by thinking of Him in the Tabernacle. Both ways are true, for after Communion, the S. Humanity is *materially* present through the *local* presence of the S. Species; at other times He is there *virtualiter* virtually, being *ever* hypostatically united to the Word. A spiritual communion, as the C. Trent [3] teaches, pro-

---

[1] John 14:6.
[2] "Virtue went out from him" (Luke 6:19).
[3] Council of Trent.

214

duces great fruit in our souls. It is our union with the Word through the *virtual* presence in our souls of the Humanity. In virtue of this virtual presence, you are by faith and love, nearer to the S. Humanity, than you are with those who are present in the room with you. For neither space nor distances exist for love.

Please pray for me; and let me know if this satisfies you, at the above address.

✠ Columba Marmion, Abb.


## XXX.  TO THE MOTHER OF A FAMILY

### SIX LETTERS

*The recipient was a Dutch Lady to whom Dom Marmion wrote a great many letters of high spiritual and doctrinal value. Unfortunately the correspondence is in French, except for the few notes in English to follow. These are included as examples of the informal style of Dom Marmion's friendly letters.*

I.

Tournai.  5 - VIII - 22.

Beminde Kind.[1] Just a word to say that God has blessed the retreat greatly, and that my health is excellent. I start for England to-morrow. (Address: 21 Elm Park Garden, Chelsea, London S.W.)

May God bless and love you. In union of grace-prayer.

✠ C.M.

II.

Maredsous.  27 . VIII . 22.

I have just got back from England after having given 2 retreats, one at Tournai, the other at Nottingham. God has blessed both wonderfully. *Many thanks* for the enlarged photos. They are perfect. I never cease to pray for you and yours. I am in good health. Our

[1] Dutch expression meaning "Dear Child."

215

retreat is 10–18.[1] Lourdes: 18–26.[2] Come!! I shall soon write more at length. May God love and bless you.

✝ C.

III.

Maredsous. 18 . IX . 22.

My dear Child,

I start in a few moments for Lourdes. I am *very busy*. I will pray for you and all your intentions with *all my heart*. A pontifical High Mass, on the Feast of St. Matthew. Your letter was a great joy, but you must not think of changing your director. God has, I am *sure*, united us in His love, giving me grace to guide you to Him. Besides we understand each other so perfectly that I can open my whole heart to you, and you to me. You can attend the reunions at Oosterhout, and still remain Oblate of Maredsous. You may certainly wear a small black scapular and cover it in white; that makes no difference. As I have quite confidence in you, I am sending you a line I just received from the Primate to show you that we must pray for A[. . .].[1] He is really good, and will not do anything wrong; but I fear he is losing the spirit of his vocation. . . .

I am so glad you are going to God in *His way*; that is, by 1) perfect *abandon* of yourself and all your interests to His love; 2) by the conscientious discharge of duty for His love; 3) by patience and silence. Would you like to get my 3rd vol. *Christ, Ideal of the Monk*? It is meant for monks, but it might interest you. Let me know. I will send one also to I[. . .]. I am so glad *our* dear E[. . .] saw Oosterhout. Good-bye; may God bless and love you as I do from my heart of hearts.

✝ Columba, Abb.

P.S. I got your card and all letters. My address at Lourdes: *La Résidence*, Lourdes.

[1] The annual retreat of the community of Maredsous.

[2] Bishop Heylen of Namur had asked him to conduct the diocesan pilgrimage to Lourdes that year.

[1] A monk who was related to the correspondent.

Lourdes. 23 . IX . 22.

Dear Child,

Thanks for your letter. I shall say the Mass for A[. . .]. You may be sure I shall be very nice and gentle. I am receiving great graces here. I am praying for you *daily*. May God bless and love you. Be patient with yourself.

✠ C.

(Visiting card)
✠ Pax

16 . X . 22.

Dearest Joke. In great haste. I shall have the 4 Masses said for your Mother-in-law at once. I am sending you the 3rd Vol. for yourself. I got such a nice letter from A[. . .]. He is furious that I was not invited. I am praying continually for *us*, as we are but *one* in J.C. I see He has taken your soul Himself in hand. He said to a holy soul I know: "I have espoused your misery and poverty, and shall make you enter into my power." This is *our* way, my Child. I am *so* busy on account of the great feast.[1] May God love and bless you, as I do from my heart of hearts.

✠ Columba, Abb.

## VI

Maredsous. 21 . XI . 22.

My dear Child,

I have just got back from Paris,[1] where I was very busy and fatigued. I can only send you a line to show you I am thinking and praying for you.

You are on the right road to God; a road which ever leads to Him, despite our weakness. It is the road of *duty accomplished through love* despite obstacles. Jesus is our strength. *Our weakness* assumed by Him becomes *divine weakness*, and it is stronger than all the strength

[1] Golden jubilee of founding of Maredsous, observed October 15–17.
[1] He had just preached a retreat to the Benedictine nuns of *Rue Monsieur*.

of man: *Quod infirmum est Dei, fortius est hominibus.*[2] This is a great, but profound truth. Our dear Lord's Passion is nothing else than this triumph of divine weakness over all the strength and wickedness of men. But for this we require great patience, and the loving acceptance of God's will at every moment. For: *Passionibus Christi per patientiam participamus.* "It is by patience that we participate in Xt's sufferings."[3] Think well over this in prayer, and you will make great progress. You must be very prudent, and take care of your health in order to perform your duty.

I have need of much prayer at present. Ever Yours in J.C.

✠ Columba, Abb.


## XXXI. TO A BENEDICTINE NUN

Maredsous. 1 - XII - 22.

My dear Child D . . .,

Your letter has greatly consoled me, for I can say with St. John that I have no greater joy than that of seeing my children walk in *truth*.[1] To be in the truth we must be in the Word, for He is truth: *Ego sum veritas.*[2] Now truth supposes us to be and to act in the essential relations which God has established for our *nature* and for our dignity of children of God. 1) Nature supposes that the *creature* remains ever in lowliest adoration before the Creator. This is so essential that *nothing* can change it. Our adoration as children of God raises our nature, but does not destroy it. Hence, when we revolt against His Will, His permissions, we are no more in our truth as creatures. 2) Our adoption as children supposes us to act ever as loving children of our Heavenly Father, to seek His good pleasure always: *quaerite faciem ejus semper.*[3] The *facies Dei*[4] is the smile of His loving

[2] "The weakness of God is stronger than men" (I Cor. 1:25).
[3] Rule of St. Benedict: end of Prologue.
[1] III John 4.
[2] "I am the Truth" (John 14:6).
[3] "Seek ye the Lord . . .: seek His face evermore" (Ps. 104:4).
[4] "The face of God."

approbation. If you keep true to this double relation, you will become more and more fixed in truth and peace.

May God bless and love you as I do from my heart of hearts.

✠ Columba Marmion, Abb.

## XXXII. TO AN IRISH NOVICE

### FIVE LETTERS

#### I.

✠ Pax                 Abbaye de St. Benoit, Maredsous.
par Maredret. 3 . XII . 1921.

My dear Child,

I am so pleased with your letter. It is so frank and open. I shall be just as frank and open with you, and so, we shall understand each other. I hate what is commonly known as *direction*, and directors *à la mode*.[1] There is often very little of God, and a lot of ourselves in it.

On the penitent's side, it means often leading the life of a mole, burrowing in the earth of your being, finding nothing but discouragement and misery; on the Director's side, loss of time, and learned discourses which lead to little or nothing.

St. Benedict loved his sister, Scholastica, dearly. He went to see her *once* a year. They spoke of God, of His love, of Heaven. They prayed much for each other. They spoke *little of themselves.*

When I met you during the retreat, I *saw*, that beneath your wild, girlish nature, there was a very deep sanctuary capable of great love; and I know that Jesus wanted that *all* for Himself. You understand this too; and the programme of the Spiritual Life, which you propose in your letter, is just what the Holy Ghost wants from you.

1. Do *all* through love.
2. For Love, work, suffer, bear up, despite monotony, just as Jesus on the Cross.

[1] Fashionable directors.

219

3. If He asks for anything, never refuse; but if it seems too hard to nature, pray, pray till He gives you the grace.

4. Keep the eye of your soul ever fixed on your *ONE* Love, for Whom you have left all. If anything comes between you and Him, He will show it to you "in the light of His Face." *Illuxit nobis in facie Xti. Jesu.*[2]

Be very open and confiding with your Mistress. Don't write to me more than once a year, unless something comes to trouble you. What I told you: "He wants you to do all for Love," came from His S. Heart. Pray for me daily, as I shall for you. May God bless and love you, and make you a holocaust of love united with your crucified spouse.

Yrs. in J.C.<br>✠ Columba, Abb.

II.

✠ Pax

Tournai. 20 . IV . 22.

My dear Child,

A holy, happy Feast. At Holy Mass to-morrow, *specially*, I shall take you, and present you to Jesus, that you may be very *faithful* to His love. He loves you *so*. When you fall into any fault, just run to Our Heavenly Father, and show Him your soul; just as a child runs to her mother to show her her soiled frock, and get it cleaned at once.

I have a great desire to make a little Saint of you. I know Our Lord wants it; and for that, all He requires is, that you do *all for love*, quite simply; and don't be astonished if you are not always as perfect as you would wish.

Let us pray for our poor Erin. I am quite ashamed of her.[1]

Your most devoted<br>✠ C. Abb.

---

[2] "God . . . hath shined in our hearts . . . in the face of Christ Jesus" (II Cor. 2:6).

[1] Reference to the Irish rebellion plus civil war at its height at that time. Dom Marmion's remark does not imply any lack of patriotism or love of his suffering country, but probably his opinion that atrocities on one side do not excuse reprisals of the same kind. See preceding letters for other references to his suffering homeland.

## III

✠ Pax

28 . IX . 22.

My dear Child,

Just got back from Lourdes [1] full of love for Mary; but so rushed and crushed with work, I can only say just a word. Your soul is on the right way. You love Jesus. *He loves you dearly.* The snobbishness is an obstacle, and He has shown it to you, to give Him the glory of your sacrifice. Like Our Lord, the deeper the misery-weakness of my children are, the dearer they are to me. Be faithful, and you will arrive at great union. It is impossible, dear Child, to arrive at intimate union with a Crucified Love, without feeling at times the thorns and nails. It is they which cause the union. You must not be discouraged when Our Lord lets you see a *little* of your misery. He bears with it always, and hides it from you; but you must see it, and feel it, before it comes out. This is painful and humiliating for a little Irish Snob.

I pray daily for you, that you may become a Saint according to His Heart. Just do your daily task *for Him*, and leave the rest to His love. He wants *you to do all for love.*

May God bless and love you, as I do from my heart of hearts.

Your Father

✠ Columba, Abb.

P.S. I shall write more at length next time.

✠ Pax

Maredsous. 21 . XI . 22.

My dear Child,

Just one little word to tell my little child how much joy her letter gave me. I see that you are going *straight* to God, by *simple*, loyal *love*. That is your way. Our Dear Lord wants you to be His, and for Him alone. He calls you to His mysterious espousals *in Faith*. He wants you as the Spouse to give yourself up to Him, and leave Him absolute Master and Spouse of your person. Don't complicate your

---

[1] I.e., on the diocesan pilgrimage he had led that year.

prayer by thinking of people in particular. Leave that to Him, except in very particular cases. As a rule, in souls, whom Jesus calls to Him, as He does yours, He invites you by His inward inspiration, when He wants you to pray for particular things or persons.

I should love to come for your Profession; but I suppose Rev. Mother must invite someone else. If she were to invite me, I would find a way of coming for a couple of days.

I am sending you my IIIrd Vol.[1] for your retreat. It is such a joy for me to guide you to Jesus. It is a great grace for you to have such a holy and enlightened Mistress of Novices.

May God bless and love you, my dear Child.

✝ Columba, Abb.

v.

✝ Pax

Abbaye de Maredsous. 23.I.23.[1]

My dear Child,

Just a little word straight from my heart to tell you I am with you in your offering. St. Paul says: *Xtus pro omnibus crucifixus est, justus pro injustis* ut nos offerret Deo.[2] What the Crucified Jesus offers His Father is ever acceptable, however miserable we be.

I am offering Mass for you on the 25th; asking Jesus to take you through the veil, that is His crucified Humanity, into the Holy of Holies.[3] During our little retreat,[4] I hope to show you what this "Holy of Holies" is. I want it to be *Our* home. "Father, says Jesus, I will that there where I am, my servant also may be." [5] I want us to pass through the veil, and to dwell there with Jesus in love.

---

[1] *Le Christ idéal du moine,* which had just been published in French.

[1] Unwittingly Abbot Marmion was writing his spiritual testament. For this letter is, with the two others sent the same day to other correspondents, the last he wrote. The same day he was obliged to take to his bed on account of the illness that was to bring him home to God just a week later, on January 30. It was he whom God was calling to "pass through the veil and to dwell there with Jesus in love."

[2] Actually this text comes from 1 Pet. 3:18." Christ . . . died once for our sins, the Just for the unjust: that He might offer us to God."

[3] See Heb. 9:11-12.

[4] Abbot Marmion had accepted an invitation to preach a retreat in the convent where the correspondent lived.

[5] John 17:24.

This programme is high, but it is our Destiny; it is *God's wish*. It is the fruit and object of the Passion of Jesus.

I am really sorry not to be at B[. . .] for your Profession; but there is no distance for those united in Xt. I want you to make this little retreat with great fervour, as it contains the programme of that journey which I am to guide you by during your life.

My dear Child, I have very deep sufferings of *heart* and soul at present; I know you pray for me, as I do *daily* for you.

Your father in J.C.<br>✛ Columba, Abb.

P.S. I expect to arrive early on the 6th,[6] so as to begin that evening. If you like to see me before beginning, you have but to call me.

[6] February 6.

# CHRONOLOGY

April 1, 1858: Joseph Aloysius Marmion born in Dublin.

January, 1874 — November 16, 1879: Philosophy studies and beginning of theology at Holy Cross Seminary at Clonliffe, near Dublin.

November, 1879 — July, 1881: Theological studies in Rome, at the Propaganda College.

August or September, 1880: Visit to the abbey of Monte Cassino.

June 16, 1881: Ordination to the priesthood in Rome.

End of July, 1881: First visit to Maredsous.

September, 1881 — October, 1882: Curate at Dundrum (Dublin).

October, 1882 — October, 1886: Professor at Clonliffe.

November 21, 1886: Entered Maredsous.

February 10, 1888: Monastic profession.

August 9, 1890: Dom Hildebrand de Hemptinne succeeds Dom Placid Wolter as Abbot of Maredsous; then in November, 1893, becomes also Abbot-Primate of the whole Benedictine Order.

1895: Dom Columba preaches his first retreat to nuns.

1899–1909: Prior of Mont-César, Louvain.

February 7, 1906: Mgr. Mercier is appointed Archbishop of Malines.

September 19, 1909: Abbot-Primate Hildebrand de Hemptinne announces his resignation of the abbacy of Maredsous.

September 28, 1909: Dom Columba is elected Abbot of Maredsous.

October 3, 1909: He receives the abbatial blessing.

February–March, 1912: Journey to Rome with Cardinal Mercier.

March 3, 1912: First audience with Pope St. Pius X.

September–October, 1912: Voyage to Germany, Austria, and Rome on business concerning the Congregation and the Order.

September 22, 1912: Second audience with St. Pius X.

March, 1913: First stay at the Monastery of Caldey Island.

April–June, 1913: Journey to Italy for the jubilee celebrations of Monte Cassino, and the election of a Coadjutor to the Abbot-Primate (elected May 13).

May 16, 1913: Third audience with St. Pius X (accompanied by the Abbot of Caldey).

June–July, 1913: Second journey to Caldey.

August 13, 1913: Death of Dom Hildebrand de Hemptinne at Beuron.

August 4, 1914: Belgium is invaded by the German armies.

September 14, 1914: Departure from Maredsous, incognito, to find a refuge for his young monks outside occupied Belgium.

Christmas, 1914: Organization of the young monks (refugees) at Edermine House, in Ireland.

February 8, 1916: Dom Marmion leaves Edermine in an effort to return to Belgium.

February–March, 1916: Seriously ill in London.

May 19, 1916: Return to Maredsous through Holland.

December, 1918 — June 2, 1919: Long journey through France, Italy, England, Ireland on business concerning Maredsous.

January 26, 1919: First audience with Pope Benedict XV.

February 5, 1919: The abbeys of Maredsous and Mont-César are separated by the Holy See from the Beuronese Congregation. They will form, with Abbey of Saint André at Bruges, the Belgian Benedictine Congregation.

April, 1919: Very serious illness in Dublin, and convalescence in Ireland.

July–August, 1919: Journey to France, Italy, England for several retreats and other business.

July 27, 1919: Second audience with Benedict XV.

June 9, 1920: Visit of Queen Elizabeth of the Belgians to Maredsous.

October 15, 1922: The Golden Jubilee of the foundation of Maredsous Abbey is celebrated, Cardinal Mercier presiding.

January 23, 1923: Abbot Marmion writes his last three letters.

January 25, 1923: He celebrates his last Mass.

January 30, 1923: He dies a holy death.

# ENGLISH BIBLIOGRAPHY

## A. Books by Dom Marmion

1. *Christ, the Life of the Soul* [1917]. Trans. by a Nun of Tyburn; London, Sands; and St. Louis, Herder, 1925.
2. *Christ in His Mysteries* [1919], 2nd ed. 1931. Trans. by an Nun of Tyburn; London, Sands; St. Louis, Herder, 1939.
3. *Christ the Ideal of the Monk* [1922]. Trans. by a Nun of Tyburn; London, Sands; St. Louis, Herder, 1926, 3rd ed. 1942.
4. *Christ the Ideal of the Priest* [1951]. According to autograph manuscript. Trans. by Matthew Dillon, O.S.B.; London, Sands; and St. Louis, Herder, 1952.
5. *Sponsa Verbi; The Virgin Consecrated to Christ* [1923]. Trans. by Francis Izard; London, Sands; St. Louis, Herder, 1925.
6. *Union with God*; according to the letters of direction of Don Marmion [1934]. Trans. by Mother Mary St. Thomas, 1935; London, Sands; St. Louis, Herder, 1935.

## B. Anthologies of Extracts
## from Published Books

7. *Words of Life*. Daily Meditations on the Mass [1937]. Trans. by Mother St. Thomas; London, Sands, 1940; Herder, 1941.
8. *Suffering with Christ* [1941]. Westminster, Md., Newman Press, 1952.
9. *The Trinity in Our Spiritual Life* [1946]. Westminster, Md., Newman Press, 1953.

10. *The Way of the Cross* [1923]. Trans. by a Nun of Tyburn; London, Sands, 1923.
11. *The Mysteries of the Rosary* [1942]. Trans. by the Monks of Marmion; Aurora, Ill., Marmion Abbey, 1949.
12. *Our Way and Our Life*. An abridged edition of *Christ in His Mysteries*. London, Sands, 1927.

## C. BOOKS ABOUT ABBOT MARMION

13. Raymond Thibaut, O.S.B. *Abbot Columba Marmion*. A Master of Spiritual Life [1929]. Trans. by Mother Mary St. Thomas; London, Sands; and St. Louis, Herder, 1932.
14. M. M. Philipon, O.P. *The Spiritual Doctrine of Dom Marmion* [1954]. Trans. by Matthew Dillon, O.S.B., 1956. London, Sands; Westminster, Md., Newman Press, 1956.
15. *Abbot Marmion*. An Irish Tribute, edited by the monks of Glenstal. Cork, Mercier Press; and Westminster, Md., Newman Press, 1948.
16. *More about Dom Marmion*. Dublin, Clonmore and Reynolds, 1949.
17. *Abbot Columba Marmion* (booklet) by the monks of Marmion Abbey. Benet Lake, Wis., Our Faith Press, 1958.

*Apart from items 15 and 17, all these are English translations of books originally published in French. The date given in brackets is that of the first French edition.*